The Last Years
of
British India

ON AUGUST 15, 1947, the rule of the British Raj over the Indian Empire came to an end. In pomp and ceremony, the legacies of nearly two hundred years of British dominion were formally handed to the newborn states of India and Pakistan. It was a day of celebration and rejoicing. It was "one of the most significant and portentous events in modern times"—yet it marked but the turning of a page in the long story of the Indian desire for independence which, having been achieved, now had to be maintained.

The primary aims of *The Last Years of British India* are to separate the facts from the myths which have been built around the granting of independence and, by presenting the first, accurate, unbiased account of what really happened, to set it in the proper historical context of the years which preceded and followed it. A leading authority on India and Indian affairs, Michael Edwardes was in that country at the time of the transfer of power. He met Gandhi and Muhammad Ali Jinnah, the strong man of the Muslim League, and portrays them and the other leaders candidly and without false piety.

Edwardes is not dazzled by the glamour of sainthood that surrounded Gandhi for the last years of his life; and while he acknowledges Gandhi's greatness as a reformer, he does not hesitate to reveal his naïveté as a political leader.

Many private and public documents not available to other writers were opened to Edwardes, and he has interviewed and questioned many of the protagonists in the struggle for independence. From his unique vantage point, he presents a cohesive, detailed assessment of facts and issues never before adequately discussed. He outlines the relationships among the Hindu, Muslim, and British leaders, the struggle by the maharajahs to maintain their power, and the role of the warlike Sikhs in the partition of the Punjab. Here, too, are all the terror and agony of the days of partition when the rest of the world, aghast, watched the spectacle of neighbors killing, raping, and plundering in a desperate effort, each to establish his own religion's ascendancy.

India and Pakistan are today enigmas in the eyes of the West. Their mutual distrust is little understood, their post-Independence policies often misjudged. Michael Edwardes' deep understanding of the problems which now face the two countries and his ruthlessly honest analysis of the decisions and influences which have shaped their attitudes make this a historically important and an exciting book, essential reading for those who would better understand this uncertain part of our world.

The Last Years
of
British India

MICHAEL EDWARDES

THE WORLD PUBLISHING COMPANY

CLEVELAND AND NEW YORK

To the memory of the men, women and
children murdered in the streets and fields
of India, who, though they did not fight
for their country's freedom, paid for it
with their lives.

Published by The World Publishing Company
2231 West 110th Street, Cleveland 2, Ohio

Library of Congress Catalog Card Number: 64-12065

FIRST EDITION

MWP664

Contents

Maps

Preface

The primary aim of this work is to place in its proper historical context one of the most significant and portentous events of modern times—the end of Britain's Indian empire. This event was not only of fundamental importance to the three countries involved—Britain, India and Pakistan. It was also the first step in the devolution of power by the once-great maritime empires to the peoples of their colonial dependencies. From Britain's actions a whole new world was born in hope, a hope that has since been frayed and tattered by tragedy and suffering. Consequently, the transfer of power in India has been subjected to the mythomania of statesmen and politicians. In British Labour circles, the act of a British Labour prime minister in granting independence to India was and still is seen in an almost religious light as the fulfilment of a long-held and often-repeated promise to end the evils of colonialism. There is some truth in such a belief, but very little, for great events are always compounded of much more than doctrine, however deeply felt it may be. The common Conservative attitude in 1947 was that the Labour government's decision to quit India was an act of treachery which was, in turn, the product of small-minded weakness. In the course of this book, I hope to show that even this apparently childish attitude was not without some grain of truth to support it.

France, Holland and Portugal, too, saw Indian independence as treasonable, a sort of stab in the imperial back, and their attempts to restrain their own colonial peoples from independence offers proof of it. The tenacity with which France, Holland and Portugal tried to hold on to their overseas dependencies has made some of Britain's ex-subjects believe that her demission of power may well have been another of those Machiavellian acts for which the British were famous—at least according to nationalist propaganda. Even a gesture as sweeping as the transfer of power in India might be part of some labyrinthine plot cooked up in Whitehall. However fatuous such beliefs may seem in cold print they should not be dismissed as without consequence. Many men have died in the past for beliefs no less foolish and unfounded, and they will no doubt continue to do so in the future.

The present work is an essay in explanation, an attempt to display and examine the many and diverse ingredients of an historical event and to disentangle them from the web of propaganda and special pleading. The actual transfer of power in India is, in one sense, only a minor part of the drama of the decline and fall of British India—as, in Sophocles' tragedy, the self-imposed exile of Oedipus is but a result of the impact of vast and complex forces. By defining the British departure from India in this way, I do not mean to diminish its importance in the historical sense, nor, for that matter, the interest which it must hold for the ordinary reader. Such interest is perfectly understandable, for many of those who were intimately involved in the moves that culminated in India's independence from Britain are still alive and have been subjected to both uncritical praise and ill-informed blame. Those who search here for new revelations may well find them. However, it is not my primary purpose to expose, but to attempt to give a reasonably objective view of what actually happened and why. This book is not propaganda for or against any of the controversial figures concerned in the transfer of power. When opinions *are* expressed, they are solely my own. These opinions are based upon facts, facts emerging out of my own knowledge—for I was present when these great events were maturing and came to fulfilment—and facts which have been given to me by the men and women involved, in one way or another, in the making of history. For those facts which are the scaffolding of the book, I must express my gratitude to the many who have willingly talked to me and answered my often impertinent questions. To record all their names would be impossible; some of my informants, in fact, have specifically asked that I should not mention theirs. I can only thank them collectively and hope that they will not feel that I have misinterpreted them or done them any intentional injustice.

The writing of contemporary history is always difficult. Much of the real material of such history is not, at least officially, available to the historian. There is also the question of how truthful one's informants are. I have taken every opportunity of checking the statements of individuals, and where no such opportunity has been available I have used my judgement to decide upon the truth. That judgement, as with all human activity, is fallible, but I have tried to reduce the margin of error to the thinnest possible line.

While preparing this work, which has taken many years of research and inquiry, I was also engaged among other projects in writing a military appreciation of another major event in the history of British India, the Mutiny of 1857. No historian of the Indian Mutiny can do without that great work, J. W. Kaye's *History of the Sepoy War*, published like the present work only a few years after the events it describes. Kaye's story too was hedged with all the difficulties of contemporary history—controversy, whitewash, and deliberate perversions of the truth. I can do no better in stating my own position than to adopt the words Kaye used in the preface to the second volume of his book:

It is probable that the accuracy of some of the details in this volume, especially those of personal incident, may be questioned, perhaps contradicted, notwithstanding, I was about to say, all the care that I have taken to investigate them, but I believe that I should rather say 'by reason of that very care'. Such questionings or contradictions should not be too readily accepted; for, although the authority of the questioner may be good, there may be still better authority on the other side. I have often had to choose between very conflicting statements; and I have sometimes found my informants to be wrong, though apparently with the best opportunities of being right, and have been compelled to reject, as convincing proof, even the overwhelming assertion, 'But I was there.'

It has often been said to me, in reply to my inquiries, 'Yes, it is perfectly true. But these men are still living, and the truth cannot be told.' To this my answer has been: 'To the historian, all men are dead.' If a writer of contemporary history is not prepared to treat the living and the dead alike—to speak as freely and as truthfully of the former as of the latter, with no more reservation in the one case than in the other—he has altogether mistaken his vocation, and should look for a subject in prehistoric times.

'To the historian,' wrote Kaye ninety-three years ago, 'all men are dead.' He might also have added that the author of that tiresome Latin tag which begins '*De mortuis . . .*' was not an historian. The dead—the legally dead, that is—have of course no redress, but the living can bring a libel action. The reader will realize from this how carefully I have checked my facts.

PART ONE

The Brightest Jewel

1 *The Brightest Jewel*

As midnight struck on 14 August 1947, Britain's Indian empire subsided into the history books. For many Indians who had struggled and waited long for the day of freedom, there was satisfaction, tempered perhaps with sorrow that the old British India had now been divided into two new nations. For the majority of India's people, however— that vast majority of hundreds of millions—the significance of the day was without reality; their poverty held more meaning for them than any of the words and deeds of their leaders. Amongst the British, engaged in giving away what Disraeli, that hard-headed imperial romantic, had called 'the brightest jewel in the British Crown', opinion was divided. For some, the transfer of India to the Indians was the final consummation of Britain's moral purpose—the education of Indians, as British statesmen had been saying for over a century, to such a level as to make them capable of governing themselves. Opinion here, too, was divided. Some—politicians and others—thought the level had been achieved years earlier and had said so consistently during the long period when they were without political power. Others insisted that the Indians had not reached the right level even in 1947, and that only ruin and chaos could follow any transfer of power.

All these differing views, even the views of those who had no views at all, played their part in the drama of the last years of British India. These views were the products of actions and ideas—and of responses to them—which had emerged over the many years of Britain's connexion with India. The simple conjuring trick played at midnight on 14 August 1947—now you see British India, now you don't—had roots reaching well into the historical past. The living who gave up their inheritance, the living who accepted the legacies, were in all they did, even in the ways they thought and felt, partly the puppets of the dead. Dead statesmen, dead political philosophers, long dead and almost forgotten events, all had exerted their pressures on the living. This chapter is about those pressures and the men they helped to make, men who, in their turn, made history.

2 *The Legislators*

Direct and undivided responsibility for the government of India was not assumed by the British parliament until as late as 1858. Before that, its authority had been exercised only through a governor-general who was appointed by the British cabinet of the time but paid by the trading organization which had made itself ruler of India. But the East India Company's administration was subject to the granting, every few years, of a royal charter. Before 1773, the Company dealt with its affairs in India pretty much as it chose, but a Regulating Act in that year signalled the first attempt of parliament to control the Company and the Company's servants in India. One of the provisions of this Act was the establishment of a Supreme Court in Calcutta designed to administer English law. Its chief purpose, in the words of Edmund Burke, was 'to form a strong and solid security for the natives against the wrongs and oppressions of British subjects resident in Bengal'. Burke's remark, the Act itself, and all the other acts concerning government in India which followed it, represent the continuing division between the legislators and the actual rulers, between the British parliament and the British administrators in India, who worked firstly for the Company and secondly for the Crown.

The British parliament sought, with varying degrees of success, to control its agents in India; parliament could make laws defining the way in which India *should* be governed, but it could not itself govern India. The reasons for this were simple. In the early days, there was the distance between Britain and India; by the time news reached London from India, the authorities in India had already acted. The British government could only confirm or condemn the *fait accompli*. As communications improved, however, with the opening of the telegraph between India and Britain in 1865 and of the Suez Canal in 1869, the control exercised by the secretary of state over his representative, the viceroy, increased according to the strength of personality of the two men involved. Nevertheless, the secretary of state in London could not control the actual everyday administration of India at any time. India was too big and the volume of administrative business too vast for the constant approval of a cabinet minister thousands of miles away. The British government, and through it the British parliament, controlled only the general policy of Indian administration; it could not direct its application in practice.

One aim remained constant throughout all the changes of policy initiated by the British parliament until the 1947 transfer of power—that Indians themselves should in some measure be involved in the governing of India. Radical and, later, socialist criticism was directed only at the speed and manner in which this involvement was to develop. Criticism by Indian nationalists took the same course until they came to realize that, as long as Indian affairs were controlled by a parliament in Britain, there would always be a limit on the extent of their involvement in their own government. This was the point at which they began to demand firstly self-government and then complete independence.

Much has been made, by apologists for British rule in India, of the statements of nineteenth century politicians that Indians would one day be self-governing—that they would demand British representative institutions for themselves and that furthermore, in the words of Macaulay in 1833, it would be 'the proudest day in English history' when they did. Although these statements, which were almost always honestly meant, have an aura of 'sometime, never (in my lifetime)' about them, and although Macaulay's view—that it would be foolish and costly to hold on to India in such a manner as 'would keep a hundred millions of men from being our customers in order that they might continue to be our slaves'—was typical of the most progressive thinking of his time, they were not motivated by British self-interest alone. Macaulay wanted to civilize—that is, anglicize—the Indians so that they would buy British goods; but he and others also saw the possibility that the Indians would come to demand British institutions too, and British institutions were the right of any really civilized man.

The British, then, began to 'civilize' India and to reform her society in what they believed to be the best way possible, by introducing English education and an English sense of values. Though essentially arrogant, the reformers were genuinely convinced that a transformation of India would benefit the Indians as well as themselves. Because reform brought about results which coincided with European self-interest, the moral aspect has often been dismissed as hypocrisy of the most unpleasant kind—exploitation disguised by humbug. But this is not true. In the continuing liberal attitude to India a desire for commercial profit was combined with real altruism. There was no question in the minds of the early liberals but that India would one day be self-governing— it would, however, be a new India transformed by Western institutions and moral values, fit to become a partner in the new prosperity that commerce would free for all.

This was all very well, but could Britain's civilizing approach to Indian society have any political parallel? Did the reformers in fact believe that representative government was possible in India? They did not. An 'enlightened and paternal despotism' was the most suitable form of government for the diverse races of India until, of course, in some distant future, the regenerative process of Western education had produced a new class, 'Indian in blood and colour, but English in tastes, in opinions, in morals and intellect'. But even when this came about, there was to be no suggestion of *representative* government, for, as Sir Charles Wood, secretary of state at the time of the Indian Councils Act of 1861, put it, 'you cannot possibly assemble at any one place in India persons who shall be the real representatives of the various classes of the Native population of that empire'. As late as 1909, Lord Morley —the then secretary of state—when piloting through the British parliament the legislation that came to be known as the Morley–Minto reforms, was emphatic. 'If it could be said,' he told the House of Lords, 'that this chapter of reforms led directly or necessarily to the establishment of a parliamentary system in India, I for one would have nothing at all to do with it.'

Thus Morley expressed once more the continuing belief that the institutions of liberal democracy were unsuited to India, that a benevolent despotism in which certain Indians could be associated, was much better than the tyranny of representative institutions which might not be—and the British believed could not be—representative in any Western sense. The vicissitudes of democracy today in the newly independent countries of Asia and Africa might well be taken as a demonstration that the 'reactionaries' of the past were not far wrong.

But the British had let loose, had in fact created, forces which in the changing climate of power after the 1914–18 War were to compel them to accept the nationalist contention that representative government for India was not only possible but desirable.

From 1861 to 1909, however, Britain's policy of expanding India's association in the government of India went virtually unchallenged; in fact, it received the enthusiastic support of most of those Indians who, because of their education, had become 'English in tastes, in opinions, in morals and intellect'.

The first constitutional advance, the Indian Councils Act of 1861, had been one of the consequences of the 1857 Mutiny in Bengal. The Mutiny showed quite clearly that, however benevolent the rulers may have been, their intentions were misunderstood by Indians, and that the government knew little or nothing of the feelings of the people. As one great Indian administrator summed it up: 'To legislate for millions with few means of knowing, except by rebellion, whether the laws suit them or not' was to say the least dangerous. With the Indian Councils Act, the British now sought access to public opinion, appointing Indians to newly-created legislative councils. These Indians—who, in fact, could express the opinions only of the Westernized few—were not elected but nominated by the governor-general and by the governors of those provinces where legislative councils were to be set up. The government thus sought the opinions of men who represented only a tiny minority of Britain's Indian subjects, a minority almost as cut off from the vast bulk of Indians as were the British themselves.

The powers of these new councils were purely legislative; they were not only barred from interfering in the control of administration, they were not even permitted to discuss it. Indian members of the councils were there for two main reasons. The Westernized middle-class had remained loyal to the British during the Mutiny and it was only proper that they should be rewarded; their loyalty seemed a further indication that Macaulay was right in hoping that, in them, lay the future of India, that, being Westernized, they would be fitted to become partners — however junior—of the British. What else they might be fitted for in the future was fortunately still a matter for conjecture, but as they were closest to the British in their thinking it was necessary to persuade them of Britain's good intentions. The rest of India was still responsive only to tyranny, but the country was ruled by a mere handful of British administrators and it was now becoming necessary to reinforce them by involving educated Indians in the structure of government. Also, it would be valuable to know their opinions. The appointment of Indians to legislative councils gave status to the Indians concerned, and proved that the government was on their side. It also proved that their interests were linked with those of the British.

The British at first encouraged solidarity among the Indian middle classes and when seventy-two Indians from almost as many parts of India gathered in Bombay in 1885 for the first meeting of the Indian National Congress, they did so with the full approval of the British government. The viceroy of the time, Lord Dufferin, thought the Congress an excellent means of tapping public opinion—though once again it was to be the opinion of a minority, even if a growing one. The first Congressmen, however, wanted more than to express their opinions; they wanted to assert their right to greater involvement in government, and they called for *representative* government and a legislature with 'a considerable portion of *elected* members'. What of course they were demanding was not parliamentary democracy but a government which represented them personally. These Western-educated middle-class Indians wanted, not association without responsibility, but active participation. Macaulay's prophecy of 1833 that Indians 'having become instructed in European knowledge . . . may in some future age demand European institutions' was being fulfilled.

The first Congressmen were by no means anti-British. They merely desired the status that their education had fitted them for and that Britain had said would one day be their reward.

The British responded with further constitutional advances in 1892. The provincial councils—though not the governor-general's central council—were allowed to discuss questions relating to administration and the budget, and the majority of 'non-official' seats (seats other than those held by government representatives) were to be filled on the 'recommendation' of such groups as municipalities, chambers of commerce and religious communities; this amounted in practice to election by such groups. But the British government and its administrators in India still believed that representative government was not suited to India and that, furthermore, there was no real question of sharing power with Indians. The British government's view, the view of the legislators, and the view of those unacknowledged legislators the political philosophers, was against such a sharing of power and against it for the best of reasons. Foremost in the mind of British statesmen was the good of the mass of the Indian people, for whom the British believed themselves trustees.

The British, however, had deliberately created a Westernized middle class in the hope that it would be in their own image, and there had appeared instead a Frankenstein monster continually demanding representative institutions as a remedy for all India's ills. The government's belief that representative institutions were unsuited to India's needs was supported by the behaviour of these articulate middle classes. When, for example, the government moved towards land reform and against peasant indebtedness to the money-lender—and it moved gingerly in the fear that Indian elected members of council, many of whom represented land-owning and money-lending interests, would impede legislation—Congress in response expressed its members' deep concern over the growing poverty of the peasant and declared that representative institutions would 'prove one of the most important practical steps towards the amelioration of the condition of the people'. This neither the government of India nor the British government in London believed to be true, and they were not prepared—for genuinely felt reasons—to allow interference with their own slow but real reforms in the condition of the peasant. They soon turned against these moderate Congressmen, whose political ideas were not revolutionary, who did not call for independence from Britain, who only wanted a slice of the cake.

Congress had become the expression not only of a minority of the Indian people, but of a minority of that minority. From 1870 onwards, there had been a considerable expansion of Western education which produced not only more university graduates but also an increasing number of men who had received some measure of English education and looked for employment as clerks. Unfortunately, there were not enough jobs for them and the unemployed malcontents turned against the British and against their more fortunate countrymen —the wealthy and established Indian middle classes who dominated Congress. The leaders of this newly-educated element demanded independence from Britain as the only way of satisfying their needs, and—feeling themselves betrayed by the 'moderates' who, merely by being moderate, were lackeys of the British and who could anyway, being without financial worries, afford to wait—they turned to revolutionary violence.

When the British realized the danger, they turned once again to appeasing the moderates. Lord Minto, viceroy from 1905 to 1910, gave it as his opinion that revolutionary activity should be stamped out and that further concessions should be given to the more moderate nationalists. The result was the Morley–Minto reforms of 1909. These reforms accepted the principle of elections for the Governor-General's Legislative Council (called for convenience 'The Centre') and for the provinces. The electoral 'constituencies', however, were still to be communities and groups. At the Centre there was to be an 'official' (representative of the government) majority, but elsewhere the 'non-officials' were to predominate. It was also decided that an Indian member would be appointed to the Viceroy's Executive Council—the cabinet of British India. On the surface, these reforms seemed to provide a considerable advance—but they were not, as Lord Morley had forcefully pointed out, intended to lead to a parliamentary form of government. On this point everyone in Britain was agreed.

It has been suggested that, Indians having had a crumb of the cake, the British should have anticipated that they would soon demand a slice. This was in fact realized by many from Macaulay onwards. The problem, however, was not how to avoid giving someone a slice, but how to decide who should have it, how it should be offered, and on what kind of plate it should be presented. The British quite naturally believed their political system to be the best there was, but they were also aware that the system had emerged in response to the demands of the British people, who had fought for it and over it. They knew from their imperial experience that it would not work in other societies.

The dilemma was a real one. The British had deliberately created a Westernized class who now claimed Western institutions. The British had often said they would provide them, and had seemed quite pleased at the thought. But now it appeared obvious that, if Western institutions were granted, the mass of the Indian people would probably suffer. The only possible answer would be to find some traditionally Indian institutions which could be adapted to fit the case. Unfortunately there were none, for the only institutions of a popular kind in

India were the village councils—which might be satisfactory for the village, but were no basis for wider local government let alone the government of the country itself.

The British approach to politics had never been very speculative or original; they had tended to adapt old ideas rather than construct new ones. Though a great deal of thought by political philosophers and others had gone into the question of British administration in India, it had all been based on the premise that despotism was the form of government best suited to India's needs, or what the British believed to be her needs. They felt a moral responsibility for ensuring the greatest good for the greatest number, but at the same time, they had a civilizing mission. The British were no fools and they could not see these two attitudes being compatible; nor could they see any precedent for making them so. Nevertheless they were unwilling to abandon either. Administration was something real, it was moral responsibility in action, and therefore the more important. The civilizing mission, on the other hand—the fitting of India for self government—was a pious hope, the fulfilment of which could conveniently be shifted on to the next generation.

Until 1914, the British could afford to take this line for their power was still unquestioned. The terrorists who threw bombs and fired revolvers at British officers did not seriously think they could bring down the British Raj. They thought that, as the Mutiny had done, they could perhaps frighten the British into reforms. In one sense, these terrorists were following European rather than English precepts; the moderates whom they despised were very English in their demands and in the gentle, reasonable way in which they put them forward. The terrorists, in contrast, had in front of them the example of nineteenth century Europe where revolution meant violence and the way to fight tyranny was not to reason with it but to throw a bomb at it. But though the British might be unsure of how to deal with political problems, there was no doubt in their minds about what to do when violence threatened.

The war that broke out in 1914, however, brought about profound changes not only in Britain's position in the world but inside Britain herself. These changes resulted in new attitudes towards her responsibility in, and to, India. In India also, new forces were emerging, forces which were to transform the nationalist movement from a minority group into a national rally and to claim the support of those very masses of whom the British felt themselves to be protectors.

After the end of the war in 1918, Britain's prestige in the world appeared not only undiminished but even enhanced. In actual fact, however, the war had enfeebled her in what was once her powerful asset, her wealth. Power is intimately related to economic strength and Britain's empire had been built—and sustained—by her dominant position in the industrial and financial structure of world trade. After 1918, this position was continuously eroded by the United States of America. After 1918, British power, already weakened from within, was to receive new challenges from the new fascist imperialisms of Germany and Italy, from the Soviet Union, and, in Asia, from Japan. These challenges would have been of little consequence if the rulers of Britain had not been compelled by vast social forces inside Britain itself to become inward rather than outward-looking.

In the last decades of the nineteenth century, Britain's strength—the period from about 1870 until 1914 was the zenith of her power—had been mainly derived from the vast quantities of surplus capital available for export and investment in Asia, and, more particularly, in Africa. This capital could have been invested at home, but only at lower rates of interest, for, in order to increase the purchasing power of the workers—essential if higher production was to be absorbed—it would have been necessary to institute labour reforms and bring about a re-distribution of the national wealth. At that time, however, social reform was anathema to private enterprise; the working classes were just another native race, to be exploited and denied a voice in their own destiny. But the time came when *this* 'native race' began to demand representative institutions and it could not be resisted. As it acquired a greater say in its own affairs, with the extension of the franchise during the 1914–18 War, it formed a powerful anti-colonial lobby. Why, the people demanded through their leaders and representatives in parliament, should there be poverty and unemployment in Britain when millions were being spent on the administration of far-away and non-white countries? Far better to give these countries self-government. Britain's newly articulate classes who had, after a long struggle, gained the right to participate in their own government, felt furthermore that Britain's unwillingness to grant the same right to Indians sprang from self-interest alone and that the excuse that democracy was unsuitable for India was merely eye-wash. The British Labour party, doomed it seemed to perpetual opposition, resurrected the prophecies of Macaulay and others and pledged itself to fulfil them. The combination of threats at home, abroad, and in India itself, turned the British government towards granting representative parliamentary institutions to India. But it preferred to move slowly, for it still considered that such a system was bad for the country. The British Labour party, however, in the light of its own limited experience, believed that liberal democracy on the British pattern was the best in the world. So did Indian nationalists, and for almost the first time they found themselves with allies in Britain herself.

The concessions made by successive British governments from 1919 until the final transfer of power in 1947 were made not so much to Indians as to the newly enfranchised classes in Britain and to that nebulous but very real thing—world public opinion. With or without the Second World War and the vast changes it produced, even the British Conservative party would shortly have been compelled by all these pressures to grant self-government to India. After 1918, it was no longer possible for any British government to permit itself to have genuine reservations about the suitability of parliamentary institutions for India. Whether real or imagined, Britain's moral responsibility for the welfare of the Indian people was of no consequence, for the questions now were not concerned with what sort of government suited India, but with how and when power was to be transferred to the Indians, and with the quickest and most reasonable way of satisfying all the pressure groups as well as, if possible, the conscience of the British.

3 The Rulers

The government of British India was unlike any other administration in the British empire. It behaved not as the government of a colony but as an almost independent state. The British parliament had always recognized this, from the days of the East India Company when difficulties of communication between London and Calcutta permitted independent action to the British who ruled in India. Edmund Burke expressed a fear that the breakers of law in India (that is, the British) might become the makers of law in England. This was not particularly likely, though the Services that ruled India had powerful lobbies at Westminster. The real danger lay in the possibility that the interests of the Indian empire might, in time, come to be of overriding import-ance. India was so big that the problems of its security were also im-mense and actions taken by the Indian government in defence of the country could have had the widest international repercussions, affect-ing Britain herself. From the Regulating Act of 1773 onwards, there-fore, the British government's primary aim was to try and exercise control, not only over India itself, but over the British who ruled there. Briefly, the fear of successive British governments in the nine-teenth century was that the British who ruled in India might become more concerned with India's interests than they were with Britain's.

This was in fact what actually happened. British administrators in India very often thought of India's interests first, even if the administra-trator's 'India' was only that of a District Officer. The British civil servants in India believed that their duty was to those whom they actually ruled, and they felt a particular loyalty to the province in which they worked; indeed, most of them spent all their years of service in one province. They criticized the central government for its interference in the affairs of the province, while the Centre, in turn, resented the interference of the secretary of state in London. There are many examples of the Centre's resistance to demands made by the minister in London. Though the government in India complained strongly on occasion to the home government, of necessity it could not do so publicly and it was therefore open to criticism by Indian national-ists as being helpless and subservient. In fact, early Congress criticisms of the cost of civil and military administration in India and of the many financial responsibilities forced upon the Indian government by West-minster were shared by the governor-general. But the government of India had no legal way of resisting the secretary of state, though it often went to considerable lengths in the attempt.

Until 1909, the British government and the Indian Services were agreed on at least one thing—that the best form of government for India was despotism. The men who ruled India saw themselves in one sense as *Indian* rulers, carrying on a traditional form of government which had operated in India before the British conquered it. But this despotism was transformed by British ideas of responsibility and 'fair play'; the administrators saw it not as an exploitive despotism but as a creative one. Very few of them believed that democratic institutions could work in India and they feared that the British parliament, desperately ignorant as its members were about India, would try to force such institutions on the country. Their attitude was based partly on administrative experience and partly upon a fear that any weakening of British authority—which the involvement of Indians in government would certainly mean—might lead to disorder. The British knew that they had the strength to suppress isolated rioting but not, perhaps, a well-organized revolt. The memory of 1857, when the native troops of the Bengal army had mutinied and, in alliance with certain princes and others, threatened British rule, was never too far away from the minds of the British in India.

The effects of material progress in India, of railways, cheap postal services, and of the spread of English as the language for the whole of India, began to produce a new sense of Indian unity. For the first time in India's history, a man of the south could feel he had something in common with the man of the north, the east, and the west. The number of British administrators was never more than three or four thousand, and below them they had a vast force of Indian subordinates. The army too was predominantly Indian. Thus, as material progress spread in India, so did the possibilities of successful revolt.

The District Officer, carrying out his duties with benevolent despotism, began to see his authority diminished by various quasi-democratic boards and councils. Partisan attitudes arose. The peasant, who had looked to the District Officer for impartiality, had done so precisely because he was not an Indian and because there were other Englishmen higher up to whom the peasant could appeal if the District Officer failed him. But as changes took place, he observed that the District Officer was being subjected to other pressures; the new district boards might include the brother of the peasant's landlord or the second cousin of the money-lender. It seemed to the peasant that such board members as these, and the sectional interests they represented, would make a fair hearing of his own case impossible. The District Officer's impartiality appeared diminished, and he could probably be by-passed by influential men. Such a state of affairs could only lead to dissatisfaction, to disaffection and unease. As the government of India at its real level, the District, was based not on a display of power but on the consent of respect, administration would not function if that respect was eroded.

This was what the rulers of India feared and they did not see how the situation could be avoided if the British parliament insisted on granting representative institutions. As long as such institutions were confined to local government, the District Officer could rely on receiving support from his own kind in the government of the province and even from the Centre; but, as reform spread to those places too, he became sadly aware that his days were numbered. He began to have fears about his future, his pension rights, the justifiable rewards of good and honest service. Young men, who had once been anxious for the opportunity of ruling India, began to think of other and safer careers. Edward Thompson, in one of his unjustly neglected novels of the twenties and thirties of this century, makes one of his characters say of the British in India: 'We neither govern nor misgovern. We're just hanging on, hoping that the Last Trump will sound "Time!" and save us from the bother of making a decision.' And this was true. Day-to-day administration went on but the British came to feel themselves caretakers rather than owners, concerned only with keeping the structure in repair and unwilling to make improvements or alterations.

In the thirty years before 1947, the administrators' attitude was that the cautious grants of representative government to India were either too big or too little, that the British should either stay with the old, well-tried system of administration or else leave the whole business to Indians and get out. Half-measures only made administration increasingly difficult. Suggestions that the constitutional reforms did not go far enough were, of course, not really meant seriously—except by a few eccentrics. The Services sought at every stage to insert into the reforms such clauses as would guarantee the executive arm of the government as much independence as possible, and they succeeded at the level which really counted—that of the District Officer. Even when there were elected Indian ministers in the provincial governments, the Englishman on the spot was still comparatively free to exercise his own judgement. It was fortunate that this was so, for it permitted the nationalists to fight the British in a fairly restricted arena and reduced the impact of political agitation on the everyday lives of the masses. Thus, despite large-scale civil disobedience and even violence, the administrative grasp weakened but did not break.

The rulers of India between 1900 and 1947 were not bad men, nor was the system they operated (and preferred) intrinsically bad. They were simply the inheritors of a tradition which no longer had a comfortable place in the world.

The system of rule had not appeared overnight but had emerged from many years of experience, experiment and failure. In fact, the form of British government in India was without precedent; the men who had evolved it had been submerged in the problems of an alien society and unconsciously took on some of the values and traditions of that society. They did much good, for their tyranny was inspired by the belief, however arrogantly expressed, that they knew what was best for India. Many of the ideas they had developed were later systematized by English political philosophers and re-exported to become the tablets of the law for British administration. Until the end of the nineteenth century, the despotism of the Indian government made it possible to carry out the most outstanding series of experiments in administration ever known. But these experiments had a certain frigidity, for they were based upon the premise that all a society's ills could be cured by efficient government. The Services who ruled India claimed that their government was efficient and the problems of the people were being solved. But in fact they were not. The administration was efficient in maintaining public order and in the preservation of internal peace. It also reduced the sources of tyranny by preventing arbitrary use of power by the native princes, or on a lower level, by the landlords. It was, however, a palliative government, not a therapeutic one. In the third decade of the nineteenth century, the British had attempted large-scale reforms in Indian society, but they had learned, through the Mutiny of 1857, that it was safer not to interfere with the totems and taboos of the Hindu world. They later learned that the new nationalism was quite prepared to use the Hindu religion in its attack on the British and to incite violence in order to preserve Hindu beliefs. In 1897, for example, British action to prevent the spread of plague was resisted on religious grounds, and a plague officer was murdered.

In the twentieth century, the men of the Services were still devoted to India and genuinely concerned with the welfare of those they ruled. Very few of the rulers of India—as distinct from the British businessmen there—thought of their job in terms of personal profit, though obviously they were not free from the normal human worries about

income, pensions, and the expense of their children's education. When
major changes came after the 1914-18 War, they felt themselves
betrayed and blamed the British government for pandering to Indian
nationalists and their allies in the British Labour party. But it was the
times rather than the British government which had betrayed them
and their self-imposed mission; now, everywhere, the dispossessed
were rising. A few of the men who ruled India tried to resist the tide of
history, and they were helped by certain politicians in Britain. One or
two, at the very end of British rule, committed what can only be
described as treason in order that their Indian friends might evade the
consequences of the transfer of power. Yet even these men behaved as
they did because they believed that what they were doing was in
India's interests. They were mistaken—and unsuccessful—but this was
another example of the peculiar, and at times passionate involvement
with India which was characteristic of the British who ruled it.

Because the men who proclaimed the virtues of British rule were
often, at least on the surface, those most interested in preserving it, their
arguments were accepted not at their real value but as the special pleading of professional reactionaries. Criticism by the socialists and the re-
form-minded was ideological rather than real, but it did reflect the
changing world. Indian civil servants did themselves no good with
their defence of 'the greatest good for the greatest number', in a world
where the achievement of political rights had come to be regarded as
the passport to a golden age. Nor was their case helped—while there
still was an Indian empire, or even after it had ceased to exist—by the
claim that members of the Indian Civil Service were some kind of
supermen, an élite of dedicated rulers. A parallel has been drawn between these men and Plato's concept of the Guardians, a disinterested
body of rulers governing only in the light of what was beautiful and
good. Most ICS men certainly believed in Plato's idea of superiority,
and they very often displayed it in the form of racial arrogance. The
men of the ICS do not need the support of such an extravagant claim,
one which has too many overtones of a pseudo-philosophic 'divine
right' to be treated seriously. Generally, they were moderately intelligent men, working under difficult conditions, who kept the administration going without resorting to overt cruelty. They were not so
much Guardians as preservers of a system that became more and more
the subject of criticism. Much of the criticism, no doubt, was ill-

informed and doctrinaire, but it represented irrational forces of great
power and complexity and it was not to be dispersed or disarmed by
statistics, or by the evidence of history, or even by appeals to the
precedents of Classical Greece.

*   *   *

There were other rulers in India besides the British civil servants.
Two fifths of India was still divided into states ruled by native princes.
The people of these territories were not British subjects and received
neither the protection of British law nor that of the British parliament.
The states existed because, in the early expansion of the British in India,
military and political exigencies had made allies of some of the native
rulers. Under various treaties, the ruling dynasties had surrendered the
management of their external relations to the British Crown, but,
generally speaking, they were free to rule themselves in any way they
wished as long as it was neither detrimental to British interests in
India nor over-stepped the bounds of toleration.

At one time, before the Mutiny of 1857, it had been the policy of the
Indian government to annex wherever possible the territories of native
princes, and the manner in which this had been done was one of the
causes of the revolt. But during the Mutiny most of the princes remained loyal, or at least neutral, and it was decided that no further
annexations would take place. The princely states, some of which were
only a few square miles in extent, were 562 in number and were scattered quite haphazardly all over India. The smaller states were forced
to accept a large measure of British control over their administration,
but the more important states were internally almost completely independent. Their relationship with the government of India operated
only through the viceroy as representative of the British Crown. The
states had certain obligations towards the 'Paramount Power', as the
Crown was called. They were, for example, obliged to supply military
forces if required for the defence of India. In the final analysis, they
were not really sovereign; their internal affairs were subject to super-
vision and the Paramount Power could intervene even to the extent of
deposing the ruler, though such intervention was very rare.

Most of the rulers of these states were Hindus but this did not mean
that their subjects were also Hindus. Kashmir, for example had some
three million Muslims and one million Hindus, but the Maharaja was

a Hindu; Hyderabad, the largest of the states—slightly larger than Scotland and England put together—had a Muslim ruler, though the Muslims were outnumbered twelve to one by Hindus. The British had a sentimental attachment to the native states, a typical nostalgia for past glories. These 'kingdoms of yesterday' claimed to be the true heirs of pre-British India, but, generally speaking, they were islands of mediaevalism out of touch with the realities of the modern world.

Until 1919, the autocratic rule of the princes was little different in principle from the government of British India, and most of the larger states had adopted British legal and administrative procedures. Originally, the states were not only isolated from the rest of British India, but also from each other; they were not permitted to combine in any way. They were, however, forced to share in a number of non-political activities. Railways were no respecters of state frontiers, and the government of India would not permit maritime states to levy different customs dues from those applicable in British India. It was not until 1919 that any suggestion was made that India should be governed other than in two water-tight compartments, and it was 1935 before any real attempt was made to involve the princely states in the concept of India as a whole.

The rulers of the states had many friends among the British who were responsible for their control, and, as British India moved towards independence, a number of attempts were made to safeguard the interests of the princes, interests which were at variance with those of the rest of India as well as with the expressed intentions of the British parliament.

4 *The Nationalists*

The great disadvantage of modern political slogans is their simplicity. They seem to mean what they say and are easily understood. Because the Indian nationalist movement used them, talked incessantly about freedom, liberty, the rights of man, and the general virtues of democracy, it was thought that the nationalists believed in these slogans and that Indian nationalism was as simple and uncomplicated as the slogans themselves. But political slogans are like the sidelights of a vehicle on a dark night in an unlit street viewed from a considerable distance. The lights—themselves recognizable and simple—do not reveal the make, shape, condition or power of the vehicle, the colour of the upholstery or the name of the driver. It might not even be a motor vehicle at all, but a horse-drawn van. Almost all the liberal-democrats and socialists in Britain and elsewhere who supported the Indian nationalists' demand for freedom observed the nationalist movement only by the glow of its sidelight slogans in the dark night of their own doctrine.

Consequently, they knew very little if anything about the true nature of Indian nationalism. Not that this mattered very much from their point of view, because support for Indian freedom was a fundamental part of the socialist campaign to assert their own political rights. Empire automatically had a class connotation. It was the symbol of middle- and upper-class privilege, of exploitation not so much abroad as at home.

During their period in the wilderness, socialists found Britain's dependent empire a valuable political weapon with which to belabour successive Tory governments. Surprisingly enough, they were not all Little Englanders, for though they believed Britain would be better off financially without responsibility for the colonies, they did not want to sever all connexion with the empire. An empire transformed into an association of self-governing dominions was the limit of their thinking, because they wanted Britain to retain in some undefined way the prestige of empire without the financial drain of ruling it. Above all, they were advocates of evolution, not revolution. This was partly the result of their English radical and non-conformist origins and partly because revolution, after 1917, was associated primarily with communism. Speeches, promises, and advice were what the socialists offered Indian nationalists. Socialist intellectuals went off to China to help fight the Japanese, or to Spain in defence of the republic. They did not go and throw bombs at British governors in India.

The attitudes of British socialist leaders and intellectuals had considerable effect upon the thinking, and action, of some of the Indian nationalist leaders. The advice they gave was always cautious, even constitutional, because they were fundamentally unrevolutionary themselves. Their influence, in fact, was to delay India's freedom rather than to speed it, for they managed to convince the intellectual leaders of the Indian nationalist movement that Britain was more likely to listen to constitutional demands than to revolutionary agitation and that, anyway, a Labour government would soon be in power in Britain and would grant India dominion status. The socialist justification for this has apparently been confirmed by events. Constitutional demand *did* bring constitutional reforms and a socialist government in 1947 *did* give India its freedom; but, as this book will show, this is only a superficial view which is not supported by analysis of the events themselves.

The struggle for freedom in India is inevitably associated with one particular organization—the Indian National Congress. But it was not in fact the only expression of Indian nationalism, though it was the principal stimulus for other streams of nationalist activity. Again, too, Congress was not a homogeneous political party but a vast rally of diverse and conflicting elements, all of which exerted their various pressures upon the leaders. Originally Congress had been founded, in 1885, with the approval of the British government in India as a kind of middle-class *durbar*. The *durbar* was an essential part of the traditional Indian concept of the autocratic ruler, a sort of levée or reception held at regular intervals when the ruler's subjects could appear in person before him with complaints and petitions.

Before the founding of Congress there had been an organized body representing Indians of wealth, social position and education. This was the British India Association, founded in 1851. Generally speaking, the British India Association was not a progressive body and its members resisted, whenever possible, any introduction of land reforms. In fact, most of the Indian educated class consisted of upper-caste men with landed interests, and the first principal conflict between the government of India and this class came when the British sought support from the mass of the people by proposing reforms in the relationship between landlord and tenant. Basically, the educated classes' demand for political reform was directed at gaining for themselves some control over government action, so that they might prevent the British from going ahead with its rather feeble agricultural reforms. It was from among members of the British India Association that most of the nominated Indian members of the legislative councils had been chosen. Most of these members represented land-owning, commercial, and professional interests, and many of them were lawyers.

The Indian Councils Act of 1892, however, brought a change in the representation of the educated classes. As there was now at least a form of election, it was the professional classes who were elected rather than

the great landowners; the reason for this was that the landed classes
were unwilling to put themselves up for election by popular vote. The
new representatives were mainly lawyers, with doctors, schoolmasters,
traders and money-lenders making up the rest. These men, generally
speaking, had little sympathy with either landlord or tenant.

It is an interesting fact that, throughout the whole of the struggle for
freedom, a large proportion of nationalists came from the legal profession, and they were possessed of a respect for law which reinforced
other pressures in favour of legitimate means of agitation. By 1899,
according to a confidential government report, almost 40 per cent
(5,442) of the 13,839 delegates to the Indian National Congress were
from the legal profession. The other large groups consisted of 2,629
representing landed interests, and 2,091 from the commercial classes.
The remainder was made up almost entirely of journalists, doctors and
teachers.

Congress, like the British India Association, was opposed to any
reform in tenants' rights, for although the legal profession might be
indifferent to landlord and peasant alike, much of Congress's financial
support came from large landed proprietors. The commercial classes
formed another interested party. They felt themselves oppressed, and
believed that British rule did not favour indigenous capitalists. They
were only partly right because, though British rule undoubtedly favoured British business undertakings and did not actively encourage the
growth of indigenous industry, development had been restricted
primarily by lack of Indian capital and enterprise. Furthermore, the
Congress attitude to industrial reform, for example, showed that its
members were no friends of the workers.

Naturally, the professional and business classes were strongly opposed
to the Indian government's financial policy, and especially to the
priority given to paying interest on loans raised in Britain and to the
charges borne by India for imperial troops and activities *outside* India.
The nationalists suggested that the cost of administration should be
reduced and that import duties should be imposed on a wide variety of
goods. They were strongly against paying taxes themselves and resisted
any form of direct or indirect taxation. The main burden of providing
revenue for the government of India rested upon those who received
least advantage from it, namely the peasant and the small trader.

The coming together of the educated classes, deprived of higher posts in the civil service which were reserved for the British, and of the businessmen who regarded themselves as discriminated against economically, was of profound importance in the struggle for freedom. It brought much-needed funds, as well as adding a further pressure in favour of non-violent reform rather than bloody revolution, for Indian businessmen also brought the innate conservatism characteristic of capitalists of all races.

This 'upper middle-class' minority—about 300,000 out of 180,000,000 in 1886—saw representative institutions as the only possible system which might satisfy its demands. It was not concerned with whether the British government was morally good or bad, but only with the fact that it was there—depriving educated Indians of their rightful jobs and profits.

If the business classes were largely conservative by nature, so too were the lawyers, who were nevertheless genuinely concerned with reform—a cautious reform in the English tradition.

After 1870, there was a considerable expansion in English education among what can only be described as lower middle-class elements, and, for them too, there was little chance of employment as the number of clerical jobs in government service or commerce was limited. It was upon these people that Westernization had a destructive effect. Being inadequately educated in an alien cultural tradition, they found themselves uneasy in their own. They became afraid of Western-style changes and saw no advantage for themselves in representative government, which they anticipated would favour the fully Westernized upper middle-class in preference to themselves.

The mass of the Indian people, on the other hand, had no such fears; there was little likelihood of too many half-educated peasants chasing too few jobs—on the contrary, they had not been educated at all. They were not uneasy within their cultural tradition. But they had a growing suspicion that their religion was in some sort of danger, not from the British but from the Westernized Indians. Most English-educated Indians, and especially those in Bengal, looked upon anything Indian —whether cultural or religious—as barbarous. They had become emotionally cut off from India and looked upon Hinduism with very much the same distaste as the British did. They sought to carry out reforms in Hindu society by legislative action. This was regarded as treasonable by orthodox Hindus and they cast about for ways to resist the challenge to their traditional order. The most obvious was to achieve political liberty, to get rid of the British, because it was the British and their influence on Western-educated Indians who constituted the main threat to the Hindu way of life. These Hindu nationalists did not believe in liberal democracy or in representative government, only in India for the Indians. They were not concerned with constitutional reforms, nor were their leaders interested in 'association' with British rule. The granting of representative institutions by the British was, in fact, something to be avoided, for such institutions would be operated by Westernized Indians, men who were no longer Hindus but bastard Englishmen. The only answer was revolution; the British must be thrown into the sea as soon as possible.

When political action and Hindu revivalism joined hands, they were to give Indian nationalism a mass appeal and to convert Congress from the narrow expression of minority self-interest into the apparent spokesman of the Indian people.

The first man to combine Hindu revivalism with active political agitation was Bal Gangadhar Tilak (1856–1920) who inspired an era of religious fanaticism and political violence which lasted until Gandhi introduced other methods in the early 1920s. But Tilak gave to Indian nationalism and in particular to Congress a sense of urgent militancy and an aim—that of *swaraj*, or independence—which was much more positive than the colonial self-government which was all the moderate leaders of his time had hoped for. Tilak can also be regarded as one of the founders of Pakistan, for he and the other revivalist Hindu leaders—and, later, Gandhi, who followed in their tradition—used the Hindu religion politically in such a way that Indian Muslims finally became convinced that it would be the *Hindus* who ruled if Congress ever came to power.

The fact that the new nationalist leaders used religion as a weapon bolstered the British government's belief that if representative institutions were granted to India this could only lead to religious discrimination. That India was made up of many races and that most of her people were backward and ignorant was not in itself necessarily an obstacle to the establishment of democratic institutions. The English, Scots and Welsh had learned to come together in a democratic state. The United States of America was an even better example of the unity of a people whose racial origins were of the most diverse. Nor had education much to do with it, for, in both Britain and America, the exercise of the vote had preceded universal education. In India, the obstacle was religious; the closest parallel is the conflict between Catholics and Protestants in Ireland, where the only solution found to the problem was partition of the country. In Ireland, too, there was violence because a religious minority feared that the government at Westminster would hand the country over to a religious majority.

In India, religious feeling was even deeper, for there religion permeates everyday life. The memory of a not too distant past also remained to inflame the Muslims, who before the British arrived had ruled India in all the glory of the Mughal empire. Under such emperors as Akbar, India had been powerful and prosperous and most of the important and valuable posts had been held by Muslims. But, with the coming of the British, Mughal power had collapsed and the Muslim community had failed to reap the advantages offered by British rule. The British seemed to be prejudiced against them and, quite wrongly, held them responsible for the Mutiny of 1857. Furthermore the Muslim community was very much concerned with religious schools and Muslims therefore did not respond favourably to Western-style education. It was not until they realized that Hindus were winning the best available jobs by reason of their Western education that the Muslims changed their attitude. Even then, they did so reluctantly and slowly.

The Muslims rapidly became conscious that they were being left behind, not only in the field of employment but also in constitutional demands. The activities of the Indian National Congress, which was composed of India's educated classes and therefore predominantly Hindu, only increased the Muslims' irritation and fear. Muslim leaders warned them that representative government on the British model could only lead to Hindu majority rule, and the growing use of Hindu revivalism for extremist political ends convinced them that Hindu rule could only result in religious discrimination. In the half-century before independence came Congress gave them little reason to change their minds.

In 1906, when it seemed inevitable that some form of representative institutions would be granted, the Muslim community formed its own political organization—the All-India Muslim League. This body never developed beyond the stage of a 'self-defence' association though it adapted its tactics to suit changing conditions. It was basically anti-democratic, but its attempts to protect the interests of Indian Muslims made it an unconscious ally of the British. The Muslim League's fight to prevent the setting-up of representative institutions, however, and Britain's anxiety to protect the legitimate rights of minorities, both served only to increase nationalist demands for independence.

The Indian National Congress blamed the British for inventing and encouraging Muslim fears of Hindu-majority rule for their own ends, but, at least as far as the legislators at Westminster were concerned, this was not the case. Although Congressmen believed the British to be engaged in deepening communal differences, on the principle of 'divide and rule', a Muslim League leader came nearer the truth when he said at the Round Table conference in 1931, 'It is the old maxim of "divide and rule". But there is a division of labour here. *We* divide and *you* rule.' With the growing strength of Congress, and the British apparently indifferent to their fears, Indian Muslims looked outside India to their co-religionists in other countries. They saw that they were not alone and, from this discovery, there grew the sense of separateness from the rest of India which led inescapably to partition.

In the meantime, the public voice of Congress still mouthed moderate constitutional demands. Its leaders ignored Muslim fears and Hindu revivalism alike. Self-government on the colonial model, such as existed in Canada and Australia, was their aim. But the moderate leaders were not only divorced from traditional India, they were also divorced from reality. Their reasonable demands neither impressed the government nor excited the public, and their failure to achieve results only antagonized the new class of young, partly Western-educated Indians who were suffering acutely from economic and social frustration. These men turned to Tilak as their leader and produced a new type of nationalism, a vernacular nationalism, which expressed its frustrations not in the English language nor in English political ideas but in the traditional vernaculars of the Hindu religion and of the Indian masses.

The strength of this new vernacular nationalism was first shown in 1905 when, for sound administrative reasons, the British decided to divide the vast province of Bengal. This plan provoked large popular demonstrations organized by the vernacular nationalists and joined later by the moderates. New methods of demonstration were used, including a boycott of British goods and the closing of Indian shops. Unlike Western political slogans, which were totally meaningless to the masses, these new methods of agitation were immediately understandable. Such methods, of course, demand men to organize them, and organizers appeared who were mostly members of secret terrorist societies. However, the success of these popular demonstrations proved to Congress that it would be possible to create a nationwide movement on a popular basis and, in 1908, Congress—which had the year before incorporated many of Tilak's slogans in its official policy—set up provincial branches for this very purpose. The boycott of British goods and the resulting demand for home manufactures incidentally convinced Indian businessmen that organized nationalism could mean profit for themselves, and an increasing number of them began to support Congress.

These changes, of course, did not receive the approval of the moderates, and the leadership of Congress was soon divided between moderates and extremists. After several years of strife and intrigue, many of the moderates left Congress. This did not mean, however, that the vernacular nationalists were left in control; other pressures were now at work which were to convert Congress into a body representing all the major interests of the Indian people. The leaders had to become such as would attract the support of all levels of the people.

The 1914-18 War supplied the stimulus for this new stage in the growth of Congress. The expansion of industry during the war increased the size both of the Indian business community and of the urban working class, although the war also produced shortages which pressed heavily upon the mass of the people. There was a short-lived co-operation between Muslims and Congress when Britain declared war on Turkey, the principal Islamic state, but the allied powers in Europe stated that one of the aims of the war was to guarantee self-determination for all peoples and this led to the British government promising India representative institutions after the war was over. This promise was not in fact made merely as part of the propaganda of war but as recognition of the growing mass support claimed by the Indian nationalist movement.

In the light of what could only be taken as concessions, as a weakening—however minor—of the British, it was all the more necessary that Congress should offer a united front. Fortunately, a leader appeared who was capable of rallying all the warring elements in Indian national-ism. This was M. K. Gandhi, a Hindu of the Vaisya caste—neither high nor low—who had been partly educated in England. Gandhi had not lost his Hindu personality because of his Western education. On the one hand, he could talk to Westernized nationalists in their own political language, and on the other, he could seem to be the expression of Hindu traditional values. Gandhi immediately saw the importance of a mass movement and that the weapon with which it might be created was the grievances—mainly economic—of the peasant. His first experiment was with peasant non-cooperation—a refusal to pay taxes—and peasant resistance of this type soon became an integral part of Congress action.

Congress organization now at last spread downwards to village level. After 1920, the lowest level Congress associations elected delegates to the next up, and so on to the level of the Provincial Congress Com-mittee. Theoretically at least, Congress was a democratic organization with clear links between the leaders and the lowliest member in the village. But this was not so in practice, for, if the principal aim of independence was to be pursued, it was necessary that the supreme executive body of Congress—the All-India Congress Committee—should have sufficient authority to overrule sectional interests. Congress was organized in such a way that there were distinct channels by which that authority could send its instructions down to the lowest level.

Mass support, however, brought its own problems because, if that support was to be held, it was necessary for Congress to champion mass demands. These were often in conflict with the demands of other groups within Congress, groups which generally speaking were more articulate than the masses. There was, therefore, constant disagreement on strategy and tactics, on programmes, and on ultimate goals. The Congress leadership was in fact compelled, during lulls between mass demonstrations, to spend more energy and ingenuity on reconciling the conflicting interests of Congress members than it did on fighting the British. If the Second World War had not come along when it did, bringing independence actually within sight, it is not altogether im-probable that Congress might have collapsed under the pressure of its parts.

That Congress did manage to present a united front to the British was due, in the main, to three things. Firstly, it used the simple

expedient of pointing to British rule as the primary source of everybody's grievances, however much those grievances might contradict
each other. Secondly, there was the figure of Gandhi—the great
indispensable—who was, for the masses, the image of Indian nationalism and, for the rest of Congress's sectional interests, the image of that
mass support without which they believed they had no hope of success.
The third source of unity, without which even Gandhi would have
been ineffective, was the growing strength of Congress organization
and propaganda.

Though, after 1920, the face of nationalism in India was very different from the one it had shown before, the old forces occasionally in
new disguises were still there, sometimes overtly, sometimes subtly
distorting the aims of the leaders. But these leaders, too, were very
different from those who had preceded them. The new men were to
face, and in the end out-face, not the British in India—for they, as the
years went by, played a progressively lesser role—but the legislators in
Westminster. The struggle was no longer to be waged in the obscurity
with which the nineteenth century and Britain's international prestige
had cloaked India. It was now to take place under the bright lights of a
growing world interest. Nor was it to be expressed in terms of a revolutionary violence directed at throwing the British into the sea. It was
to be a much more subtle and perhaps, in the long run, a more dangerous affair for India herself. Congress, under the leadership of Gandhi,
chose to assault not the military power of the British in India, but the
conscience of the British people, to try to make them so ashamed of
what they were doing that they would voluntarily give up their Indian
empire. It was perhaps the most improbable strategy that has ever been
offered to a nationalist movement—and it seemed to work. Why it
did so will be made clear as the events of the last years of British India
unfold.

5 The People

Statesmen, politicians, and historians often refer in their speeches and
writings to 'the people' as if this was some homogeneous mass possessed
of one voice proclaiming the desires of the collective will, and one pair
of feet marching inexorably towards one collective goal. Essentially,

however, no politicians and very few historians believe that 'the people' have much to do with the making of history. They are the instrument on which great men play the themes of their greatness, or the backcloth of the stage on which the hero declaims his dramatic role. But very little more. In the case of historians, this attitude partly results from the difficulty of analysing the motivations of all the diverse elements that make up a 'people', and partly from the even greater difficulty of assessing the importance of these motivations in the pattern of history.

People, however, do exert immense pressure upon the course of events. In the story of the last years of British India, the people of both Britain and India played a decisive though ill-defined and often un-recognized part. In the present century, the masses have come to influence events in a very special way for which there is little or no historical precedent. Generally speaking, before our own times authority maintained a studied indifference to the interests of the people as long as they remained quiet. One of the first concerns of the success-ful revolutionary who had made use of the people and their grievances to precipitate change was to neutralize the violence he had himself incited, to cut the people out of the calculations of politics while leav-ing them in its vocabulary. But, as the twentieth century dawned, the place where the desires of the masses could be expressed changed from the barricades to the halls of parliament. The masses became, in fact, respectable, part of the system of government, and authority could no longer rely on their indifference. In Britain, the strengthening voice of the working classes demanded a better standard of living, even at the expense of disposing of an empire, and in 1947 a 'people's government' in Britain finally had to make a choice—between hanging on to India or getting out. The choice it made was the choice of the British people. That choice was not, however, made consciously; there was no mass expression of popular opinion about India's freedom, for the majority of the British people were indifferent to the issue. But there were other issues about which they had positive, even passionate, hopes, and any attempt to retain India would have prejudiced their fulfilment. The government, in effect, had no choice of its own and, even if the Con-servative party had been in power, it too would have been forced to recognize the fact. The British people ceased to be interested in the British empire, in its glories, responsibilities, virtues or vices, because they were concerned with their own welfare above all others and were at last in a position to demand that their wishes be given priority.

The people of India, too, had begun to express themselves but they were denied the respectable, the parliamentary, means of doing so. There was no outlet for their opinions but agitation. In Britain, the working classes had sought a means of demanding the solution of their economic grievances, and they had found it already present in the British political system. In India, after 1920, the masses turned to Congress. On the surface, this seems both simple and natural. It had its parallels in Europe and America. There have been peasant revolts and industrial upheavals throughout history—all with sound economic bases. But the parallels are not exact. In Europe, the working class achieved entry into the political system because the individuals who made up that class had some identity of interests, and there was nothing in the social order, or in their religion, to inhibit them from organizing themselves to express those interests. In India, the situation was very different. There the social order was divisive, seeking to separate each man from all except those inside his own group. The Hindu religion sanctified the existing social order by saying that a man's position in it —the caste to which he belonged—was fixed irrevocably by forces outside his control, or that of anyone else. Acceptance, not social action, was, and to an alarming extent still is, the basis of Indian society. It was Gandhi, with the success of his first civil disobedience campaigns, who showed the peasant that economic grievances could be remedied by action. In doing this, he not only gave Congress the means with which to fight the British but opened a crack in the armour of the Hindu social order.

The two peoples—of Britain and India—had a profound effect upon the forces which controlled their destiny, and in at least one sphere, they were unconscious allies. Both were engaged in a struggle against the same privileged class, the British who ruled in Britain and who also ruled in India. From the British people's point of view, the Indian empire ceased to exist because they became indifferent to its symbolic image. As long as they remained without a voice in their own destiny, the British people accepted the glory of an empire on which the sun never set and from the possession of which some glamour rubbed off upon their shabby lives. But when they saw, or believed they saw, that its very existence was a brake upon their own progress, they became indifferent to its mystique and called for its abandonment, disguising their self-interest under the cloak of democratic slogans. In India, the British had continued to rule only by consent. In the case of the articulate classes, this had been the consent of respect; for the mass of the people, it was the consent of indifference. If man's position was ordained by the gods, what did it matter who ruled? But the respect of the Indian middle class did not survive the end of the First World War, and in the twenty years that followed, the masses ceased to be indifferent. As the British people stopped being interested in their empire, the people of India began to be conscious of their country, and came to believe that their economic problems did not result from the will of the gods but from the policy of the British.

PART TWO

The Struggle

'NON-VIOLENCE . . . does not
mean submission to the will of
the evildoer. . . . It means the
putting of one's whole soul
against the will of the tyrant.'
M. K. Gandhi

'WE HAVE to live in the present.'
Subhas Chandra Bose

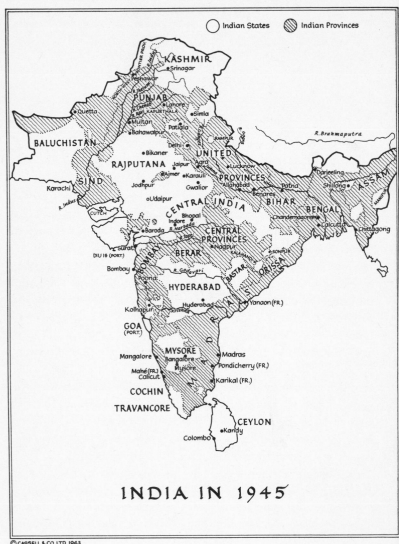

INDIA IN 1945

1 For Moral Effect

The war that broke out in Europe in August 1914 brought about a
truce in nationalist agitation against the British; there was in fact an
outburst of enthusiasm which seems today, in the light of subsequent
events, almost incomprehensible. But many nationalists thought that
helping the British would result in a victory which might bring some
tangible reward. This belief was encouraged by the allied statesmen's
insistence that the war was being fought to make the world safe for
democracy, and self-determination for all peoples was the battle cry;
unfortunately, the Indian nationalists were naïve enough to believe this
applied to them. At that time, nationalist opinion was directed towards
achieving self-government within the British empire and this, they
thought, was comparatively little to ask. Recruits flocked to the army
—some 1,200,000 volunteered—and there were spontaneous contribu-
tions to war loans and the like. The British reduced their garrison in
India to 15,000 men, and many British administrators going off to
fight handed over their jobs to Indian subordinates. In this way, two of
the nationalist demands—the reduction of the 'army of occupation'
and more, higher posts for Indians—were unintentionally granted.

But, like everyone else, Indians believed the war would soon be
over and, when it dragged on, popular enthusiasm waned. This was
partly due to the government's inability to make use of its newly found
popularity. The British government, intent only upon governing
whether Indians liked it or not, was unable to channel enthusiasm into
productive endeavour. Recruiting declined, and money was no longer
freely lent. The British government in India, being composed mainly
of men with no experience of, and little inclination to learn, the
mechanics of modern government, had never been particularly

efficient. It could rule by thumb but it was not very good at organization. Before 1914, there had been a number of serious administrative breakdowns; the requirements of war intensified inefficiency, and soon the Indian army in Mesopotamia found its supply lines from India in hopeless chaos. The government was compelled to impose restrictions and pressures upon Indian businessmen which soon convinced them that they should—in the interests of their own business—support the nationalist movement. Further, the war against Turkey—whose ruler was the Caliph of Islam—seriously disturbed Indian Muslims, and in 1916, Tilak, who had modified his more revivalist views, was able to persuade the Muslim League to join Congress in the 'Lucknow Pact'. The success of Tilak also eliminated the influence of the moderates in the nationalist movement and certainly made it easier for Gandhi to change the direction of the movement when he succeeded Tilak in 1920.

The Lucknow Pact brought considerable nationalist activity throughout India, and the government in London, worried about the course of the war in Europe as Russia seemed about to collapse, decided that some holding action must be taken. Obviously, repression was out of the question—there were insufficient British troops available for the job. A carrot must be substituted for the stick. There was ample excuse for London to interfere in the Indian government's affairs – a government which, in the words of E. S. Montagu, secretary of state for India, had proved itself 'too wooden, too iron, too inelastic, too antediluvian, to be of any use for . . . modern purposes'. This speech naturally pleased Indian nationalists who had been saying the same thing for some time.

When Montagu arrived in India in October 1917 to see for himself, he was received by some nationalists almost as a liberator. It was the first time that any member of a British government had gone to India to find out the opinions of Indians themselves. The result of the secretary of state's inquiry was published under the title of 'Report on Indian Constitutional Reforms' in the summer of 1918. This document has been overshadowed by the failure of the reforms it advocated, but it enshrined a new and quite revolutionary idea—that it was, in the words of Gladstone, 'liberty alone which fits men for liberty'. For the first time, the flatulent rhetoric of Macaulay was pushed aside and a declaration of faith in the ability of the Indian people to operate responsible self-government was explicitly stated. The report, in fact, rejected the strictures Lord Morley had made at the time of the 1909 reforms and expressed a belief that parliamentary government could work in India. This change of attitude stemmed firstly from the natural belief that liberal democracy, as practised in Britain, was the best of all forms of government (and it had already proved impossible to convince Indian nationalists that there might be a better), and secondly from the fact that parliamentary government was what the nationalists were asking for. If a carrot was to be used, there was no doubt that it had to be a real one.

Unfortunately, fine phrases do not of themselves create a workable system. There remained still the problem of minorities and, in particular, the fear of the Muslims that representative government would mean Hindu domination. In India, these fears had to some extent been allayed by the Lucknow Pact—which had necessitated concessions by both sides—in which Congress had acquiesced to the establishment of separate electorates for Muslims. Britain's attitude, however, was complicated by that often misunderstood love of the underdog which is characteristic of the British approach to politics. In spite of the Lucknow Pact many British statesmen firmly believed that a Hindu majority *would* discriminate against smaller groups if it had the opportunity and they consequently sought to give constitutional protection to these groups. In his report, Montagu felt himself justified in keeping separate electorates, but only for the largest minorities—the Muslims and Sikhs. When, however, his Act passed through the British parliament in 1919, separate representation was extended to Indian Christians, Anglo-Indians (Eurasians), and Europeans. These additions almost certainly resulted from members of the Indian Civil Service lobbying powerful interests in Britain. By continuing the principle of separate electorates, the administration hoped to keep the nationalist movement divided and to maintain its own assertion that the Indian National Congress was *not* representative of the wishes of all the Indian people. When the final Act was promulgated, the government of India was able to relax in the knowledge that the actual effect of the reforms would be to leave authority where it had always been—in the hands of the British.

The major change brought in by these reforms was embodied in the principle of 'dyarchy', the division of powers, encumbered rather than supported by a delicate system of checks and balances. The centra l executive remained responsible to no one but the secretary of state i n London, but legislation was in theory to be the function of a new central assembly and a council of state, both with elected majorities but including also an 'official' or nominated bloc. Any legislative authority which these bodies might have, however, was rendered nugatory by the fact that such legislation as they might refuse to pass could still be 'certified' by the viceroy and thus become law. The provinces were also to have legislative councils, and certain responsibilities were to be assigned from the Centre to provincial control. This devolution covered both finance and administration and in some measure the provinces became self-governing, though real power—in revenue legislation and the control of the armed forces—remained at the Centre. Administration at the provincial level was divided into two areas; 'reserved' subjects, including finance, justice and the police, remained under the control of the governor, while the 'transferred' subjects, such as education and public health, were entrusted to ministers responsible to the legislative council. The franchise was restricted by a sliding scale of property qualifications, which meant that the number who could vote in provincial council elections was over five million, in elections for the central legislative assembly nearly one million, and in the case of the council of state a select group of some seventeen thousand. The population of India at that time was over three hundred million.

The nationalists, however, were divided over these reforms. Some— though not very many—welcomed them as 'the Magna Carta' of India but the majority believed that they did not go nearly far enough. One of those who thought the changes indicated a new British attitude to India was Mahatma Gandhi, but events were soon to destroy his faith in the solemn pledges and promises of the British government.

The period between Montagu's visit and the actual passing of the Act had witnessed events in India which have a parallel only in the after effects of the Mutiny of 1857. The government of India had begun to feel itself menaced by revolutionary activity, though in fact this illusion was only the product of efficient nationalist propaganda. Nevertheless, the government felt itself handicapped by the existing security regulations, and set up a committee under Mr Justice Rowlatt to inquire into what it called 'criminal conspiracies', that is, terrorist activities. The Rowlatt report was published shortly after the appearance of the Montagu–Chelmsford report, and together they made rather odd reading. On the one hand, the British at Westminster were envisaging some delegation of powers, while on the other, the British in Delhi were reinforcing their authority with all the apparatus of the police state—trial of political cases without jury, and the weapon of summary internment. Naturally, Indians saw this as giving with one hand and slapping down with the other.

The end of the war had brought back the old administrators—sullen with the prospect of slow promotion after the excitements of war, but determined to treat the war as merely an interlude in the happy superiority of British life in India. To Indians, no longer convinced of their inferior position, it seemed that the worst features of the British occupation came back with the old administrators, and that the Sedition Acts which followed the Rowlatt report were to usher in a new period of repression. To the apprehensions of the educated classes was now added a further dimension of unrest, this time amongst those who had previously been unaffected by the nationalist struggle.

The influenza epidemic which raged in Europe in 1918 had swept across India and resulted in some twelve million deaths. In 1918, too, there had been a poor harvest and a consequent rapid rise in prices. Indian soldiers, who had been rather hastily demobilized for fear that they might use their weapons against their officers, had taken their grievances back to the villages. In the cities, despite enormous profits made by industrialists both British and Indian, wages were kept low while the conditions under which the workers lived became progressively worse.

Feelings of unease produced the semblance of a united front against the government. Among the peasants, no real sense of the national struggle as such ever appeared. To this day, they form an inert mass, shifted sometimes into activity by a man capable of giving direction to inchoate feelings of oppression. Such a man was Mohandas Karamchand Gandhi, who had returned to India from South Africa in 1915. As late as July 1918 he was still a moderate, believing that the achievement of equal partnership within the empire would constitute 'freedom'. He even took part in recruiting campaigns for the Indian Army, but the end of the war and the return of old, familiar faces to the administration convinced him that India had been tricked into giving her support to Britain's war by specious and empty promises. Furthermore, like many other Indians, he thought that President Wilson really believed in self-determination for all and assumed that the only great non-imperial power in the world would look with sympathy upon India's aspirations. Unfortunately, the allies never intended self-determination to refer to anyone outside Europe, where the splitting up of Austro-Hungary demanded some high-flown justification.

Under Gandhi's leadership, Congress now began a campaign against the so-called Rowlatt Acts. Their straightforward provisions were distorted by extensive propaganda throughout the countryside into the most ogreish of interferences in the life of the people. Rumours were spread that under one provision the Acts required inspection of a man and a woman before marriage, and that under another they restricted to two the number of plough-bullocks a peasant could own. Once again, Tilak's belief, that any lie was justified if it helped the national struggle, was to gain political currency. Gandhi added to the revolutionary movement two singular techniques, both essentially derived from the Hindu traditional conceptions of *Satyagraha*, the vow to hold to the truth, and *Ahimsa*, the doing of no harm. From these he produced the idea of passive resistance and its instrument, the *hartal*, a day of fast and suspension of business which was the equivalent of a strike in an industrial society but at the same time a traditional Hindu method of protest. The use of these ancient weapons for modern ends was Gandhi's prime contribution to the technique of revolution.

In March and April 1919, the pressures of unemployment and high prices, the return of soldiers to the insecurity of their former lives, and the renewed arrogance of returning officials, precipitated outbursts of popular indignation, very few of which were the products of extremist organization. Rioting was almost entirely confined to the Punjab and western India, and the mobs who attacked isolated Europeans and government buildings did not appear to have either leaders or specific objectives. Most of the rioting in Delhi, Lahore, Amritsar and elsewhere, was characterized by racial hatred. The government arrested Gandhi on his way to the Punjab in April, and this provoked a riot in the mill town of Ahmadabad, where he was well known and loved. He was released and helped to restore order.

On 15 April, martial law was declared in the Punjab in consequence of a deed which became one of the great rallying cries of Indian nationalism. Amritsar, a city of some 300,000 inhabitants and the chief religious centre of the Sikhs, stands about 250 miles north-west of Delhi. There, on 10 April, two nationalist leaders were arrested and deported. A large crowd attempted to enter the European cantonment and, on being turned away, began rioting in the city. Two banks were attacked, railway stations set on fire, four Europeans were murdered and others attacked, including a woman missionary who was left for dead. The military, under one General Dyer, restored order and all public meetings and assemblies were declared illegal. Nevertheless, on 13 April a meeting gathered in a large enclosed space known as the Jallianwalla Bagh. When he heard of this, General Dyer went person-ally to the spot with ninety Gurkha and Baluchi soldiers and two armoured cars, with which he blocked the only exit. Then, without warning, he ordered his men to open fire on the densely packed crowd, and, on his own admission, fired 1,605 rounds before he withdrew, ordering the armoured cars to remain and prevent anyone from leaving or entering the Bagh. Official figures gave 379 dead and 1,200 wounded. Dyer's action was approved by the provincial government. The following day, a mob rioting and burning at another spot was bombed and machine-gunned from aircraft. On 15 April martial law was declared and not lifted until 9 June. During this period, Indians were forced to walk on all fours past the spot where the woman missionary had been attacked, and, according to the report of the Hunter Commission which inquired into the disturbances, public floggings were ordered for such minor offences as 'the contravention of the curfew order, failure to salaam to a commissioned officer, for disrespect to a European, for taking a commandeered car without leave, or refusal to sell milk, and for similar contraventions.'

The commission of inquiry from whose report this quotation is taken was set up in October 1919 with four British and four Indian members. Three of the British were members of the civil service, and the Indians were men of moderate opinion. All criticized the actions of General Dyer—but in such mild phrases as 'unfortunate' and 'injudi-cious'. The Indian belief that the old repressive ways were again to be imposed was reinforced by General Dyer's testimony, for he made it clear in his evidence that he had gone down to the Jallianwalla Bagh with the intention of setting a ferocious example to the rest of India.

'I fired and continued to fire until the crowd dispersed, and I consider this is the least amount of firing which would produce the necessary moral and widespread effect it was my duty to produce if I was to justify my action. If more troops had been at hand, the casualties would have been greater in proportion. It was no longer a question of merely dispersing the crowd, but one of producing a sufficient moral effect from a military point of view not only on those who were present, but more especially throughout the Punjab.'

Though the government of India vehemently dissociated itself from such a policy of intimidation, Dyer was expressing the general opinion of most of the civil and military in India. Dyer was removed from his command, but his actions and presumably his motives were supported by a large section of the British press as well as by members of parliament and others, and a sum of £26,000 was subscribed as a testimonial for this fine example of a gallant British soldier. It is not difficult to understand the very special position that the massacre of Amritsar holds in the minds of Indians. In British–Indian relations, it was a turning point more decisive even than the Mutiny. Henceforth, the struggle was to permit of little compromise, and the good faith of British concessions was always to be in doubt.

The affair at the Jallianwalla Bagh certainly had 'a moral effect', particularly upon Gandhi. For him, there was now no possibility of compromise with the British and he declared that 'co-operation in any shape or form with this satanic government is sinful'. The last years of British India were ushered in to the sound of General Dyer's guns.

2 Non-cooperation

Gandhi's reaction to government oppression was essentially emotional. The affair at the Jallianwalla Bagh quite rightly assaulted his conscience. His response was to develop a system that might be called 'conscience in action' and, because it was successful, Congress never became a truly revolutionary movement; Gandhi remained round its neck like the Ancient Mariner's albatross inhibiting its actions, dividing its purpose, confusing the genuine revolutionaries and ultimately ensuring the partition of India. The explanation of the latter is simple. Gandhi had no liking for politics, though of necessity many of his ideas were expressed in political terms. He was a religious reformer whose main pre-occupation was with changing the Hindu social order. British government, in his opinion, was not only immoral but alien and he believed that reform could only be brought about with the support of an Indian administration. He had no faith in Western liberal democracy, an extremely nebulous view of the nature of modern government, and very little awareness of the mainsprings of economic life. But he was a man who could exercise almost hypnotic influence upon the most diverse of characters, and his main effect on them was to drain away any revolutionary fervour they might have had.

Gandhi chose his lieutenants with great care, for, despite his mystical approach to life, he was an unerringly shrewd judge of men and events. To organize Congress into an efficient and militant machine for his reformist purposes, he chose a man of peasant stock, who, although he was Western-educated, was still near enough to the mass of the Indian people to be accepted by them. This was Vallabhbhai Patel, who represented a new type of nationalist—the party organizer—and whose work in welding Congress into a whole ensured that when independence finally came it would stand the strain of transition from nationalist movement to political party. The other leader was Jawaharlal Nehru, a Harrow-educated aristocrat with Fabian-socialist ideas. Nehru was valuable because he was a Brahmin who at the same time was 'progressive' in a Western sense and could rally the more modernist young men behind him. Gandhi's choice was astute. Patel was not a thinker but a worker. Nehru was a thinker but not really a man of decisive action. The British feared Nehru because of his background and his socialism but they made the mistake of thinking he was an extremist. Gandhi knew better and, though Nehru often criticized Gandhi for his reactionary ways, he never broke away from him into genuine revolutionary activity. With these two men behind him, Gandhi could carry on with his great experiment in mass action. Only one outstanding personality took a different and violent path, and, in a sense, India owes more to him than to any other man—even although he seemed to be a failure. In the period between the wars, although he became president of Congress, his influence was small. It was only after the outbreak of war with Japan in 1941 that the drama of Subhas Chandra Bose was to begin.

In 1920, India was in a ferment. Indian Muslims were angry over the terms of the peace treaty with Turkey, and Gandhi, now the dominant figure in Congress, sought to create out of this anger a united front against the British. The instruments that Gandhi chose were 'non-cooperation' and 'civil disobedience'. For his first act of non-cooperation, Gandhi tried to persuade Congress to boycott the elections under the new constitution. There were, however, plenty of moderate nationalists—now established in a new Liberal party—willing to stand for office so the boycott proved to the the first stage not so much of 'non-cooperation' as of positive assistance to the British administrators in India. Nothing could be better from their point of view than that the new assemblies should consist of men dedicated to slow constitutional advance. From the Congress viewpoint, the boycott was an utter failure. In disgust a number of Congressmen, lead by C. R. Das and Pandit Motilal Nehru, formed a new *Swaraj* (freedom) party within Congress and fought the 1925 elections.

Gandhi's first exercise in 'civil disobedience', though successful, soon degenerated into violence and he called off the campaign. The violence however, could not be called off and after a particularly ferocious rebellion by Muslim peasants in South India, directed not against the government but against Hindus, the fragile thread of self-interest joining Hindus and Muslims snapped. Extremists from both sides now began to organize large-scale rioting, and, from 1922 onwards, bloody conflicts between Hindus and Muslims became a regular feature of Indian life. Gandhi antagonized Congress by publicly confessing the failure of the civil disobedience movement and he was only preserved from utter defeat by being arrested by the British. He was sentenced to six years imprisonment, but was released on grounds of ill-health after serving only one.

Gandhi's contribution to the nationalist movement after his release was almost entirely confined to praying and advocating the virtues of hand-spinning. Though the latter was given a certain propaganda value by the boycott of foreign cloth and the weaving of home-spun as a sort of nationalist uniform, it was essentially an example of Gandhi's *naïveté* about economics. Certainly it had little value in the struggle against the British when Gandhi insisted that one of the qualifications for membership of Congress would be proof of spinning a fixed quota of yarn. Many thought Gandhi's preoccupation with spinning ludicrous. As the great Bengali poet, Rabindranath Tagore, replied when Gandhi advised him to use the spinning wheel for half an hour a day. 'Why not eight and a half hours if it will help the country?'

The British felt that they had little to fear from Gandhi himself, for they soon recognized him for what he was—an anti-Western reformer. As long as Gandhi was in control of Congress, they knew they had an ally. As long as civil disobedience remained non-violent, it did not greatly worry the government. Who was hurt by non-cooperation anyway? Only the Indians. Gandhi's whole aim was to minimize violence; the government's was the same. They were still capable of suppressing a few outbreaks of small-scale violence, but if once Gandhi ceased to dominate Congress, the machine he had built up might well be used by more dynamic and violent people. A full-scale rebellion could not be crushed. So the government obliged Gandhi by treating him with considerable respect—jailing him occasionally to keep up appearances—while they took much more positive action against terrorists and those Western-style revolutionaries whom they really feared.

The *Swaraj* party, which won a number of seats in the elections of 1925, soon found itself corrupted by close association with the administration, and some of its members even became prepared to accept office. This was a long way from the party's original intention of making government impossible by holding up legislation. In 1926 the leading *Swarajists* left the assemblies. Congress, in Gandhi's words, was 'passing through midnight gloom'.

Attempts to embarrass the British from within the assemblies had failed. Civil disobedience had been called off when it reached the edges of rebellion. Gandhi, who had sought to blackmail the British through an assault on their consciences, had been repulsed. 'An Englishman,' he had once told an English friend, 'never respects you until you stand up to him. Then he begins to like you. He is afraid of nothing physical, but he is very mortally afraid of his own conscience if you ever appeal to it and show him to be in the wrong. He does not like to be rebuked for wrong doing at first; but he will think it over and it will get hold of him and hurt him till he does something to put it right.' In this, as in many of his other beliefs, Gandhi was wrong. In India, the moral content of British rule could not be reached by blackmail, for it had become petrified into a system. In Britain, there was merely indifference. In fact, the conscience of the British would have been much more quickly aroused if there had been widespread rebellion in India and a consequent attempt to suppress it. Gandhi and his methods were not understood. All that was recognized was that he was harmless.

In November 1927, the *Times of India* wrote of the 'completeness of the Congress collapse, the utter futility of the Congress creed, and a total absence among Congress supporters of a single responsible political idea'. And this seemed to be the truth.

3 Marking Time

The continuance of Hindu–Muslim conflict gave what the nationalists believed to be a further proof that religious antagonisms were being used by the government for its own ends. The viceroy, Lord Irwin, in his address to the legislative assembly in August 1927, warned Indians that self-government could only lead to civil war. That the viceroy further suggested calling a conference in an attempt to bring Hindus and Muslims together, seemed only a Machiavellian ruse. A conference was held but it produced nothing more than admirable sentiments. Congress appealed for toleration and, in the streets of the cities, Hindus and Muslims went on murdering each other.

But other events were in the air. The Act of 1919 had provided for a commission of inquiry after ten years to review the working of the Act. In November 1927, the commission arrived in India. The date had been brought forward primarily because it seemed possible that a Labour government might be in office in 1929, and at least one member of the Conservative cabinet actually believed that the Labour party meant what it said about India's right to self-government. Far better, thought Lord Birkenhead, the secretary of state for India, to set up the commission early and give the impression that the Conservatives too were interested in India, so interested as to be prepared to bring forward the date by nearly two years. It was this same Birkenhead who had been the only member of the cabinet to oppose the reform of 1919, and he was determined that there would be no more if he could help it. So that the commission could be kept as much on his side as possible, it had to consist of members of the British parliament. The Labour party co-operated by choosing only obscure back benchers as their representatives. But one of these was a certain Clement Attlee, and his experiences were to have direct effect on the decisions he took nearly twenty years later as prime minister. The chairman of the commission was Sir John Simon, a lawyer delighting—if such a warm attitude can be attributed to such a cold temperament—in the passionless world of legal precedent. He was an ideal choice, for it was unlikely that even the vaguest suggestion of any sort of radical view would ever cross his mind.

The British in India were delighted at the all-British composition of the commission. Indians, on the other hand, held it to be racial discrimination. It seems probable that senior British officials hoped the exclusion of Indians would provoke criticism from the Hindu Congress, to which Muslims would react by supporting the commission, and that in turn, Congress fears of Muslim influence would prevent Congress from boycotting it. If this was indeed so, it merely confirms how little the administration understood the immense change that had taken place in Indian nationalism since 1919.

Gandhi remained quiet but Congress did not, for it viewed the commission as an insult that could be used to revive Congress purpose once again. The younger Nehru put forward a number of resolutions in the Madras session of Congress, and all of them were passed including one which called, not for dominion status but for independence. Nehru, however, suspected that his resolutions were accepted because they were not understood, and he was probably right. In the meanwhile, virtually all shades of Indian opinion had united against the commission. The Muslim League, however, was divided, and one group headed by M. A. Jinnah supported a Congress decision to boycott the commission. 'Jallianwalla Bagh was physical butchery,' he said. 'The Simon Commission is the butchery of our soul.'

The government of India, now seeking some way to appease Indian opinion, suggested that the commission should associate itself with a body of representatives from the Indian legislative assemblies. The London *Times* thought this too generous, and even Attlee apparently thought it perfectly reasonable. The nationalists rejected it. But in the first two months of its visit, the commission was met by only a rather half-hearted boycott, and a less refrigerated personality than Simon might have broken it with a little display of human warmth. He had not, however, been chosen to be friendly to Indians. He even believed that the government of India was hostile to him, as it did not prevent such demonstrations as there were. However, this calm did not last and demonstrations increased. A time bomb was set off in a train when the commission arrived in Bombay, and the police began to act against demonstrators. In one scuffle a veteran nationalist, Lala Lajpat Rai, who was already fatally ill, received a blow and died soon afterwards.

The commission continued its 'blood-red progress', as Gandhi described it, throughout India, understanding little of what they saw. Congress published a report calling for immediate dominion status and outlining, in considerable detail, the sort of constitution the nationalists required. The report was submitted to an All-Party conference in August 1928 and immediately resulted in a schism. Jawaharlal Nehru and his friends would not vote for it as it would commit them to the demand for dominion status. The report's attempt to solve the 'communal' problem only exacerbated it, and the Muslims now closed their ranks, demanding the continuance of separate electorates and a federal constitution in which Muslim-majority areas would have complete autonomy.

Gandhi had viewed the report as the instrument of an 'honourable compromise' with the British, yet the instrument had broken even before it could be used. But once again the character of the younger Nehru displayed its weakness. Under pressure from Gandhi, he agreed to wait and see if the British would accept the report by the end of 1929. If they did not, then would be the time to organize civil disobedience. This was a tactical error, for it served a warning upon the government of India without having any effect upon the government in London. The Muslim League also took it as a warning. Jinnah now became the dominant figure in the League and the road to the partition of India opened up. 'This,' said Jinnah, 'is the parting of the ways,' and he was right. Hindu-Muslim conflict was to continue to the very end and its legacy still divides India and Pakistan today.

Lord Irwin, the viceroy at that time, was a deeply religious man who reacted emotionally to what he believed to be the essentially moral content of Gandhi's ideas. He was prepared to meet him—'taking tea with treason', as it was described—and to attempt to discuss issues with him. Gandhi, however, made the mistake of thinking that Irwin's religion would inhibit him from behaving as the head of an administration responsible only to the British parliament. Irwin was the prisoner of the system and, in the final analysis, basically without real power of decision. Nevertheless, Irwin's reasonableness convinced Gandhi that his own methods were right. The government, however, believed that Gandhi was no longer in control of the nationalist movement. It therefore prepared itself for the coming battle. The situation was in fact growing more dangerous every day and was worsened by considerable industrial unrest behind which the government believed there was communist influence. The government of India arrested a number of communists, including two Englishmen, and after a series of dubious legal manoeuvres designed to ensure that the men would be convicted, brought them to trial. The arrest of the communist leaders, however, made little difference to the organization of terrorism which was in progress, and the government was in fact faced with a revolutionary conspiracy, though it was not as yet unduly alarmed. But it made its preparations and kept a watchful eye, through informers and spies, on the various nationalist organizations.

Irwin had learned that the key to an evolutionary approach to Indian self-government was Gandhi, and that he should make some approach to strengthen Gandhi's position. The iron hand was not to be put aside—on the contrary, it was to be displayed; but a velvet glove was needed to hide its nakedness. Irwin's first step was to make a statement unprecedented in viceregal history. He stated that he had a 'double duty', that is, to carry on the king's government and to serve as an intermediary between India and Britain. He saw no incongruity in saying this. Irwin suggested to London that Indians should be associated in some way with the discussions on the Simon report, and that a declaration should be made that dominion status for India was also the goal of the British. London accepted the principle of association but was not prepared to make any statement about dominion status. In May 1928, Birkenhead made it quite clear to Irwin that the government was not prepared to commit itself to any such pledge.

In the summer of 1929, the second Labour government in Britain's history took office under Ramsay Macdonald. Shortly before taking office, the new prime minister had declared 'I hope that within a period of months rather than years there will be a new dominion added to the Commonwealth of our Nations, a dominion which will find self-respect as an equal within the Commonwealth. I refer to India'. Now everything seemed set for Indian self-government. Labour leaders had actually talked of it. In October 1929, Lord Irwin reiterated in a rather vaguely worded announcement that dominion status was indeed the goal. Trust between Indians and the British, which had been thought irrevocably dead, now, like some Lazarus, revived. Gandhi praised Irwin's sincerity and called for a positive response. Irwin called a conference of various nationalist leaders, including Jinnah. It met on the same morning as a bomb destroyed part of the viceregal train. Gandhi stated that Congress members were there only on the assurance that a conference would be called to frame a dominion constitution. Irwin was not empowered to promise this. Congress leaders went away, realizing at last that the rhetoric of politicians out of office bears little resemblance to their policy when they achieve it. As one Congress leader had said even before the Labour government took office, 'first we believed in the British officials as a whole; then in higher officials; then in the viceroy; then in the British government; then parliament; then in the Labour party. All have failed. Now we can only believe in our own efforts'.

4 Stage Lightning and Teapot Thunder

Congress decided to have nothing to do with the so-called Round Table conference which the British Labour government had decided to summon in 1930. It now demanded independence without any qualification of dominion status and decided upon a campaign of civil disobedience, but these resolutions were passed in face of considerable opposition which was overcome only by the still immense prestige of Gandhi. 'I have but followed the Inner Voices,' he proclaimed, and there were none authoritative enough to question whether he had heard the Voices aright. The real questioning took the form of continued terrorist activity—which frightened Congress more than the government.

On 26 January 1930, at gatherings throughout India, the Congress flag was unfurled and a pledge of independence taken. Generally speaking, this symbolic act was greeted with no great enthusiasm. One distinguished Indian civil servant described the whole business as 'stage lightning and teapot thunder' and he was not far wrong.

Gandhi had thought long about the nature of the first act of civil disobedience. He had learned that, to rouse the masses, it was necessary to use some symbol they could easily recognize. There was no point in slogans about dominion status, because the masses had no idea of what that was. Gandhi hit upon the salt tax. The production of salt was a government monopoly and, in 1930, half the retail price of salt represented tax. Everybody used salt, everybody paid the tax. Why not incite the masses to break the monopoly by making their own salt? Gandhi sent a letter to the viceroy informing him that, if by 11 March he had not accepted eleven proposals, Gandhi himself would break the salt laws. Irwin refused to receive such an ultimatum. On 12 March, Gandhi marched off from Ahmadabad to the sea, expecting to be arrested on the way. But the government of India decided to try non-cooperation itself and instructed the provincial governments not to arrest Gandhi. If the law *was* broken, only Gandhi's lieutenants were to be arrested and the Mahatma himself was to be denied martyrdom. Finally, Gandhi reached the sea, ceremonially made his uneatable salt— and broke the law. The act received great publicity abroad, especially in America where it appeared to have overtones of the Boston Tea Party. The government of India, however, had not sent a single policeman to watch this symbolic act. On the same day, salt was made at about five thousand meetings throughout India; Congress gave five million as the official number of those involved, but anything in India can draw a crowd and it is certain that the majority of those who attended the ceremonies did so as casual onlookers.

The government went on quietly arresting some of the leaders— Patel on 7 March, Jawaharlal Nehru on 14 April—but Gandhi remained free, even though the government called his acts 'rebellion'. The administration did not even deny Congress permission to use the telegraph and the mails. There was no doubt that the government sought to protect Gandhi's control over the civil disobedience movement by eliminating those it thought might give the movement a violent direction and by acting with moderation so as to keep the effect of the salt march within bounds.

In part, the government's policy was a success, for Gandhi's campaign had so far inhibited other action. Gandhi's hold on the masses seemed to drain the vigour from more intelligent and dynamic minds. Though all the essential motives for modern rebellion existed in India at this time—chronic unemployment among the educated classes and squalid living conditions for the industrial proletariat—1930 was a year almost entirely free from labour unrest; Gandhi canalized revolt into quiet channels, and when he shook his fist, it contained a moral maxim, not a gun. The authorities were instructed by the government not to use the military to disperse crowds: Jallianwalla Baghs in every town might be an incitement to uncontrollable violence. The police had to handle things with as few strong-arm tactics as possible. Congress, of course, claimed 'police brutality', but most of it was exaggerated—justifiably so, for it was useful propaganda.

Concealed behind the façade of Gandhi's great campaign, there were men who felt that general rebellion was the only way of getting rid of the British, and these men were preparing to strike a blow. In Bengal, with its tradition of revolutionary violence, an armoury was attacked and eight men were killed trying to defend it. On the other side of India near the north-west frontier, the city of Peshawar exploded into violence after the arrest of Abdul Ghaffar Khan, a Congressman known as the 'Frontier Gandhi'. Troops had to be called in and heavy casualties inflicted. Even worse, two platoons of a native regiment of the Indian Army refused to go to Peshawar to shoot their unarmed brethren. The ugly spectre of mutiny, a spectre the British had never been free from since 1857, now seemed to rise again. On 24 April, conditions were so bad in Peshawar that the British were no longer in control of the city and it was not until British troops and aircraft arrived twelve days later that the city was reoccupied.

The government of India at last decided that it had to arrest Gandhi, because the impression was growing, mainly amongst government servants, that the administration was being weak. In fact, there was not much purpose in keeping Gandhi out of jail any longer. The peasants who were his instruments were all busy in the fields reaping the spring harvest and were certainly not going to desert that for mere civil disobedience. Early in the morning of 5 May, Gandhi was unobtrusively arrested. There were a few demonstrations—serious ones in Delhi and Calcutta—and the remaining Congress leaders called on all Indians to intensify the campaign. The government, freed from the moderation necessary when backing up Gandhi, replied with sharp oppression—five years' rigorous imprisonment for failing to give information to the police, seven years and a heavy fine for carrying a Congress flag. The velvet glove was certainly off.

The government of India, however, soon found its attention diverted to what looked like a new frontier war, for the Muslim tribesmen of the north-west were on the march again and there was considerable rioting in towns in the North-west Frontier Province. The government, on the advice of a Muslim member of the viceroy's council, offered local self-government and secretly encouraged the spread of propaganda which smeared Congress as a Hindu body, so helping to intensify Muslim separatism. The government believed, though no adequate proof has ever been forthcoming, that Congress had incited the tribes and paid them large sums of money. It seems highly unlikely that such was the case, but the government was beginning to see Congress, like the devil, under every stone and behind every disorder. The government even went further; it declared the All-India Congress Committee an unlawful association, and arrested Motilal Nehru, the Congress president.

The arrests did not halt violence, which continued all over the country though, generally speaking, at such a level as to be fairly easily controlled and suppressed. The boycott on foreign goods, which assured Indian businessmen that nationalism was good for them and their businesses, flourished while the import of piece goods and cigarettes dropped to nearly a quarter of the previous year's figures. The government could do very little about this though, in Bombay, it confiscated Congress buildings and property. Larger bodies of police were raised—the British could still rely on plenty of recruits despite Congress propaganda—collective fines were imposed upon villages, and young offenders whipped.

In June 1930, the publication of the Simon report had been received in India with enthusiastic indifference. In fact, its reception in Britain was much the same; it is, after all, rather futile to be concerned over the future of a stillborn child. The Labour government dissociated itself from the report by announcing that Sir John Simon would not attend the Round Table conference, and the prime minister did not bother to consult even those Labour members of Parliament who had been on the commission! The problem now before the governments of Britain and India was how to get Congress to attend the coming Round Table conference.

5 Round Table and After

The first step had already been taken. The new government's virtual rejection of the Simon report seemed a good omen to Congress. Those moderate nationalists who had staked their all on slow constitutional development now tried to mediate between the Indian government and Congress. Gandhi, visited in jail, stated his terms. He was prepared to call off civil disobedience if in return the government would release political prisoners convicted of crimes other than violence, restore sequestrated property, refund fines, and not enforce the salt laws; on constitutional issues he demanded a number of safeguards. The Nehrus, in jail together, refused to countenance Gandhi's terms without first discussing them with him. To this the government consented. But, under the influence of the Nehrus, Gandhi's attitude stiffened; he said the government must recognize India's right to secede from the British empire, and that a responsible Indian government must be formed. Of course Irwin could not accept such terms, for he could not in any circumstances commit the British parliament. It was up to Congress to attend the Round Table conference and persuade the legislators.

It was Jawaharlal Nehru who was responsible for the hardening of the Congress attitude. There seems little doubt that Gandhi himself was prepared to compromise, but Nehru was obviously not anxious for a settlement; he must have known that the revised demands were asking the impossible. His attitude was partly due to the fact that he had lost faith in the British Labour government which, despite its fine phrases in opposition, seemed very little different from the Conservatives when it was actually in power. He was, too, unwilling to accept the mediation of those moderate nationalists whom he despised as lackeys of the British.

In November, the first Round Table conference met in London. The Indian delegates, carefully chosen, represented every special interest from the princes onwards—except the only effective nationalist organ, Congress. Obviously, the conference could be of little value and in fact it brought about nothing except a new stage in the relationship between the princes and British India. But one thing the conference made clear, that all the delegates (including the princes) wanted responsible government in India. Congress, it seemed, was not alone; even those elements whom the British thought to be 'on our side' echoed Congress demands.

Irwin made an appeal to Gandhi, inviting him to co-operate in placing 'the seal of friendship once again upon the relations of the two peoples, whom unhappy circumstances have latterly estranged'. The sensation that resulted from this was caused not by its almost classic understatement of the real state of relations, but by the fact that it was made at all. Official opinion was shocked; the viceroy's words seemed almost treasonable. But the appeal was really only another expression of governmental support for Gandhi in his role as neutralizer of rebellion. It was precisely keyed to his emotional understanding—hate put aside, earnestness displayed, a 'change of heart' for all to see. This was exactly what Gandhi had foretold would take place, that the conscience of the British would be awakened. The Labour prime minister, Ramsay Macdonald, followed Irwin's appeal by stating a new policy for provincial autonomy, a federal legislature, and safeguards for minorities during a transitional period only. This seemed adequate enough. Not to the Nehrus; but the government was concentrating on Gandhi.

On 25 January 1931, Gandhi and the more important Congress leaders were released from jail. To many British this was an outrageous act, implying that sedition had become respectable. Congress, however, accepted the release as a gesture of genuine goodwill. Gandhi explained 'I am hungering for peace, if it can be had with honour'. 'Honour' is a curious word, especially when used in conjunction with 'peace', but to Gandhi it meant 'respect', and that was what seemed to be offered. Also, Congress was wearying of civil disobedience. The government did not seem to have been weakened by ten months of agitation, authority still remained in its hands, and the disease of religious conflict among Indians had—instead of being stamped out—in fact become more acute. Perhaps Gandhi was right after all.

Given power by the weakness of Congress but deprived of the counsel of Motilal Nehru—who had died in February 1931—Gandhi stated his terms to the viceroy. He complained against 'police excesses' and demanded an inquiry; the viceroy, however, replied by appealing to him to forget the past and think of the future. Gandhi was apparently not prepared to do so but, when matters seemed to have reached a deadlock from which neither side could break out, the moderate nationalists persuaded Irwin to invite Gandhi to come and talk to him.

The meeting that took place was almost entirely concerned with the past, and on all major current issues the viceroy was unyielding. Gandhi, however, was not. 'I succumbed,' he said later, 'not to Lord Irwin but to the honesty in him'; in doing so, Gandhi ignored the instructions to be firm that had been given him by the Congress Working Committee. The Indian government nevertheless conceded the right of peaceful picketing under certain conditions, and ordered provincial governments to take the first step towards releasing political prisoners. Gandhi agreed to stop the boycott of British goods and to halt civil disobedience, which had almost come to a standstill anyway; when this had been done, the government was to abandon punitive ordinances, cease prosecutions, and make a number of other concessions.

On the surface, it seemed that the viceroy had won all the advantages, particularly since Congress had agreed to attend the Round Table conference in London. But Congress also gained—in prestige. The pact appeared as one between equals and implied acceptance of the fact that Congress spoke for at least a large proportion of the Indian people. Most British opinion in India considered that the viceroy had been foolish to parley with an already defeated enemy who was only playing for time. They did not realize what a brilliant tactical advantage Irwin had achieved in the results of the parley. Neither did the government in London. The Conservative opposition—naturally enough, for its instincts were imperialist—became restive at Baldwin's support for Irwin, a support which was in fact based more on personal esteem than on approval of the viceroy's policy. Discontent within the Conservative party was so strong that attempts were made to dislodge Baldwin from the party leadership, and Winston Churchill resigned from the shadow cabinet in protest against Baldwin's acceptance of the way in which the viceroy had let down 'the majesty of Britain'.

In India, opposition was growing against Gandhi, but it was not particularly powerful. Nehru opposed the settlement, but he soon gave in, and a number of really dynamic Congressmen, who might have made things very uncomfortable for Gandhi, were not free to do so; among these was Subhas Chandra Bose, whom the government kept in jail throughout the negotiations. Many nationalists thought the amnesty for prisoners was too narrow in scope and that those convicted of murder should also be freed, or should at least have their death sentences commuted. Gandhi did in fact discuss with Irwin the case of one Baghat Singh, but he was not able to win any concession. Although moderation would have been publicly wise, Irwin could not risk rousing British opinion in India any more than he had already done by his settlement with Gandhi. It has also been suggested that Gandhi put forward the request for clemency in a half-hearted way and this may well have been true, for his hatred of violence was so acute that it inhibited him from pressing the case of Baghat Singh with any great enthusiasm. When the execution took place, Gandhi sensed the emotional atmosphere, and condemned it as 'a first-class blunder'. But Congress was not much concerned with Baghat Singh, and he was soon forgotten.

The government, in its desire to encourage Gandhi, withdrew its special ordinances *before* the civil disobedience campaign had actually been called off, and there followed a period of considerable confusion. Ambiguous statements filled the air and each side interpreted them in its own particular way. The fact that the so-called Delhi Pact had been made in a cloud of emotion did not contribute to verbal precision. But one thing at least was clear. Gandhi had established a firm basis for Congress *co-operation* with the British and, despite the events that succeeded the agreement, the British government also was more firmly committed to co-operate with Gandhi. Irwin had achieved a stay of execution—for the British—while Gandhi had succeeded once and for all in diverting Congress from any truly revolutionary path.

Congress met, in a 'festival atmosphere', at Karachi and it was decided that Gandhi should attend the next session of the Round Table conference. But changes, none for the better, were taking place in the political climate. Irwin had been replaced in April 1931 by Lord Willingdon, who has often been contrasted unfavourably with him but who differed from him only in technique; in war, though a general may change his tactics to suit changing situations, the strategic rules which guide him remain the same. In August, the Labour administration at Westminster had given way to a so-called 'National' government, which was really Conservative. Ramsay Macdonald remained prime minister, but he was no longer anything more than a compliant prisoner of the Conservatives.

Gandhi, who went off to London with, as he put it, only God as his guide, found the conference preoccupied with the problem of minorities, and, in particular, that of the largest—the Muslims. When Ramsay Macdonald addressed the delegates as 'My Hindu and Muslim friends', Gandhi interrupted with 'There are only Indians here'. Though the prime minister retaliated by changing his form of address to 'My Hindu friends . . . and others', Gandhi had stated his position and he clung dogmatically to the thesis that Hindu and Muslim were one and that Congress—whom he represented at the conference—was the only body which could speak for all India. He would therefore offer no constructive suggestions for reconciling differences with those who spoke for other interests. His mystical attitude was not well received, especially as he appeared to have little or no awareness of the problems involved; he seemed to think that, by ignoring them, he proved they did not exist. The only precise statement he made was that if India received self-government she would not necessarily leave the British Commonwealth. Those at the conference who represented minority groups, especially the Muslims, demanded that separate electorates be retained. Gandhi, whose indifference to reality had by now antagonized everybody, was firmly against it. The British government, seeing no possibility of sensible discussion on this point, announced that it would itself make a decision on the problem of minorities. Gandhi's reply was to leave for India.

While Gandhi was in London, unrest and terrorism had continued in India. When he returned to Bombay he found that a number of Congress leaders, including Nehru, had been arrested. 'Christmas gifts from Lord Willingdon, our Christian viceroy,' remarked Gandhi bitterly. He tried to see the viceroy, but refused to accept Willingdon's conditions.

Congress now determined to revive the civil disobedience campaign and, in reply, the government arrested Gandhi, Patel, and, over the next few months, some eighty thousand others. Congress itself was declared illegal and so were many other organizations associated with it. The velvet glove was off again.

The viceroy had displayed to the world that the British were still in control. The British in India—and the 'National' government in London—were pleased. They believed that Gandhi was no longer needed to help run the country. Furthermore, the Congress party's sense of purpose had been considerably eroded by Gandhi's 'accommodation' with Irwin, and the new civil disobedience campaign was a failure. Acts of terrorism and communal violence still took place, but the mass of the people had had enough of living at the centre of a whirlpool. By the middle of 1932, a sullen peace had descended upon India.

Gandhi now threatened a fast to the death if the British government went ahead with its declared plan to keep separate electorates for minorities. The government was unimpressed and, in September 1932, Gandhi began his fast. Nehru and other Congress leaders felt this to be too big a gesture over too small an issue—what was the point of dying for anything less than freedom? But their opinions made no difference. Gandhi continued his fast, gave it up, then began another.

In Britain, the secretary of state for India remarked smugly 'The interest of many Congress leaders has now been diverted from self-government to Mr Gandhi's campaign against Untouchability'. The Untouchables, the lowest classes of Hindu society, were denied entry to temples, the use of the same wells as caste Hindus, and were generally discriminated against both socially and religiously by the rest of Hindu society. The Simon commission had estimated that they made up some 30 per cent of the population, and it was now the British government's intention to protect their interests, like those of the Muslims, by reserving seats in the legislative assemblies exclusively for representatives of the Untouchables. Gandhi, the religious reformer, was particularly concerned with altering their status (or lack of it) in Hindu society, and his overriding preoccupation with reform shows most obviously in the fact that he was willing to abandon action against the British in favour of a campaign against Untouchability. Gandhi came to an agreement with the Untouchable leader, Dr Ambedkar that the offer of separate electorates for Untouchables would be rejected.

In May 1933, shortly after his release from prison because of ill health, Gandhi officially called off the civil disobedience campaign, which had in any case ground almost to a standstill. There was much criticism of his action, or rather of his lack of action. Subhas Chandra Bose, away in Europe for medical treatment after being released from jail, condemned Gandhi as 'an old, useless piece of furniture', and issued, in conjunction with the veteran Congress leader, Vithalbhai Patel (also in Europe at the time), a statement which described the ending of the civil disobedience campaign as 'a confession of failure' and called for a new leader to replace Gandhi. Nehru—still in jail—was torn between irritation at the superb irrelevance of Gandhi's actions, and his own weakness in face of the Mahatma's 'irresistible charm and subtle power over people'.

There was no doubt that the majority of the Westernized intellectuals in Congress resented Gandhi's reactionary views, but there was very little they could do about him even if they wanted to. The very fact that they were intellectuals, with European-style left-wing opinions, was against them. The majority of Congress members did not even understand what these men were talking about, and those who did were usually businessmen who automatically reacted against the very mention of the word 'socialism'. The left wing too was convinced that the support of the masses was the key to political change. That support they could not hope to win by themselves; even today, Nehru's dominating position in the eyes of the Indian masses is not a product of his socialist ideas but of the fact that he is the chosen heir of Gandhi. The equation was inescapable—Congress needed mass support to justify its claim that it spoke for India, Gandhi had mass support, therefore Gandhi must equal Congress. A socialist party *was* formed in 1934 but it called itself the Congress Socialist party and remained within the movement, proliferating manifestoes but totally unable— and basically unwilling—to challenge Gandhi and the right wing for the leadership of Congress.

Other and subsequently victorious opposition to Gandhi was, however, in the making. Between 1933 and the 1936–7 elections, which began a new stage of constitutional reform, the Muslim League was transformed from an organization designed to protect a religious minority into one pledged to the creation of a separate Muslim state. The Muslims believed that the British were now determined in the not-too-distant future to grant representative government to India, and their fears of Hindu majority rule once again revived. In 1934 the League was reorganized by a new leader, Muhammad Ali Jinnah, whose main concern was to create for himself in the Muslim League the commanding position he had failed to achieve as an erstwhile member of Congress. At this time, Jinnah saw himself as a sort of Indian Ataturk, but he was rather vague about what was to be done. He first put forward the 'two nation' theory, that Muslims were not just of a different religion from Hindus, but that they had a separate personality and were, in fact 'a nation'. It is very unlikely that Jinnah at this time actually envisaged the possibility of any partition of India, but he gave the Muslim League a 'modern' ideology, however vague, and a positive *political* platform in place of negative religious fears.

Congress leaders of all shades looked upon Jinnah as a monster. To Gandhi he was a challenge but not an important one as yet, for Gandhi quite rightly believed that Jinnah did not speak for the Muslim masses. To Nehru, and others who felt like him, Jinnah was a reactionary anti-democrat, a demagogue using religion for his own purposes. Congress propaganda even suggested that Jinnah was a creature of the subtle British. But Jinnah was not in the pay of anybody. He was only taking a mortgage upon his own destiny. This cold, highly-Westernized lawyer passionately wanted recognition for the greatness he thought was in him. At one time he had believed that he could make his mark in Britain; he had even hoped to become a Privy Councillor, but the British failed to see the superman behind the elegant façade. Jinnah was not really interested in the Muslims of India and their problems. He was determined to prove that *he* could not be ignored. And he was to succeed in becoming 'the key to Indian freedom'.

In the mid-1930's, however, Congress was not particularly interested in Jinnah. It merely took an insulting and negative attitude towards him and the Muslim League—an attitude which did much to consolidate Jinnah's position.

6 *A New Charter of Bondage*

While the affairs of the nationalists remained in some confusion, the mountain of British parliamentary method continued to gestate and, to the surprise of everyone and the regret of many, the mouse it brought forth was larger than anyone had expected. The proposals became law as the Government of India Act of 1935.

The 1935 Act incorporated all the stages of constitutional development up to that date, and added two new principles: that a federal structure should be organized and that popular responsible government should be set up in the provinces. Under the terms of the Act, new provinces were to be formed and Burma was to be separated from

India and given a new constitution following the lines laid down in the
Act of 1919. In India, dyarchy—with its 'reserved' subjects—was to be
maintained at the Centre, and the overall authority of the British parliament was to be undiluted. Dyarchy was, however, abandoned in the
provinces and an almost completely responsible parliamentary government, based upon a considerably wider franchise, was established. The
federal provisions of the Act had been designed to incorporate the
princely states into the new system of government; but the princes
would not co-operate, and nationalists viewed the federal proposals
as an attempt to perpetuate British rule by playing on the nationwide
divisions between special-interest groups. The part of the Act which
incorporated the federal provisions never, in fact, came into force.

Indian reaction to the new reforms was basically unfavourable.
Even moderate leaders saw them as undesirable and nationalists were
quick to describe the Act as a 'slave constitution' and 'a new charter of
bondage'. The British, on the other hand, saw it as the last stage before
dominion status. The Muslims, of course, were sure it contained the
threat of Hindu majority rule. But in spite of their fears, the Muslim
League decided that 'the provincial scheme of the constitution should
be utilized for what it is worth'. The League thus made it clear that it
did not intend to be deprived of the chance of winning some sort of
power in areas where there was a Muslim majority.

Congress denunciation of the Act was not unanimous. Nehru, who
was elected president in 1936, said: 'It would be a fatal error for the
Congress to accept office. That inevitably would involve co-operation
with British imperialism.' But a large body of opinion in Congress
believed that refusal to accept office would merely be playing the game
according to British rules.

Gandhi, at this eventful time, was not even a member of Congress.
He had 'deserted politics' in September 1934, ostensibly because, as he
wrote in his letter of resignation, the more intellectual Congressmen
'were hampered' by an 'unexampled loyalty' to him which prevented
them from opposing him. Nevertheless, as Nehru put it, Gandhi
'could not rid himself even if he wanted to of his dominating position';
indeed, Gandhi had left Congress partly to demonstrate just that. But
he also wanted to prove to left wing elements that *they* could not control the Congress machine nor win the loyalty of the masses. During
the arguments over the 1935 Acts, Gandhi was off marching through

the countryside, active in schemes of village welfare. His spirit, however, remained behind to influence decisions.

Although Nehru believed that Congressmen should not accept office, he did not mean that they should boycott the elections under the new Act. It was decided to postpone any public statement about accepting office until after the elections had taken place. When they did take place, the results gave Congress absolute majorities in five of the provinces. In general, the electorate voted not for individual candidates but for a party; most votes for Congress candidates were a vote for Gandhi, and most Congress victories were in Hindu-majority constituencies. One thing the elections did prove—Congress did not speak for all Indians, and certainly not for most Muslims.

The size of the Congress vote, however, surprised everybody including Congress. Somewhat overwhelmed by this display of popular approval, the party overruled Nehru. It *would* take office. Nehru, with his familiar casuistry, argued that this did not imply a change of policy. 'The opinion of the majority of the Congress today,' he said in July 1937, 'is in favour of acceptance of office, but it is even more strongly and unanimously in favour of the basic Congress policy of fighting the new constitution and ending it. . . . We are not going to be partners and co-operators in the imperial firm. . . . We go to the assemblies or accept office . . . to try to prevent the federation from materializing, to stultify the constitution and prepare the ground for the constituent assembly and independence . . . to strengthen the masses, and, wherever possible, in the narrow sphere of the constitution, to give some relief to them.'

But Congress would take up the office to which it had been elected only under certain conditions. The governors of the provinces, who in special circumstances had the right to veto legislation, must guarantee not to do so. It seemed that, by making this condition, Congress was trying to break the constitution even before taking office. A compromise was reached, however, one in which Gandhi (now returned from the countryside) again discerned the honesty of motive which he had first seen in Lord Irwin. What actually happened was that Congress had observed that, during the three months in which the Act had already been in force without Congress co-operation, those ministries which had taken interim office exercised a large measure of real power. The majority of Congress members wanted the perquisites of that power and did not intend to be baulked of them by left wing intransigence. Once in power, Congress soon began so show signs of enjoying it and forgot the main issue of national independence by becoming, in Nehru's words, 'involved in petty reformist activities'.

Congress was not a political party in any Western sense, nor, when it accepted office, did it operate in Western democratic terms. It had declared its aim as, not to work the constitution, but to destroy it and thus bring independence nearer. But Congress had been elected on a platform which contained the promise of specific social and economic reforms and, when its ministries took office, they found themselves under pressure from their constituents to get on with the job of translating the promises into reality. This brought a dilemma. To institute radical changes could only lead to the alienation of some special-interest group essential to Congress unity. Agricultural reform would have meant antagonizing landlords, industrial legislation would have threatened Indian big business. On the other hand, failure to initiate reform would imperil the masses' support of Congress. Furthermore, it would be a denial of Congress's avowed reasons for claiming that Indians could rule themselves better than the British. The strains inside Congress soon became severe and there is no knowing what might have happened if the outbreak of the Second World War had not given Congress ministries an excellent excuse to resign. Otherwise, mass disillusionment would inevitably have grown and Congress itself might well have split.

Meanwhile, for a limited period, Congress leaders were in a position to control their members. They used coercion where possible and expulsion when necessary. The organization which had been built up by Vallabhbhai Patel facilitated dictatorship by the Congress Parliamentary Board. In fact, the board was so powerful that it functioned as a sort of central government. The authoritarian control exercised by the board further convinced the Muslim League that, should a federal India ever emerge, the central government was sure to be Congress dominated and would try to continue to coerce the provinces.

Many Congressmen resented being bullied from above and tried to force the Congress leadership into following a programme of radical reform. One in particular, Subhas Bose, saw behind this authoritarian rule the deadening hand of Gandhi, the Congress dictator. Bose had been out of India at just the time when he might have been able to form a new and dynamic party, and after his return from Europe he had been put in jail again. By the time he was released, Gandhi was back at the head of Congress, although he was still not officially a member. Bose, through his writings and speeches, had now become a national figure—at least among the younger, left-wing members of Congress—and Gandhi decided that the best way to neutralize this new opposition, while at the same time convincing the more progressive members of Congress that their place was still within the movement, was to make Bose president of Congress.

In 1938, Bose took office. Gandhi, it seems, believed he could convert the fiery revolutionary to his own non-violent views. He was wrong. In 1939, Bose stood once again for president against Gandhi's wishes and, after a bitter contest, defeated the candidate whom Gandhi had favoured. Gandhi now turned the technique of non-cooperation, not against the British, but against Congress's own president. Bose was forced to resign.

Many Congressmen including Nehru were soon condemning Bose as a fascist, but Bose replied that if fascists meant Hitlers, super-Hitlers, or budding Hitlers, 'then one may say that these specimens of humanity are to be found in the Rightist camp'. He now attempted to found a new left wing organization, the Forward Bloc. This failed. It was, however, by no means the last that India was to hear of Subhas Bose.

Gandhi, whom so many both in India and abroad believed to be compounded only of sweetness and light, had, by the use of his over-whelming prestige and the sort of intrigue one would expect from Tammany Hall, succeeded in disposing of the only real opposition to his leadership.

7 The Mad World of War

In April 1939, Bose was gone but the likelihood of war in Europe had taken his place as a threat to Congress. Bose himself welcomed the possibility of conflict because a blow to Britain in Europe would undoubtedly weaken her grasp on India. Other Congress leaders had no such clear-cut vision of the future. Gandhi and Nehru apparently had no desire to take advantage of Britain's troubles. Gandhi's sympathies—'from a purely humanitarian standpoint', he said—were with

Britain and France. Nehru, with his touching faith in democracy as not practised by the British in India, was an opponent of fascism.

On 3 September 1939, the viceroy—as was undoubtedly his right—declared India at war with Germany and promulgated a number of ordinances granting himself special wartime powers. The viceroy's action did no more than underline the fact that in spite of the 1935 Act, effective power still lay with the British, and that Indians themselves even in matters concerning their life and death—did not count very much and had no right to be consulted. Congress demanded that Britain should immediately state her war aims and their meaning for India; if the reply was satisfactory, then Congress would co-operate. Nehru had declared that Congress was 'not out to bargain', but it had obviously stated a price for its support.

Gandhi, characteristically, appealed for unconditional support for Britain. The whole of his political philosophy was conceived, not in terms of defeating the conquerors of India, but of converting them; without the British, everything that Gandhi stood for was bereft of meaning. If Britain were to be defeated, India might well find herself under another conqueror, one who would have little patience with the Gandhian approach to politics. Gandhi, however, made it clear that the sort of support he had in mind was not practical but moral. Congress followed up Gandhi's statement with a demand for the immediate declaration of Indian independence!

Other parties were also attempting to bargain with the British. The Muslim League courteously informed the government that, though it condemned Nazi aggression, it required an assurance that no decision should be made about India without the approval of the League. 'The Muslim League,' it stated categorically, was 'the only organization that can speak for Muslim India.'

All Britain was prepared to offer anybody was a promise that, at the end of the war, she would 'be prepared to regard the scheme of the Act [of 1935] as open to modification in the light of Indian views'. The government in India, however, was prepared to make what it obviously considered a major concession; it would establish some sort of consultative body which would include the viceroy and representatives of various Indian political groups. Though this offer was not unreasonable in the light of the realities of the time, it was obviously too vague to be acceptable to Congress. By 15 November 1939, all the Congress provincial ministries had resigned. Jinnah described this as 'a day of deliverance and thanksgiving', and the Muslim League ministries remained in office.

Despite the Congress action, attempts at compromise continued. In March 1940, Gandhi stated 'Compromise is in my very being. . . . The basis of my fight is love for the opponent'; but love or no love, the chance of compromise was non-existent. Britain once again repeated that dominion status was the goal for India—after the war. Congress found this unsatisfactory; it wanted independence and the right that Indians themselves—not the British parliament—should decide what sort of government they would have. The main obstacle to compromise was the peculiar love–hate relationship between Congress leaders and the British, a relationship rather like that of a long-married couple who say they want a divorce, yet who are so used to each other's ways that they are reluctant to part. But there was another, stranger, obstacle. Over the years of struggle, a fear of freedom had grown up in Congress. Its inability actually to win that freedom had reinforced the inertia of naturally peaceful men. The Congress leaders had virtually grown old in failure. Now that the world outside had broken into the closed room of Indian nationalism, they were frightened of what it might do to them.

Gandhi wanted Britain to win the war so that the British could leave India as a clear consequence of his campaign to convert them. Above all, he needed the reassurance of their conversion to prove that he had been right all along. If a new and ruthless tyranny were imposed upon India—which would happen if Germany won the war—it would mean that non-violence would have to give place to genuine revolutionary methods. Jawaharlal Nehru, too, hoped that Britain would win. He was not prepared to help her do so, but, though revolutionary in speech, he was no more a revolutionary in fact than the bourgeois leaders of the British Labour party.

During the Congress session held at Ramghar in March 1940, the old demands were repeated although the situation had changed. Congress now met under the shadow of the blitzkrieg in Europe; it seemed that Britain would soon be overrun by Germany and that British rule in India might collapse as a result. In their fear that India might have to face an enemy invasion, Congress leaders turned against Gandhi, the apostle of non-violence, and a new resolution was finally passed in July 1940, pledging Congress support for the war effort. Only, however, in return for a national government. This resolution marked the end of an era. Mr Rajagopalachari, who was later to become the first Indian governor-general, phrased the epitaph bluntly. 'The Indian National Congress,' he said, 'is a political organization pledged to win the political independence of the country. It is not an institution for organizing world peace.' Yet again, Gandhi withdrew from Congress.

Meanwhile, the Muslim League had not been inactive. Jinnah had rejected an approach by the then Congress president, a Muslim named Maulana Azad, with these crude words: 'Cannot you realize [that, as president of Congress] you are made a Muslim show-boy, to give it colour that it is national and deceive foreign countries? The Congress, is a *Hindu* body.' Jinnah had already made it clear that he now envisaged a separate Muslim state. 'Muslims,' he proclaimed in March 1940, 'are a nation according to any definition of a nation, and they must have their homelands, their territory, and their State.'

In August 1940, the British made another offer which differed on a number of points from those which had gone before. Now the government was prepared to invite a number of representative Indians to join the viceroy's executive council; to set up a War Advisory Board; to continue to give full weight to the views of minorities; and, after the war, to set up a representative body to decide on a new constitution. In substance, it offered the same as had been offered by Lord Irwin eleven years before!

Minority parties, including the Muslim League, welcomed the 'August Offer' though all made conditions for their acceptance. Congress, however, did not welcome it, for the government had merely repeated that the final goal was dominion status, and this was not acceptable to Congress. Nevertheless, a curious 'sporting offer' was made by Rajagopalachari on 27 August; he undertook 'to persuade my colleagues to agree to the Muslim League being invited to nominate the prime minister', and to form an administration if the British would agree to establish a provisional national government forthwith. Whether this was meant seriously is open to question, but Rajagopalachari may have deluded himself into thinking that he actually could 'persuade' his colleagues. Even with this intervention, there was no likelihood of the British accepting any Congress ultimatum.

It had only been a few weeks before Congress turned once again to

Gandhi and invited him to re-assume the leadership. Congress thought negotiations were about to take place and that they would need him; they were wrong. The British were not prepared to establish a national government in India, and in this they were not unreasonable, for they were responsible for India's defence and could hardly be expected to regard the techniques of non-violence as having any practical value in the face of aggression. Gandhi now called for civil disobedience, although not on a large scale. The government had declared it an offence to make speeches against the war, so Gandhi decided that someone must make an anti-war speech. On 7 October, one Congressman did so, was arrested, and sentenced to three months' imprisonment. The government did not leave it at that. They also arrested Nehru. He, however, was sentenced to four years. By the end of November 1940, some five hundred more who had offered civil disobedience joined him in detention.

The arrests caused very little stir, partly because the government of India had forbidden newspapers to report the civil disobedience campaign. Congress nevertheless pursued its policy, and by the end of January 1941 another 2,250 were in jail. By August, the number had risen to 20,000, although only about 13,000 were actually behind bars. This figure was very small compared with the total membership of Congress, and many Congressmen were coming to believe that the campaign was not a success. Gandhi, however, would have none of this. His 'moral protest' was a 'token of the yearning of a political organization to achieve the freedom of 350,000,000 people'. Many Congress leaders wanted to call off the campaign but Gandhi insisted that it should continue.

Outside Congress, the minority parties continued to issue statements. The Muslim League, though Jinnah's leadership was not altogether unchallenged, expanded its ideas about Pakistan. League members expressed opinions highly critical of the British. No action was taken against them. League governments continued in three of the provinces, ostensibly fully committed to the war effort but, in fact, not being particularly co-operative. Moderate Indians tried to bring about some sort of unity but they held the confidence of no one, not even the British. There was unresolvable deadlock. The British refused to consider granting any form of popular government until the various forces in Indian political life became reconciled. Of this, there was really no possibility since neither Congress nor the Muslim League genuinely desired control at the Centre. And the British were well aware of it.

The government in London continued to reiterate its promise of full dominion status for India after the end of the war, but such status—it was implied—could only be granted to a united India. There is no doubt that the British government, which was now made up of representatives of all British political parties under the premiership of Winston Churchill, still reflected the continuing Conservative attitude to India—pragmatic enough to realize that a transfer of power from Britain to India must one day take place, but nevertheless conditioned by a sense of Britain's historic mission. Britain had created India out of a collection of warring states; it did not intend to destroy that creation by dividing India when the time came to leave. This belief—emotional perhaps, but genuinely held—was shared by the Labour party, but neither party really understood the nature of the nationalist yearning for freedom. Not necessarily freedom at *any* price, but certainly not freedom at a price dictated by Britain. Indian nationalists were concerned with their own struggle for status and could hardly be expected to care whether or not Britain's historic mission was justified. They regarded this—to them, morbid—insistence on 'unity' as a deliberate attempt by Britain to perpetuate British rule by emphasizing the divisions within India. L. S. Amery, the then secretary of state, gave Indian nationalists a watchword for unity—'India First'—which provoked Gandhi into one of the few realistic statements he ever made. 'Let them [the British] withdraw from India and I promise that the Congress and the [Muslim] League will find it to their interest to come together and devise a homemade solution for the government of India. It may not be scientific; it may not be after any Western pattern, but it will be durable.' He then went on to make a surprising comment. 'It may be that, before we come to that happy state of affairs, *we may have to fight amongst ourselves.* But if we agree not to invite the assistance of any outside Power, the trouble will perhaps last a fortnight.'

The significance of Gandhi's suggestion lay not in the possibility of a fight, for by that he probably meant only argument, but in the implication that there might be other forms of government for India than Western-style democracy. Not, however, that it mattered very much what was said by either party. All the arguing was no more than a shadow-play. Indian nationalists did not trust the British government, who, in turn, did not really understand what motivated the nationalists; the administrators and rulers in India were not much concerned with either, and simply got on with the job of ruling.

But there were some who saw that, by encouraging Muslim intransigence, they might delay the granting of even dominion status. Jinnah began to receive, and accept, advice from very high levels in the administration. Some believed that the Muslim League's demand for Pakistan could be used to influence both the British Conservative and Labour parties; neither of them wanted to see a divided India, and so long as deadlock was maintained, neither would be likely to transfer power to India. Those, however, who thought that by encouraging the desire for division they could perpetuate Britain's presence in India, were as on most other occasions out of touch with the times. The Indian nationalists shared with the Indian Civil Service a narrow, parochial view, believing that the only factors involved in the imperial equation were Britain and India. They could not have been more blind.

Congress was further convinced of the untrustworthy nature of Britain's intentions by the slowness with which the terms of the so-called August Offer of 1940 were put into practice. It was not until July 1941 that the composition of the new viceroy's council was announced. There were to be eight Indians out of thirteen members, but though all were men of standing and experience they did not represent in any way the main streams of Indian nationalism. Consequently, from a nationalist point of view, they could be no more than puppets of the British.

A few weeks later, something occurred which seemed to confirm that Congress fears were not without foundation. The doctrine of self-determination expressed by President Wilson during the First World War had not applied to colonial peoples, and it now appeared that the 'Atlantic Charter' of the current war was also to be denied them. Indians had welcomed the statement in the charter which claimed that the British and American governments respected 'the right of *all peoples* to choose the government under which they live; and they wish to see sovereign rights and self-government restored to those who have been forcibly deprived of them'. But Prime Minister Churchill hastened to make it quite clear that this clause referred only to Euro-pean nations and that India was 'quite a separate problem'. He was undoubtedly right, but once again a declaration of war aims appeared to have overtones of racial discrimination. Nothing, it seemed, had changed between the two wars.

The secretary of state repeated the promise that India would be able to choose its own form of government after the war, but he could hardly expect Indians to believe him. Even the promise itself now sounded ambiguous to Indian ears, although no one had really ques-tioned it before. It had stated that Indians were to be 'primarily responsible' for making their own constitution; but did that mean the same—as Amery insisted—as those words in the charter, 'the right of all peoples to choose the government under which they live'? Who was *secondarily* responsible? If there *was* someone, and the phrase implied that there was, then the 'right' was diminished. Even moderate leaders began to have doubts, not about British sincerity but about what exactly the sincerity referred to. Almost everybody now had some reservations about Britain's trustworthiness.

On 4 December 1941, the government of India unexpectedly released its Congress prisoners, including Azad and Nehru. Three days later, the Japanese attacked Pearl Harbour.

*   *   *

It would be quite wrong to assume that everyone in India was con-cerned in the problems of politics. The Indian peasant remained virtu-ally untouched by controversy and argument; for him, life was too near the edge of death, and his main concern was with the struggle to stay alive. Many educated Indians still served loyally in the legislatures and in the Civil Service. Recruits for the Indian Army—the majority of them Muslims—flowed in, and elements of that army were fighting in Africa and the Middle East. Indian factories turned out war materials and other goods in ever-increasing quantities. Indian workers took their increased wage packets thankfully and remained quiet.

But while India behaved normally and the political parties wrangled, one Indian leader set off in search of what he believed to be the only way of forcing the British to leave India; Subhas Bose, who had been arrested again in July 1940, had come to the conclusion that the Axis powers were more likely to win the war. But were they to be trusted to give disinterested help to Indian nationalism? Bose thought that Russia would probably be more altruistic. He determined to leave India and find out. But first he had to get out of prison. Knowing that the British would be most unlikely to let him die in jail, he announced that he proposed to starve himself to death, and having resisted forcible feeding, he was finally released to await his trial at home. When the day arrived, Bose could not be found. He was on his way to Moscow.

But Bose got no further than Kabul. There his attempts to contact the Russians were unsuccessful and he finally turned to the Italians, who promised him a passport. After a difficult journey, he arrived in Berlin in March 1941. Soon, a new voice was to be heard over the radio, a voice that called Indians to rise and help those who were willing to help them. Until Japan entered the war, however, Bose could do little except broadcast and try to form an Indian legion from among prisoners of war in Germany. As 1942 dawned, Bose's call to Indians was reinforced by the Japanese sweep towards the gates of India. Tokyo radio, and transmitters in Siam and Singapore, announced that the armies of Nippon were coming to free India from British tyranny. Singapore and Rangoon had fallen to the Japanese, the British Navy's largest ships had been sunk. It seemed that deliverance was imminent.

Deliverance was not particularly welcome, however, especially to Indian nationalists. One of the justifications of British rule, and the one which no one questioned, was that it had protected India from outside invasion; now it seemed that India was to suffer simply for being part of the British empire. The British tried to rally Indians to defend their country. But many asked, why should Indians respond to the call if Japan was in fact winning? If Japan *was* winning, it would be madness to antagonize her.

Again, however, the majority of Congress leaders rejected Gandhi's policy and called for some sort of co-operation with the British. But though Gandhi's pacifism now no longer seemed acceptable to them, he succeeded in destroying any possibility of co-operation with the British by nominating the uncompromising Pandit Nehru as his successor. Congress remained divided.

The threat of a Japanese invasion had brought no sign of compromise between Congress and the Muslim League. The League's official organ, *Dawn*, proclaimed 'Pakistan is our deliverance, defence, destiny.

... No amount of threats [from Congress, not the Japanese!] or intimidation will ever deter us from the chosen path. .... Pakistan is our
only demand ... and, by God, we will have it!' With the characteristic short-sightedness of all Indian nationalists, the League was apparently more concerned with fighting Congress than with resisting the
Japanese.

During this period of unease, Congress was overhauling its organization and preparing for every eventuality by setting up a parallel
government of its own, ready to take over when the British collapsed.
The extreme reactionary organization, the Hindu Mahasabha, its
temper rising against the Muslims, defied them to come out and fight.
It also demanded full independence from the British, but promised in
the meantime to co-operate with them in the defence of India. The
political groups of India screeched at one another while the Japanese
marched on. India, in Nehru's words, was caught up in the 'mad world
of war and politics and fascism and imperialism'.

8 A Post-dated Cheque

One Congress leader, Rajagopalachari, publicly called for 'whole-
hearted resistance' to the Japanese and the 'transfer of full responsibility'
to 'a council of national leaders'. Furthermore, he warned the people
of his own province, Madras, they must be prepared to die in defence
of their country. Rajagopalachari also made an approach to the Muslim
League, but Congress did not approve his sense of realism.

The views of the principal nationalist leaders at this time were as
confused as they had ever been. Gandhi at least was consistent; he
meant to meet the Japanese with the same loving non-violence that he
thought was working against the British. His *naïveté* was sublime—
and characteristic. Nehru, who found fascism emotionally frightening,
was aware of the utter irrelevance of Gandhi's approach; but for
pacifism Nehru sought to substitute non-cooperation with the British
—and this was only replacing one *naïveté* with another. Jinnah was so
preoccupied with his own ambitions that he was indifferent to everything outside them. Bose, the only one with a clear-cut view of the
world, was far away in Europe nurturing his plans to liberate India
from outside.

Into this anarchy of purposes, the British once more inserted an offer. On 11 March 1942, four days after Rangoon fell to the Japanese, Winston Churchill announced that Sir Stafford Cripps, a socialist member of the British war cabinet, would go to India 'to satisfy himself upon the spot, by personal consultation, that the conclusions upon which we are all agreed and which we believe represent a just and final solution, will achieve their purpose'. The real desire of the British government was, in Churchill's words, 'to rally all the forces of Indian life to guard their land from the menace of the invader'. This represented little more than a hope that the government would receive moral support; all that the British required was a truce from controversy. This turned out to be more than Indian nationalism was prepared to give.

The reason for the attempt being made at all can be seen in the composition of the British war cabinet itself. The government of India, now rather rattled by the threat of invasion, wanted to arrest all the principal Congress leaders and was confident that it could do so without sparking off serious trouble. This idea was duly suggested to London. Some members of the cabinet there, however, were not convinced that the government of India was as efficient as it pretended to be, and Labour ministers were also pressing for a last effort to reach a compromise with Congress. War or no war, the British Labour party did not relish being involved in the suppression of Congress, without at least some attempt at reconciliation. Furthermore, they believed that Congress would accept a reasonable offer. In the interests of cabinet solidarity, it was agreed that the attempt be made. Furthermore, there was considerable pressure from the United States, always emotionally opposed to British imperialism even if she was an ally of Britain. Churchill felt it necessary to make a gesture, and Cripps was sent to India.

The 'Draft Declaration' that Cripps took with him repeated the terms of the August Offer of 1940, but it went much further on a number of points. It conceded India's right to leave the British Commonwealth if she wished. This implied that 'dominion status' now meant the same as 'independence'. Also conceded was the unambiguously-stated right of India to decide upon a new constitution. The framing of it was to be solely, not 'primarily', in Indian hands. When the constitution had been decided, India was to negotiate a treaty with

Britain in order to guarantee 'British obligations'. These obligations were now considerably diminished in number; fair treatment for business interests was not to be made a condition of the transfer of power, nor were British residents in India to be classed as a 'racial or religious minority'. As for British financial claims against India—times had changed and it was now Britain who owed India money (because of war purchases) rather than the other way round. The offer was also made that there should be an interim system of government, and the declaration invited the 'leaders of the principal sections of the Indian people' to join. Cripps, at a press conference, made it quite clear that the British proposals meant 'complete and absolute self-determination and self-government for India'.

The choice of Cripps as negotiator was astute. He was an upper-class socialist and the British Labour party had always forcibly put forward India's case for freedom—except for the two occasions when it had been in office. But Ramsay Macdonald was now conveniently forgotten and Cripps, a somewhat puritan figure, had an obvious sincerity which immediately appealed to Indians. On the other hand, however, everything he said was always conditioned by one over-riding factor. The main bulk of the British pledge could not be redeemed until after the end of the war. Also, Cripps was to some extent tainted by association, for he was a member of a cabinet whose head was the reactionary Conservative and arch-enemy of India's freedom, Winston Churchill.

Cripps talked to representatives from virtually every facet of Indian political life, but there was one party which could not be amenable to discussion—the Japanese army. While Cripps was still talking, the Japanese dropped bombs on Indian towns. Though talks continued in India, though innumerable avenues were explored, there was no real will towards agreement. The Japanese were at the gates and it seemed only a matter of time before they battered them down. The intervention of Colonel Johnson, representing in some obscure way the inter-ests of the American president, Franklin Roosevelt, only clouded the issue. What could the United States do to help India, when America too was fighting for her life?

Cripps and those elements in the war cabinet who supported him were undoubtedly sincere, but it is questionable whether anyone else was. Churchill had made his gesture of appeasement to the United

States and to the Labour members of the war cabinet. It was a gesture
without real meaning. Whether or not the Draft Declaration was
accepted by Indian nationalists, the fundamental problems of India's
defence would be unaffected; even if they refused to co-operate at all,
experience had shown that Congress was unlikely to act as an efficient
fifth column for the Japanese.

Indian nationalists of all shades were unwilling to accept promises
redeemable only in the distant and rather gloomy future. Faced with
the strong possibility that there would be a successful Japanese invasion
of India—an invasion which would probably bring Subhas Bose with
it—many felt it better to have no truck with the British. If the nationalists had really wanted immediate self-government, they would have
tried to arrive at some compromise amongst themselves. No such
attempt was made. In fact, the divisions became even sharper than they
had been before. Fundamentally, all the counter-proposals and arguments put forward by the various nationalist organizations were a
bluff. Why, as Gandhi is reported to have asked, accept 'a post-dated
cheque on a bank that was obviously failing'? Far better to save their
energies and reputations for negotiation with the Japanese.

This was, in the pattern of the times, an extremely sensible view.
There might be a number of sophisticated nationalist leaders who
genuinely hated the fascism and militarism of the Japanese, but there
was an overwhelming majority who were quite prepared to win
freedom with the help of the Asian power which had struck the first
successful blow against Western imperialism. Japan's actions in China
were hardly pleasant from any point of view, but Indian nationalists
had a notoriously narrow view of the world outside India. 'Asia for the
Asiatics', the Japanese trumpeted, and it was a cry which automatically
provoked a response. Pressure upon the nationalist leaders was immense, and there was no possibility that they would be allowed to
accept less from the British than they thought they stood to gain from
the Japanese.

When Churchill received news from India that the Cripps mission
had failed, he is reported to have danced around the cabinet room. No
tea with treason, no truck with American or British-Labour senti-
mentality, but back to the solemn—and exciting—business of war.

9 Quit India

The Cripps offer was so reasonable—in any other circumstances than those under which it was made—that Indian nationalists were forced to disguise their real motives for rejecting it behind virulent criticism of the proposals themselves. Jinnah attacked the Draft Declaration because 'Pakistan was not conceded unequivocally, and the right of Muslim self-determination was denied'. But Congress remained the League's first enemy; if the British had conceded immediate independence, the new government would have been a 'Fascist Grand Council, and the Muslims and other minorities . . . entirely at the mercy of Congress'. Congress chose to attack Cripps personally as the agent of British reaction—in which they were not altogether wrong. The Cripps mission, said one Congress newspaper, was 'the result of American pressure. It was a stage-managed show to buy off world opinion and to foist pre-concerted failure on the people of India.' Pandit Nehru found it 'sad beyond measure that a man like Sir Stafford Cripps should allow himself to become the Devil's Advocate'.

At the meeting of the All-India Congress Committee held at Allahabad in August 1942, a resolution was passed which stated that if the Japanese invaded India they would be met by non-violent non-cooperation. The wording of the resolution concealed rather than revealed Congress policy. In fact, Congress was preparing for negotiations with the Japanese when they arrived. A police raid on the All-India Congress Committee offices discovered notes, by Gandhi himself, for a draft resolution assuring the Japanese 'that India bore no enmity' to them and that 'if India were free, her first step would be to negotiate with Japan'. Pandit Nehru had apparently protested against the wording but had, as so often before, given in. In fact, he was no longer in a position to influence the Committee. Rajagopalachari, still campaigning for a sensible settlement with the Muslim League, resigned from Congress, but only seven of his colleagues followed him. Gandhi had turned his face against any compromise with the League. Congress, he maintained, still spoke for India and no one else could. Let the British give up and 'leave India in God's hands', said Gandhi, once again displaying his indifference to the real world. Have no fears about the communal problem; it was the British who created it, and when they go it will go with them. Anarchy, internecine warfare, may follow 'for a time', but 'from these a true India will arise in place of the false one we see'.

Gandhi, however, could not maintain his extremist position with any consistency. Allied forces, he had conceded, would be permitted to remain in India 'for the sole purposes of repelling a Japanese attack and helping China'. Furthermore, 'India's ambassadors' would go 'to the Axis powers not to beg for peace, but to show them the futility of war'! Ambiguous phrases and contradictory nonsense continued to roll out, but one clear-cut threat emerged, to use 'non-violent strength' against the government. Gandhi himself did not seem particularly worried that non-violence might once again degenerate into violence. 'If,' he had said in July 1942, 'in spite of precautions, rioting does take place, it cannot be helped.' Now the talking was over. It was to be open rebellion. But these words of Gandhi's further isolated Congress from the rest of India, for they seemed to say that he was ignoring the welfare of the very people he claimed to represent.

The moral collapse of the Congress leadership was a sorry sight. Under the threat of a Japanese invasion, the really revolutionary elements in India had begun moving into the open, and it seemed that Gandhi had taken over their slogans in a desperate bid to maintain his position. He knew there were other Indians waiting to claim his mantle, men who had always preached violent revolution and who now seemed about to be proved right. Obsessed as he was with a belief in his almost divine role as saviour of India, Gandhi intended to lead India to freedom even if he had to use means which were the negation of all he had previously stood for. Those who listen too often to 'inner voices' are driven into a world of horrifying fantasy, and the Gandhi of 1942 was no exception. In August, the All-India Congress Committee declared a 'mass struggle' to force Britain to quit India. Their decision was welcomed by Gandhi in these words:

'The voice within me tells me I shall have to fight against the whole world and stand alone. . . . Even if all the United Nations oppose me, even if the whole of India tries to persuade me that I am wrong, even then I will go ahead, not for India's sake alone but for the sake of the world. . . . I cannot wait any longer for Indian freedom. I cannot wait until Mr Jinnah is converted. . . . If I wait any longer, God will punish me. This is the last struggle of my life.'

But he was not to have the opportunity to struggle, for, next day, he and the whole working committee, as well as a number of other Congress leaders, were quietly arrested. Gandhi's parting shot was a plea for non-violence, but 'keep the nation alive even at the risk of death', he added.

When news of the arrests became public, non-violence broke out with brickbats and knives. The government proclaimed a curfew and prohibited meetings of more than five people. Congress was once again declared illegal and the British set about suppressing what appeared to be a full-scale rebellion. Extreme nationalists indulged in extensive sabotage, while professional gangsters and religious fanatics took advantage of the unrest to murder and loot. By the middle of September, 250 railway stations had been destroyed or seriously damaged and 550 post offices attacked. A large section of the railway system was put out of action and communications were interrupted to such an extent that the army on India's northern frontier was deprived of its main channel of supply. Police stations and government buildings were set on fire, and many Indians still working for the government were threatened if they did not join the rebels. A number of those who refused were murdered.

The government used British troops and aircraft against mobs, machine-gunning crowds from the air on at least five occasions.

Though the rebellion was undoubtedly organized, it was not well planned. It did not trigger off a national uprising because too many influential elements in the country not only held aloof but actively supported the government. The first phase of large-scale sabotage and violence had been suppressed by the end of August, and the second phase, of isolated outbreaks, was virtually over by the end of the year. The failure of the Congress campaign gave great satisfaction to Conservative circles in Britain. Had they not been right in always maintaining that Congress did not represent the mass of the Indian people? One thing had become clear from the rebellion, so Churchill said in the House of Commons in September 1942, and that was the 'non-representative character' of Congress and its 'powerlessness to throw into confusion the normal peace of India'.

Labour and Liberal members of parliament criticized Churchill's words and demanded that the Congress leaders be released from jail. They also condemned the rebellion, however, though it is highly unlikely that any of them appreciated the tangled motives that lay behind it. Officially, the Labour party could do little; like everyone else in Britain at that time it was primarily concerned with Britain's own life-and-death struggle with Germany and Japan. Clement Attlee, the deputy prime minister, made it clear that no government would be prepared 'to negotiate with a people who are in rebellion'. In any case, the Cripps offer expressed Labour views with reasonable accuracy, and in spite of a number of improbable 'solutions' offered by certain Labour members—including the suggestion that a distinguished Indian be appointed as the next viceroy and an invitation be sent to the principal Allies to mediate'—there was really very little difference between Labour and Conservative opinion. Attlee, in a speech at Aberdeen on 6 September, used phrases which, with only the slightest modification, had been used by practically every British statesman for the previous two decades. 'We have made,' he said, 'many mistakes in our treatment of the Indian problem but we have given India more than a century of internal peace and good government and have in the last twenty-five years made immense progress towards Indian self-government. Further progress was held back by disagreement among Indians and by the difficulties of introducing democracy into a country of 300,000,000 people at all stages of civilization.'

There is no doubt that, apart from a few (though highly influential) diehards, most British politicians believed that Indians should rule themselves. Forty years before, Lord Curzon—the last great viceroy in the nineteenth century tradition—had said 'in Britain there are no two parties about India'. He was still right in 1942. From a Conservative point of view, the Indian empire was a wasting asset, and all parties were agreed that democracy was the only possible system of government for Britain to leave as the legacy of her rule, and that it must be left only to an undivided India. It was, however, obvious even to the stupidest of politicians that to hand over to an Indian government dominated, as it would inevitably be, by Congress could only lead to civil war. The British had not been prepared, and no political party would have countenanced the attempt, to examine other forms of government which might be better suited to India's problems. By 1942, it was too late. And in India, Congress—which stood to gain power in a democratic system—would also have refused to consider other forms. The twin essentials of democracy and an undivided India resulted in a deadlock which was unbreakable, and the diehards whose spokesman was Winston Churchill could therefore offer something they knew would never be acceptable. It was the insistence of both Conservative and Labour upon the virtues of democracy which made the partition of India inevitable and, with it, the death of hundreds of thousands of innocent people during the period of vivisection.

In India, Gandhi began a fast in order to force the government to release him from jail. The Muslim League reiterated its demand for recognition of the principle of partition. The Hindu Mahasabha described Gandhi's fast as 'bound to be futile, detrimental and suicidal' and called for an 'active movement' to compel Britain 'to defend the integrity of India against Pakistani Muslims'. Many solutions were offered to help break the continuing deadlock. The secretary of state for India, L. S. Amery, said in the House of Commons, 'It is for Indians themselves to find the way' out of the deadlock. Hardly a practical proposition under the circumstances.

By the end of 1943, India was comparatively quiet; a few acts of sabotage took place, a number of terrorists were loose in the country-side, but on the whole those nationalists who were not in jail had given up their efforts to take advantage of the absence of Congress. But there were sinister signs of further communal trouble. The Muslim League's demands for partition grew louder and louder, and the phrases it used were larded freely with threats. The government was remarkably for-bearing, for the speeches of the League leaders were undeniably incite-ments to communal violence. Membership of Congress fell but that of the Mahasabha, firmly communal and militant, rose. Other com-munities—the Scheduled Castes Federation, which represented some 15 per cent of the population, and the Sikhs, among others—began to take on a marked political edge. It seemed that the knives were being sharpened.

10 Jai Hind!

The fight for India's freedom was now to take place outside India and the actions of one man were to have profound effect upon the future. In India itself, the political situation appeared so quiet that the viceroy, Lord Linlithgow, who had held office since 1937, was replaced in

October 1943 by a soldier, Lord Wavell. Though the new viceroy quickly expressed his hopes that 'I can better serve our cause and India as a civilian', there was little doubt that his appointment was to be part of a new command structure designed to carry on the war against the Japanese. Wavell also said 'There is certainly no intention to set up anything in the shape of military rule', but in fact such an intention would have been superfluous as the emergency regulations promulgated by the government of India were already the equivalent of martial law. The Indian government had now a great soldier as its head and the reason for this was obvious. Politics were to take second place to the demands of war. The British government no longer seriously considered the possibility of a political settlement with Congress and, with the Japanese now on India's north-east frontier, it was determined to concentrate on immediate problems.

A few months before Wavell took over, Subhas Bose had arrived in Tokyo after a journey by submarine and aircraft which lasted eighteen weeks. His period of waiting in Germany was now over and he was making preparations to ride to Delhi with the Japanese army. The Japanese had already encouraged Indian prisoners of war in Malaya to organize an 'Indian National Army'. In this, they had been helped by another Bose, Rash Behari by name, who had founded an Indian Independence League in Japan as far back as 1916. But the Japanese had merely sought to utilize the League for forward intelligence and sabotage while the Japanese army moved into India. It was Subhas Bose who was to turn both the League and the National Army into a genuine revolutionary movement aimed at liberating India from the British. Subhas had already acquired the aura of a hero, even in the eyes of nationalist circles in India itself. Gandhi, the professional of non-violence, had hailed him (now that he was at a safe distance) as a 'patriot of patriots'—but, Gandhi added, 'misguided'. One British Labour newspaper, on the basis of Bose's broadcasts from Berlin, had feared that it was 'not opportunity knocking at our door . . . it is history battering it down'. Subhas seemed the embodiment of dynamic action, with even Gandhi now apparently supporting him. In October 1943, as Wavell reiterated the British promises of 1942, Bose was proclaiming a 'Provisional Government of Free India' in Singapore. 'Jai Hind [India forever]!' he had cried, and the words soon became a greeting between Indian nationalists. The British, however, remained silent on the subject; 'If only,' Bose said bitterly, 'they would abuse us!' But many Indians knew of his activities from broadcasts and propaganda, and ironically enough it was to be the British who, though they ignored him during the war, were to make him a legend after his death. The ghost of Bose was to inhabit the conference rooms four years later as India moved through the last days of British rule, and in death he was to have the success denied to him in life.

The actual performance of the Indian National Army when, with the reluctant approval of the Japanese, it finally set foot on Indian soil and raised the Congress flag, was of comparatively little importance. The British were by then on the offensive and the INA shared in the débâcle of the Japanese army in Burma.

Events in India were also on the move again. In May 1944, Gandhi had been released from jail on grounds of ill health, although the government was still not prepared to release the other Congress leaders. Gandhi, the government insisted, had been let out only because his health was in danger. This was merely the excuse for releasing him, and the real reason was rather different. Despite Gandhi's apparent conversion to violence in 1942, the government was convinced that he had now returned to his old ideas and could therefore once again be used as a mediator. It was, however, necessary to keep him away from the influence of more inflammatory Congress leaders such as Pandit Nehru. If Gandhi could arrive at some arrangement with the Muslim League, it might still be possible to hand over power to a united India. One of Gandhi's first acts after his release was to visit Jinnah. The Mahatma's stay in prison had perhaps brought a belated sense of reality, for he offered Jinnah a formula which envisaged the possibility of partition; but there must, he insisted, be a provisional government at the centre for a transitional period. In spite of this offer, there was no possibility of compromise with Jinnah. He could play too well upon Muslim fears that once there was a central government it would be dominated by Congress, who would make it their business to see that the provinces could not secede. Jinnah had smelt the coming of freedom and was not prepared to give way on anything. Unlike many Congress leaders, Jinnah did believe that the British really meant to leave India. They had by implication conceded the principle of Pakistan. Why then should he compromise when all he had to do was wait?

Gandhi had failed and the government was not prepared to co-operate any further. It did not even bother to re-arrest him. Labour members of parliament in London, sublimely ignorant of the real nature of India's troubles, still called for the one thing that was impossible—the formation of a national government in Delhi. All this did was convince Jinnah that he was right in refusing to compromise. Most Labour members thought that Indian nationalists distrusted Britain and that if this distrust could be removed all other problems would fade away. But the really dangerous distrust was between Indian and Indian, Congress and League, Hindu and Muslim, and to resolve it was beyond the power of Westminster. When it seemed that the end of the war and a British victory were in sight, all parties in India began to prepare for the final struggle. The Japanese no longer appeared as the probable liberators of India. Subhas Bose no longer threatened the old-guard leadership of Congress. The question now was whether the promises of the Cripps mission were genuine or not.

On 14 June 1945, Lord Wavell, who had been recalled to London for discussions, returned to India. The British government no longer included Labour ministers. The war in Europe had been over since May and a general election was soon to take place. The proposals which Wavell took back to India in an attempt to break the old political deadlock had, however, been framed by the wartime coalition cabinet. The principal advance over the Cripps offer of 1942 was that the viceroy's executive council should be entirely Indian except for the viceroy himself and the commander-in-chief. The council would give equal representation to Muslims and Hindus. Wavell also announced that a conference would be called at Simla to discuss the proposals and that Congress leaders would be released from jail and invited to attend.

The Simla conference did take place, but it was what happened outside that was decisive. Congress assumed that the division of seats in the executive council between Muslims and caste Hindus was to be on a religious rather than a political basis. Congress maintained that it (Congress) was a *secular* body and would of course nominate Muslim members of Congress for the Muslim seats. Jinnah, however, was not prepared to accept this interpretation. The Muslim League, he claimed, was the sole representative of Muslim interests; consequently, the Muslim seats in the council should be filled by members chosen by the Muslim League. To this the viceroy could not agree, since the division of seats *was* intended to be purely religious. Jinnah refused to continue the negotiations and the first Simla conference broke up in failure.

Not that this mattered very much, Congress thought, for by now a new government had taken office in Britain. Churchill and the Conservatives had been rejected by the British electorate and the Labour party had been swept to power with a large majority of the seats in parliament. Would Labour fulfil its often reiterated pledge to give India her freedom? On 15 August, as the war with Japan ended, the speech from the throne at the opening of parliament at Westminster contained these words: 'In accordance with the promises already made to my Indian peoples, my Government will do their utmost to promote in conjunction with the leaders of Indian opinion, the early realization of full self-government in India.' The words themselves were not very inspiring. 'Full self-government' did not sound like independence. Three days later, in a hospital on the island of Formosa, terribly burned after the crash of an aircraft taking him to Japan, Subhas Chandra Bose lay dying. 'Tell my countrymen,' he said, 'India will be free before long.' Soon his name and the tales of his exploits were to help convert the emptiness of 'full self-government' into the reality of independence.

PART THREE

The Victory

'I NEVER thought it would happen. I never expected to see
Pakistan in my lifetime.'
                    M. A. Jinnah

'HISTORY SEEMS sometimes to
move with the infinite slowness
of a glacier and sometimes to
rush forward in a torrent.'
                    Lord Mountbatten

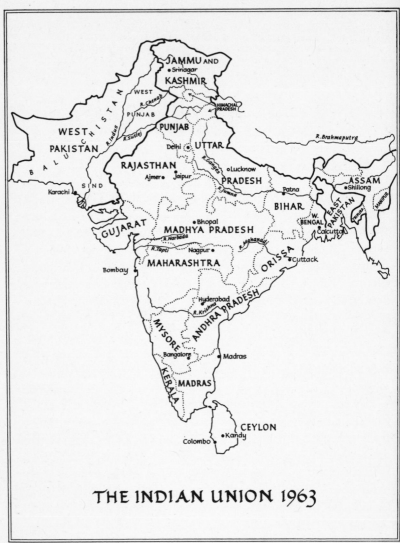

THE INDIAN UNION 1963

1 Dramatis Personae

With the Labour party now in power in Britain, hope grew in India that self-government might really be only just around the corner. But that hope was conditioned by past experience. It seemed likely that the Labour government meant what it said, but this was not absolutely assured. The Labour government must be made to see that it was essential to grant India her freedom, not only in fulfilment of Labour promises but also in the interests of the British people. From the Congress point of view, this called for a new approach. On the one hand, the Labour government must be persuaded of the political sophistication of those to whom it would be handing power, and on the other it must be made quite clear that the alternative to freedom was violence.

This new approach meant that Gandhi had to be relegated to the background, for he was hardly a symbol of political maturity. While freedom had seemed far away, he was necessary both to Congress and the British. Now it was Nehru the socialist, charming and flexible, who was to fill the picture. Labour ministers would respond positively to his civilized Western point of view; they could treat him as an equal. Gandhi, like some Indian Rousseau, was of another century, another and incomprehensible dimension, a man who spoke in the language of the pre-industrial world. As socialism had been spawned by industrial capitalism, it could hardly listen with patience and understanding to the spokesman of a back-to-nature philosophy. This was, in effect, the end of Gandhi as a moulder of events. The mediator was no longer needed, the saint with his phalanx of illiterate peasants could be put aside. It was now the time for civilized negotiation between men who spoke the same unapocalyptic language. The stake was not freedom itself—for this seemed to have been agreed—but the pattern of that freedom. Nehru now spoke for Congress.

In order to convince the British that violence was still possible, Congress needed a second spokesman, to play another role that Gandhi could not play. Just as the British had not feared Gandhi, the reducer of violence, they no longer feared Nehru, who was rapidly assuming the lineaments of civilized statesmanship—even elder statesmanship—in response to the changed situation. The British, however, still feared Subhas Bose or, rather, the violence he represented. Congress concluded that the British administration in India, numerically wasted and no longer sure of itself, could be frightened by the old threat of another mutiny or of large-scale violence into advising the government not to procrastinate. Unfortunately, India in 1945 seemed calm and peaceful. The mass of the people was once again indifferent. There was nothing to hand with which popular indignation could be excited, no Jallian-walla Bagh nor anything remotely resembling it. But members of Bose's Indian National Army were returning to India and to their old regiments. So were the Indian prisoners of war who had joined the Indian Legion raised by the Nazis. The death of Bose was now public knowledge and he had acquired a halo of martyrdom and apotheosis. Congress leaders, who had hated and feared Bose, were not at first anxious to use the INA as propaganda. After all, Bose had actually fought and died in an attempt to free India; the surviving Congress leaders had merely gone to jail. Then the British government in India decided to court-martial certain INA officers for making war against the king-emperor. This decision at first received the support of Congress until it began to realize that the trial could be made a focus of popular indignation. Thereupon, Congress set up a defence committee for the INA officers. Counsel for the accused included Pandit Nehru himself.

The trial was the last display of ineptness by the British administration in India, the final proof—if at this stage such proof was needed—that the Services who ruled India had, like the Bourbons, forgotten nothing and learned nothing. The decision to prosecute was taken on the sole initiative of the Indian government. That it was agreed to and tacitly supported by the government at Westminster merely demonstrated the doctrinaire attitude towards India which dominated the Labour party's thinking. In practice, the Labour government knew as little about the realities of India as its predecessors had done.

With the assistance of the government of India, Bose and the INA—
of whom millions of Indians had never heard—now became household
names. The trial was held at Delhi in the Red Fort, which had once
been the palace of the Mughal emperors. 'The trial,' Nehru wrote
afterwards, 'dramatized . . . the old contest; England versus India. It
became in reality not merely a question of law . . . but rather a trial of
strength between the will of the Indian people and the will of those
who held power in India.' The prisoners were found guilty and sentenced to be transported for life to the penal islands, but the commander-in-chief, General Auchinleck, very sensibly remitted the
sentence of transportation. This remission was regarded by many as
an acquittal under duress.

The government of India had hoped, by prosecuting members of
the INA, to reinforce the morale of the Indian Army. It succeeded only
in creating unease, in making the soldiers feel slightly ashamed that
they themselves had supported the British. If Subhas and his men had
been on the right side—and all India now confirmed that they were—
then Indians in the Indian Army must have been on the wrong side. It
slowly dawned upon the government of India that the backbone of
British rule, the Indian Army, might now no longer be trustworthy.
The ghost of Subhas Bose, like Hamlet's father, walked the battlements
of the Red Fort, and his suddenly amplified figure over-awed the
conferences that were to lead to independence.

The spectre of Subhas Bose also frightened Jinnah. Once again
Congress and the Hindu masses seemed to have been galvanized out of
their torpor. The threat of Hindu majority rule now seemed greater
and more immediate than ever before. But Jinnah saw clearly and
alarmingly that his dream was about to be fulfilled. Freedom was near,
and the key to that freedom was in Jinnah's hand. Just as the thousand-
year Reich had been merely the sublimation of Hitler's dream, so
Pakistan was the sublimation of Jinnah's. To both these men—and they
had surprisingly much in common—the end was of considerably less
importance than the adventure of the means. For Jinnah, the Muslims
of India were the *Volk*, and the defeat of the Mughal empire had been
their Versailles. Out of the simple fears of a religious minority he had
created the image of a nation oppressed, which only he could liberate
from the dark shadow of subjection. Just as Hitler was not taken seriously because of the absurdity of his philosophy, so neither Congress

nor the British had ever really taken Jinnah seriously. They thought he was only a communal politican who could be coerced or even bribed by promises and disclaimers. Instead he was beyond reason, a daemonic figure, remote in his own dreams, ascetic except in the emotional tenderness he felt for 'his people'. Jinnah had not concerned himself very much with the form of Pakistan, and his ideas were always rather nebulous about what his people's 'homeland' was to be. It was 'Pakistan', the symbol, that was important to him and in the end he left the geographical problem for the British to solve. If Jinnah sometimes seemed willing to compromise it was, like Hitler, only that he might create further confusion amongst his enemies, for he thrived upon disruption. He delayed India's freedom because he did not wish to be faced with the reality of Pakistan. When it became obvious that the British were going to leave India, he played out his part and remained disruptive until the end.

There were other Indians who played minor roles in the drama. Not the least of these were the criminals, known as *goondas*, who incited religious riots and then profited from them by murdering and looting. The religious zealots, both Hindu and Muslim, spoke their bloody lines. Some of the princes, conspiring with English friends to keep and enhance their states, added their contribution to the tragedy. But they were only lesser characters.

There were the two viceroys, Lord Wavell and his successor who finally negotiated the transfer of power, Lord Mountbatten. Wavell's role was comparatively small, for, without any justification whatsoever, neither the British prime minister nor the Indian leaders trusted him. In fact, Wavell's virtues made him unsuitable for the office of viceroy. He was blunt in the face of deviousness. He still thought that, as viceroy, his was the ultimate responsibility for what went on in India. He was a caretaker who refused to act like one. He believed, and no reasonable person can deny that he was right, that he had a double purpose—to carry out the British government's policy for the devolution of power, and to ensure that, in the meantime, the government of India did not neglect its responsibilities to those it still ruled. Unfortunately, the times were not reasonable, nor was there a precedent for the events in which he had become enmeshed; no great empire had ever negotiated itself away after emerging victorious from a major war. Wavell was naïve enough to think that everyone should be as honest as himself and that India's leaders should be thinking of India and not of themselves. But his was the *naïveté* of a great human being, and his greatness has been too much overshadowed by the reputation of the man who took his place.

Lord Mountbatten's advantages over Wavell were considerable. He was extrovert, handsome, and had a natural charm. A relative of the king-emperor, he brought with him to India some of that mysterious glamour of royalty which appeals so much to Indians. Unlike Wavell, who had been shuffled out of military command by the prejudice of Winston Churchill, there shone around Mountbatten's head the aura of victory against the Japanese and of heroic action in the Navy. Furthermore, his mind was uncluttered with prejudices and he believed himself uninvolved. He had the kind of mind capable of viewing the transfer of power as a military operation, to be carried out with despatch and a sort of clinical insensitivity. He came to India with one overwhelming advantage—it was publicly known that he would be the last viceroy. Nehru thought he was a 'straightforward English socialist', a sort of Philippe Egalité in naval uniform. Wavell, on the other hand, had been tainted with the guilt of that earlier government of India which had clapped Congress leaders in jail in 1942.

In London, at the centre of all things, there was the not very imposing figure of the new socialist prime minister, Clement Attlee. Just as Nehru had been shocked into socialism by the condition of the Indian peasant, so Attlee had been by the condition of the British working class in the East End of London. The British Labour party attracted a surprising number of such men from upper middle-class families, who, because of the superior education and the self-assurance of their class, naturally gravitated towards leadership. For many of them, the Labour party, with its strong non-conformist background, resembled a sort of secular Salvation Army. But apart from their socialism, there were no other similarities between Nehru and Attlee and none whatsoever between the parties they led. Attlee was no revolutionary, his socialism was slow and cautious. Unlike Nehru, he was an exceptionally good judge of men and events. He had always supported the orderly, somewhat schoolmasterish British approach to self-government for India. But this had been at a time when Britain was still powerful, still able to carry out her obligations. Times had now changed. Britain had emerged from the war seriously weakened and would need all her resources for her own recovery. Attlee was above all very conscious that, as the first Labour prime minister with a working majority, his primary responsibility was to those who had elected him to office. Labour voters were demanding a new deal and the fulfilment of long-stated promises. It seemed that Britain could be remade into a socialist paradise and all pressures for doctrinaire reform were upon the prime minister. The Labour party was prepared—had in fact been conditioned over the years—to sacrifice India in order to create a new Britain. It is one of the coincidences of history that as a party came to power ready for sacrifice, there appeared to sensible men no alternative but sacrifice. One sacrifice was to beget another. In India, the Congress party was forced, because there seemed to be no acceptable alternative, to sacrifice its dream of a united free India.

Of the factors that made up the equation of British India, two now counted for very little: those who actually ruled, and the people of India. The British element in the Civil Services had dropped to nearly half what it had been in 1935. The Indian Army, which had grown vastly during the war, had now about 11,400 British officers but would have only 4,000 by 1947. The proportion of Indian officers would naturally increase to fill the gap. The British members of the ICS became more concerned with their own future than with that of India. A few, out of a rather distorted sense of duty, were to play a minor and essentially treasonable game with some of the Indian princes, but most were anxious only to pack up and go home.

The people of India, apart from those butchered in riots in the back streets of the cities, got on with the job of scraping a living. They were, it seemed, not needed in the last act, though they and their leader, Gandhi, would be kept on call. They still had the Mahatma moving amongst them to divert their minds to other and more comprehensible things than the comings and goings of strange men at Delhi.

Nor did the British people have any active role to play. As we shall see, however, one of the factors that contributed to the speed at which the transfer of power was finally made was the Labour government's desire to see that they did not become active.

2 Three Wise Men

Though the Simla conference had produced nothing of value except a restatement of Jinnah's claim for Pakistan—a claim which practically no one, at least in Congress, took seriously—one thing had been agreed. Elections must be held in India as soon as possible. Both Congress and the League needed the election results as public proof of their power and their representative character. Certainly, elections were long overdue. The Central Assembly had been elected as far back as 1934, and the provincial legislatures in 1937. Everyone agreed that by now these bodies were totally unrepresentative of the electorate. In fact, the government would have been wise to have held the elections *before* the Simla conference; then Congress and the League would have been able to base their claims on up-to-date foundations, and it is possible that the conference might have had a rather different outcome because of that. The excuse, an essentially sound one, had been that elections were impossible under wartime conditions. On 21 August 1945, however, the government announced that elections would take place as soon as possible.

Before the actual date for them was set, the viceroy, Lord Wavell, was recalled to London for consultations with the new Labour government. On his return, he brought with him very little comfort. The Labour government seemed to think that the Cripps offer of three years earlier was still sufficient. After the elections, it was announced, the viceroy would take steps to bring representative Indians into his Executive Council, and a constitution-making body would be convened as soon as possible. There was no mention of 'independence'— only the usual phrases, eroded of meaning by constant repetition over the years: 'self-government', 'full self-government', 'early achievement of full self-government', and so on. It was obvious that the new Labour government was still thinking in terms of dominion status, of 'free and equal partnership'. It was as if a new stepfather had decided to give his grown-up son a separate set of rooms in the family mansion, when what the boy really yearned for was a place of his own away from parental control. Congress quite understandably described these anaemic proposals as 'vague, inadequate and unsatisfactory'. Most political parties in India felt the same way. Perhaps the most soul-destroying thing of all was that there was to be no *immediate* change. For example, the old ministries which had resigned in 1939 were not to be allowed to form interim governments in the provinces in the period before the elections. Nor was the very restricted franchise—only 10 per cent of the population had voting rights—to be enlarged. It looked as if the Labour government was not only offering the same old proposals but the same built-in reasons for rejecting them. It seemed to be a false dawn.

Nevertheless, the parties began to build up their organizations and to frame their election promises. The Muslim League, characteristically, was not much concerned with a detailed and constructive programme. For the League there were only two fighting issues—Pakistan, and the proof that the Muslim League was the only organization that could speak for the Muslims of India.

Congress made it clear that its programme was based on the 'Quit India' resolution of 1942, and that it would contest the election 'to show that the inevitable result . . . must be to demonstrate the over-whelming solidarity of opinion of the voters on the issue of inde-pendence'. Flicking Jinnah aside, the statement loftily continued: 'Therefore in this election, petty issues do not count nor do individuals nor sectarian cries—only one thing counts: the freedom and indepen-dence of our motherland from which all other freedoms will flow to our people.'

These were admirable sentiments, no doubt, but they only partly concealed a widening division in the ranks of the Congress leadership. Hindus and Muslims were divided in Congress as elsewhere. The president of Congress, Maulana Azad—himself a Muslim—said that Congress *did* accept the principle of self-determination, 'even to the extent of separation under certain circumstances'. He personally, however, thought the division of India would not be to Muslim advantage. In any case, if separation was desired, the present provincial boundaries would have to be redrawn. Muslim League newspapers, already condemning Azad as a traitor, now accused him of advocating a 'maimed, mutilated Pakistan'. Hindu Congressmen, led by Patel, would have none of Azad's 'reasonableness'. For Patel, there was not going to be any partition of India on religious grounds. The usual confused rigmarole now emanated from Congress spokesmen. Freedom must come to a *united* India, they insisted—though, of course, Congress 'cannot think in terms of compelling people'! Confusing phrases implied confused thought, and obscure language and conditional clauses satisfied no one. But one thing was sure. The bulk of Congress was not prepared to compromise with the Muslim League.

The result of this war of words was that the elections were fought, not over independence, but on the issue of a united India or a divided one. Whatever Congress had hoped to gain by contesting the elections on an independence platform was doomed to failure—the communal issue became paramount, and the emphasis on independence, by which Congress had tried to divert the electorate from the communal problem, soon had serious repercussions on the peace of India. The INA trials were used by Congress propagandists to glorify the right to rebel against foreign rule, and Pandit Nehru called on the people to prepare 'for a mass battle for freedom'. This and many other inflammatory speeches by Congressmen increased unease, encouraged rioting, and convinced the Muslims that Congress was in a warlike mood. Was Congress only pretending to threaten the British while it really meant to threaten the Muslim League? It seemed likely.

Congress leaders demanded that the British get out and leave the communal problem to them. 'Civil war if need be' formed the theme of many speeches. The general implication was that if Jinnah wanted Pakistan then he would have to fight for it.

The British government now became concerned over real violence, for rioting and disorder were rife and there was a threat of more. The new secretary of state for India, Lord Pethick-Lawrence, after repeating that elections were an indispensable step towards self-government, announced in December that a parliamentary delegation representing the three major British political parties would go to India in order to assure Indian leaders of Britain's sincerity. This dazzling offer seemed finally to prove that the Labour government was incapable of any new approach. It talked like its predecessors and it acted like them. Wearing the straitjacket of precedent, was it not likely to think in the same antique and often-discredited terms? The announcement was treated with an almost unanimous lack of enthusiasm. The delegation was not only composed of nonentities, it did not even have instructions to make an official inquiry nor submit an official report. Where an imaginative and dynamic gesture was called for, all the Labour government could think of doing was to send a second-rate goodwill mission.

The elections, fought over the real issues of unity or division, revealed that Congress and the Muslim League did have overwhelming support from the Hindu and Muslim communities respectively. Congress won all the elective seats in the Central Assembly except those reserved for Muslims, which were won by League candidates. In the provinces, Congress increased its representation over the 1937 results and won absolute majorities in eight provinces, and in the remaining three it was the second largest party. The Muslim League which, in 1937, had won only 108 seats out of the 492 reserved for Muslims, now captured 428, although in two of the provinces—Assam and the North-west Frontier Province—which were claimed by Jinnah as part of Pakistan-to-be, Congress had gained absolute majorities. In the remaining three provinces that were to make up the proposed Muslim state—Bengal, Sind and the Punjab—the League, though the largest single party, did not have an absolute majority. From these results, it may appear as if the League had failed even in the heartland of its chosen territory. But this is not really true, as the number of seats allotted to Muslims under the 1935 constitution was less than it should have been in relation to the size of the Muslim population. The new voting pattern, however, made it clear that other minority parties were of little consequence. India was divided between Congress and the Muslim League.

For Britain at least the elections seemed to simplify the problem. She had always maintained that it was her unavoidable duty to protect the minorities, but it was now clear that she could not protect them all. Henceforth the smaller communities must remain on the periphery. Britain could no longer concern herself with their welfare. The problem, in fact—as had always been the case since Jinnah became leader of the Muslim League—concerned Hindus and Muslims only. Clement Attlee voiced this realization in the House of Commons in March 1946. 'We cannot make Indians responsible for governing themselves,' he said, 'and, at the same time, retain over here the responsibility for the treatment of minorities and the power to intervene on their behalf.' One of the basic tenets of British rule in India—that its justification rested in protection of the weak—had been washed away at the polling booths. The British government could no longer delude itself with the moral arguments of the past. The problem had now been brought home to the government as it had to the Indian voter. Unity or division. To those, all things must be subordinate.

The British government recognized that it would have to make some positive gesture if there was to be any solution at all. Pressures, both overt and secret, were growing. Indians seemed incapable of constructive decision. The only answer was to produce a detailed plan which could be argued over and modified if necessary; but the Labour government was as enmeshed in the old mystique as the Conservatives and Liberals who had gone before. It was not as yet ready to capitulate to the terrible logic of Indian reality. The Labour party was determined to rid itself of India—but not of history. It was perfectly willing to dissolve the empire, but not to break it up. None of its members wanted Britain to become only a tiny island off the coast of Europe, and it occurred to them that a great Commonwealth could have as much, if not more prestige than a dependent empire. India had been the visible symbol of British greatness. An independent India would naturally assume the old British role in Asia. If the business was to be handed down, it had to be handed down as a unit. Attlee announced in February 1946 that a Cabinet Mission of three wise men would visit India. These were Sir Stafford Cripps, president of the board of trade, Lord Pethick-Lawrence, secretary of state for India, and A. V. Alexander, first lord of the Admiralty.

The choice, on the surface at least, was not particularly exciting. Cripps, the 'Devil's Advocate' of 1942; Pethick-Lawrence, a generous, honest man whose reputation appeared to be founded on an early involvement in the suffragette movement; and Alexander, a party stalwart whose career gave no indication that he could contribute very much to the solution of a complex and alien problem. Their cabinet rank, however, rather than the men themselves was an indication of the importance the government attached to their visit. To Indians, it seemed that the British government at last was serious. To reinforce this impression, Attlee announced that the mission's purpose was to set up a constitution-making body and a representative Executive Council. They would take to India with them no British proposals for the form of the constitution—that was for Indians themselves to decide, without interference. Furthermore, there was now no question of dominion

status. If Indians wanted to remain within the Commonwealth, it was
to be their choice and theirs alone.

Among these unambiguous statements, one cryptic remark was to
stand out like a sore thumb, and it is not too fanciful to say that it
provided one of the reasons for the mission's failure. 'We are very
mindful,' said Attlee, 'of the rights of minorities and minorities should
be able to live free from fear. *On the other hand, we cannot allow a
minority to place a veto on the advance of the majority.*' If this had any
meaning at all, it was directed against the Muslim League. 'The issue is,
to give a simile,' Jinnah remarked, 'walk into my parlour, said the
spider to the fly, and if the fly refuses it is said that a veto is being
exercised and the fly is being intransigent.' Did the British government
still think of the Muslims as a minority, when for all these years Jinnah
had been proclaiming that they were a nation? The mission, on the day
after its arrival in India, tried to eradicate this unfortunate impression,
but it is doubtful whether they succeeded in doing so.

Cripps and Pethick-Lawrence—Alexander was merely a pas-
senger—soon became aware of the tragic realities of the Indian political
scene. They listened to many different points of view, and what they
heard only reinforced the actuality of the Hindu-Muslim confrontation.
Would there be a civil war if Britain left, having handed over power to
a Congress-dominated Centre? If there was a civil war, there were
men and nations who might take advantage of it. Britain's wartime
honeymoon with Russia was over and the old fears had returned. In
Tsarist days, Russia had always been the main threat to India, and only
the strength and unity that Britain had imposed had protected the
country from invasion from the north. The Soviet Union, which had
revived a good deal of Tsarist legend to boost morale during the war,
might also revive the Tsarist dream of conquering India. Even if this
thought were merely a nightmare, civil war would be sure to affect
British business interests in India just when they were most needed to
bolster the tottering economy of a war-exhausted Britain. But the
solution of partition seemed almost as hazardous as leaving India to
Congress. The Indian Army would have to be divided; so would the
public services. There would be an unavoidable period of administrative and military chaos which might be almost as bad as a civil war.
Nevertheless, the mission was forced to choose between two evils, and
it seemed to them that partition might well be the lesser.

To the problem that faced the Cabinet Mission there appeared to be only one key, and that was held by Muhammad Ali Jinnah. But what did he want? Pakistan, the League claimed, must comprise the whole of the provinces of Assam, Bengal, the Punjab, the North-West Frontier Province, Sind, and Baluchistan. If this was conceded, however, it would mean that the new state would also include large areas where Muslims were in fact in a minority. The alternative—to slice off the Muslim-majority areas from the rest of the Punjab and Bengal— would only create other problems, for, in both provinces, there was a common language and a common tradition shared by both Muslims and Hindus. To divide the Punjab would also mean cutting in two the homeland of some four million Sikhs, who could hardly be expected to view the prospect with equanimity. Furthermore, Pakistan itself would thus be divided into two halves, each with a dangerous frontier, and with eight hundred miles of India in between. From any reasonable point of view, it would be something of an abortion. But this was hardly the time for logic—reason had been blown away in the growing storm of emotion. Congress was demanding that Britain should 'Quit India', while the League demanded that she should 'Divide and Quit', implying that Britain should not leave until she had imposed partition, by force if necessary. In the meanwhile, however, the League was pre- pared to join a reformed Executive Council, although only on the understanding that Congress would accept the principle of partition and that there should be two constituent assemblies, one for Pakistan and the other for the rest of India.

The solution offered by Congress was the old one—let Britain with- draw and India would settle her own problems. The Labour govern- ment, however, was even less likely to accept this solution than the Conservative administration had been. If India exploded into civil war, the Labour government would be held responsible—just as, years later, the Belgian government was to be held responsible for the tragedy of the Congo. The Labour government might just manage to justify its actions in Britain—though even this seemed unlikely—but in the eyes of the world it would appear to have been callous and indifferent to the sufferings of those who had depended upon it. Some Congress- men suggested—and it showed that there was a sizeable body of opinion that had very little faith in the ability of Indians to settle their own problems peacefully—that the Pakistan issue might be submitted to some international tribunal. But did this really offer a way out of the deadlock? What if neither side agreed to accept an outside award? Who was going to impose it? Certainly not the British, who were in a hurry to leave. There was no alternative; the mission would have to search for some sort of workable compromise.

Congress itself occasionally seemed ready to explore the possibilities, but it spoke with conflicting voices. Some of its leaders were so inconsistent that it was impossible to know what their opinions really were. One day Nehru would proclaim that he was 'prepared to view with respect a demand for Pakistan if it is made after the freedom of the country had been achieved'—a statement both reasonable and accommodating. But a few days earlier, he had said that 'Congress is not going to agree to the Muslim League's demand for Pakistan under any circumstances whatsoever, even if the British government agrees to it'. Patel, too, declared that there could be no compromise on Pakistan, yet remarked that Congress would be prepared to give 'the fullest autonomy possible in the areas in which Muslims are predominantly in the majority'. But, he added, 'subject to a strong Centre'. There is little wonder that Jinnah found it easy to keep up Muslim tensions and fears.

Once again it was to be Maulana Azad who suggested the basis for a compromise. The formula he offered was deceptively simple. There should be, he said, full autonomy for the provinces in a loose federation, with a central government responsible only for defence, foreign affairs and communications, although the provinces should be able to cede powers to the Centre in order to allow overall economic and administrative planning. The mission's view—it was really that of Cripps, who had a brilliant analytical mind unsullied by the emotions of ordinary men—was that the last part of the suggestion, the ceding of powers to the Centre, would not work for purely functional reasons. The mission then departed for a short holiday in Kashmir, expressing the naïve hope that while they were away the two parties might arrive at a settlement for themselves. When the mission returned and found that no such settlement had been achieved, it began once again the weary round of talks with Congress and League leaders.

The result was a new proposal very little different from that suggested by Azad—there would be a central government responsible for defence, foreign affairs and communications, and the provinces would be divided into two groups, one predominantly Hindu and the other Muslim. The mission invited Congress and the League each to send four negotiators to explore the possibility of an agreement on this basis. This they did, and the conference opened at Simla on 5 May 1946. The delegates seemed to be treating the proposals seriously, and the mission supplied a mass of data outlining the details of how such an arrangement might work. It was all highly ingenious—on paper. A sort of lawyer's brief for a test case in a legal textbook.

If the proposals had been accepted they would not have worked, because the Centre would have been weak and divided. The plan could only have functioned if the continuing goodwill of all parties was guaranteed, and it was most unlikely that, even if initial goodwill could be created, it would survive more than the first few months of independence. To even the detached observer, the plan looked like a clever trick by which Britain might slip out from under the burden of choice.

Surprisingly enough, it seemed that both Congress and the League were approaching the proposals with unprecedented seriousness, but in reality the two parties were speaking different languages and had no interest in understanding each other. Any suggestion of a strong central government was anathema to the League but axiomatic for Congress. Later, the mission tried to claim that both parties had been 'prepared to make considerable concessions' but it was deluding itself and the public in saying so. Congress *had* apparently agreed to provincial groupings, but only if there was to be a strong Centre. The League was prepared to submit to a central government, but only if it was weak. In reality, no concessions had been made at all. Reluctantly, the mission was compelled to announce the failure of the Simla conference.

The mission, however, had not reached the end of its resources and, with the approval of the British government, it proposed its own immediate solution. The statement contained one paragraph which read: 'We [the mission] are unable to advise the British government that the power which at present resides in British hands should be handed over to two entirely separate sovereign states. . . .' Instead it proposed an Indian Union, very much as before, with autonomy for the provinces. The provinces were to be 'free to form groups'. A new idea was that there could be reconsideration of the arrangements every ten years, but the main virtue of the proposals lay in their outline of a way in which the constitution-making body might be set up. The mission also advocated the immediate formation of an interim government. Fundamentally, in fact, what they now offered was not a solution but the machinery for arriving at one. The statement ended with a claim that the plan offered a way for India to attain independence 'in the shortest time and with the least danger of internal disturbance and conflict'. The alternative, it said, could only be 'a grave danger of violence, chaos and even civil war'.

The mission's attempt—and basically it was no more than this—to substitute action for talk was, to its surprised satisfaction, received favourably by both Congress and the League. Gandhi, with inapposite rhetoric, hailed the plan as containing 'a seed to convert this land of sorrow into one without sorrow and suffering'.

Both sides, inevitably, interpreted the proposals to suit themselves. Congress said that the clause on grouping meant that each province could choose either to join the appropriate group or to stay out. The League, on the other hand, believed the clause meant that grouping would be compulsory. This analysing of words was yet another example of the different ways in which the British and Indians treated the language—the British with characteristic looseness, and the Indians with dictionary precision. 'Free to form groups,' said the lawyers of Congress, implied freedom not to form groups. The mission said this was not what they meant; it was their intention that grouping should be compulsory.

Nevertheless, the mission seemed to have achieved a major breakthrough. The Muslim League accepted the proposals on the understanding that grouping would be compulsory, and Congress announced that it was prepared to co-operate in setting up a constituent assembly.

Congress did question a number of points, one of which was the right of Europeans to representation in the constituent assembly. Because of the special provisions of the Government of India Act of 1935, Europeans were to be entitled to representation vastly out of proportion to their number. In Bengal and Assam, for example, twenty-one thousand Europeans would, on the present basis, elect as many members as would seven million of the rest of the population. In any case, Congress said, if Indians were to be solely responsible for deciding their own future, why should the European community have any representation at all? The mission replied that it was not prepared to deprive Europeans of their vote. When the elections were held, however, the Europeans did in fact abstain from voting. Congress also protested against British troops remaining in India during the interim period before independence, although it was later to be thankful for their presence.

Other political groups in India were outspoken against the proposals, for they seemed to ignore all but Congress, League and British interests. The Scheduled Castes Federation declared that the plan's vague provision for their protection was 'absolutely illusory and unworthy of serious consideration'. The Sikhs of the Punjab, foreseeing the liquidation of their homeland, stated that 'no constitution will be acceptable to the Sikhs which does not meet their just demands and is settled without their consent', and they began to prepare themselves to resist partition. The Hindu Mahasabha rejected the 'principle of regionalism based on communalism' and its agents stepped up their incitement of religious violence. The princes, on the other hand, who had been told that after British paramountcy lapsed they would be able to negotiate their own position with the successors, accepted the proposals with some qualifications.

The Cabinet Mission seemed justified in its satisfaction with the Congress and League attitudes to the setting up of a constituent assembly. For the first time, Jinnah appeared openly co-operative, though he had repeated that a 'sovereign Pakistan' was the 'unalterable objective of the Muslims of India'. In reality, however, he had not changed his attitude, only his tactics. Not for one moment did he believe that the Congress tiger had given up its hope of swallowing the Muslims. Soon he was to have his judgement confirmed.

Maulana Azad, who had at least shown real awareness of the depth of Muslim feelings, relinquished the office of Congress president to Pandit Nehru. Though inconsistent by nature, on one issue Nehru was totally consistent; he did not like Jinnah and the Muslim League. He genuinely hated parties based upon narrow religious motives. To him, communalism was a monster, whose head was the League and whose claws were stained with the blood of innocent men murdered in the sordid streets of the cities. Jinnah he viewed with contempt as the fascist demagogue he was. Nehru believed, against all the evidence— including the voting figures in the last election—that Jinnah had no real backing. Ironically enough, it was Nehru's contempt for the strength of the Muslim League that helped convince the British that partition was necessary if a civil war was to be avoided.

Nehru had inherited the mantle of Gandhi, but he also spoke as the rational exponent of a rational socialism, and his distaste for Jinnah struck a chord in both the left and right wings of Congress. At this critical time, however, he displayed a total lack of statesmanship. Congress, he replied to a journalist, who asked him whether his party accepted the Cabinet Mission plan in every detail, was 'completely unfettered by agreements'. How pleased Jinnah must have been; Congress was working for him—and in double shifts. Enemies of Nehru today, from Congressmen who would like to see his influence destroyed, to employees of Lord Beaverbrook, have condemned him for this and other statements made at this time. On Nehru has been placed a large part of the blame for the partition of India. His contempt for Jinnah has been unfavourably contrasted with the pragmatic intelligence of Maulana Azad. But blame will not be so readily apportioned by those who have followed the history of the Hindu-Muslim conflict in the early pages of this book. The gap between Hindu and Muslim was by now unbridgeable, and Nehru's speeches were not the isolated remarks of one leader. Hundreds of others were saying just the same thing, although Westernized intellectuals like Nehru did not reach their conclusions by the same process as the majority of Congress. It just so happened that the progressives' distaste for religion disguised as politics in the end added up to the same thing as reactionary Hindu dislike of Islam. In the main, Congress *was* a Hindu party inadequately disguised behind a secular mask.

Congress assisted Jinnah in his campaign for Pakistan, and its spokesmen supplied him with the bulk of his propaganda. But it was age-old fears that sustained him, fears concerned with murder and oppression and not with Western political shibboleths. The mistake of many people at the time, and of most commentators later, was to believe that Jinnah's main aim was to create a new state of Pakistan, when in fact all his actions were negative, directed at *preventing* an undivided, Congress-dominated India. In dealing with him, the Azads and the Rajagopalacharis—honest, reasonable men searching for honest, reasonable solutions—had no hope of success. Fanaticism cannot be opposed by reason. Jinnah could afford to seem accommodating at one moment and intractable at the next, but at no time did he make an actual concession, nor did he have any intention of honouring a promise. Nehru may have exhibited petulance and conceit, but even if he had dispensed nothing but sweetness and light it would have made no difference to Jinnah. It could only have resulted in delaying independence while the British searched for a solution it was no longer possible to find.

Discussions over the composition of the proposed interim government, which had been going on simultaneously with the controversy over the constituent assembly, made it clear that the League—while apparently accepting the long-term proposals for setting up a constituent assembly—was not really being co-operative at all. The nub of the problem still concerned the allotment of seats between the various parties and interests. Wavell had tried to get agreement on a Centre composed of Hindus and Muslims in equal proportions plus representatives of the minorities. He had suggested five representatives from Congress, five from the League, and two from the minorities. Congress, which had reluctantly approved the principle of parity at the Simla conference of 1945, was in 1946 not prepared to accept it. Wavell now put forward an ingenious compromise—a council of thirteen consisting of six Congress representatives, of whom one must be drawn from the 'scheduled castes', five from the League, and two from the minorities. Thus parity would actually be maintained between Hindus and Muslims, yet Congress would have one more seat. But there was no hope that the League would be duped by this sleight of hand. Jinnah said that when the five: five: two formula had been offered to him the viceroy had assured him that it was final. Wavell denied this. Jinnah responded by offering to put the new formula to his working committee only *after* Congress had agreed to it. Congress, however, would have nothing to do with it. The deadlock continued.

Again, the Cabinet Mission and the viceroy tried to get things moving by publishing their own proposals and inviting the parties to accept them. But the mission's proposals were only another variant on Wavell's last offer: six Hindu members of Congress, including one from the 'scheduled castes', five from the League, one Sikh, one Indian Christian, and one Parsee. The mission excused its lack of originality by saying that its proposals were designed only to settle the composition of the interim government and implied no commitment for any other occasion. The statement, as always, ended with a clause (paragraph 8) so phrased as to allow different interpretations of its precise meaning.

'In the event of the two major parties or either of them proving unwilling to join in the setting up of a Coalition Government on the above lines, it is the intention of the viceroy to proceed with the formation of an Interim Government which will be as representative as possible of those willing to accept the Statement of May 16th [concerning the constituent assembly].'

Congress and the League reacted to the proposals in the way that any intelligent person would have expected. Neither of them was taken in by the mission's juggling with figures. The League complained that it would be in a perpetual minority, Congress that there was parity between Hindus and Muslims. Both parties had other objections but these paled into insignificance when the newspapers reported that Congress contemplated appointing a *Muslim* Congressman to one of its seats. To this provocation, Jinnah reacted by insisting that Muslim League representatives must be the *only* Muslims. This of course Congress could not accept, because it would be an admission of the truth of Jinnah's contention that Congress was a Hindu organization and not the secular national party it claimed to be.

Rejecting Wavell's argument that the nominations of a Congress Muslim to a Hindu seat would be most improper, the Congress Working Committee met on 25 June and officially refused the viceroy's terms for an interim government. It had really no alternative but to reject Jinnah's challenge to its claim that it was an organization representing the whole of the Indian people. The working committee also officially announced that, though it accepted the Cabinet Mission's proposals for setting up a constituent assembly, it did so only on the basis of its own interpretation of what these proposals actually meant.

The mission was now faced with two acceptances hedged by all manner of variable reservations. But it believed that if it could get the League and Congress together in a constituent assembly, good sense would prevail and some reasonable settlement would be arrived at. It was obvious that the mission was living in a never-never land of its own devising, although there may have been an excuse for this. Cripps and Pethick-Lawrence were tired men, anxious to get home and participate in the remaking of Britain as a socialist paradise. It was the height of the hot weather in India, the season when the Delhi climate has a stifling, searing embrace, and the mission had been negotiating at high pressure for nearly three months in an atmosphere heavy with unreality. Cripps and Pethick-Lawrence decided to assume that, despite the reservations, Congress and the League had genuinely accepted the scheme for setting up a constituent assembly. But the League had not yet stated its position on the question of an interim government. Jinnah, the mission, and the viceroy met on 25 June, when Jinnah was told that Congress's rejection of the interim government proposals meant that, under the terms of paragraph 8, the whole scheme had broken down, but that the viceroy would be prepared to re-open negotiations after a short interval. Elections for the constituent assembly—the body which was to frame a constitution—were however imminent and it might be as well to get them over first.

Jinnah went straight from this interview to a meeting of the Muslim League Working Committee. There he told members that he interpreted paragraph 8 to mean that, if the League accepted the proposals for an interim government, the viceroy was bound to form one, *even if it excluded Congress*. Jinnah accused both the mission and the viceroy of a breach of faith and demanded postponement of the elections for the constituent assembly. As preparations for these were already far advanced, the viceroy wrote briskly to Jinnah that: 'We do not propose to postpone them.' He also appointed a caretaker government to function until such time as the political leaders could agree on the composition of a new one.

The Cabinet Mission left India on 29 June under the impression that, despite everything, at least a constituent assembly would come into being. It carried with it to Westminster the air of unreality in which it had operated in India, for both Cripps and Pethick-Lawrence claimed in the British Parliament that the mission had been a success. But apart from a very doubtful acceptance of a constituent assembly, the mission had produced no change in the attitude of the two major parties. Congress was not prepared to move an inch from its position that power must be transferred to a united India. The League was still determined that this should never happen. The wise men from the West had brought no instant panaceas in their baggage, nor even a great deal of understanding of the problems they were supposed to solve. But at least one thing was now indisputable—the British really meant to leave India, and within a very short time. Even this, however,

created new problems, for there was now no incentive towards compromise between Congress and the League. There would be no need
for a war of independence against Britain, only for a war of succession,
a fight over the inheritance. The possibility was no longer rebellion.
It was civil war.

3 The Menacing Shadows

While the Cabinet Mission had been in India there had been compara-
tive peace in the narrow streets of her crowded cities, but the peace was
only an insecure lid on a bubbling pot. Other happenings, however,
were to have an effect on the Labour government's future plans, for
the trustworthiness of the armed forces—on whom a great deal of the
responsibility for any peaceful transfer of power would ultimately lie—
came into question. In the middle of January 1946, the British authorities, who had always feared the possibility of revolt in their Indian
units, were shocked by a mutiny amongst the British. The ground and
maintenance units at Dum Dum airport near Calcutta and at other
RAF stations in India and the Middle East mutinied over delays in
repatriation and demobilization. The great majority of the men were
civilian conscripts, anxious only to be freed from the petty restriction of
service life, who apparently believed that a Labour government—*their*
government—should do something about it. They offered no violence to their officers, for their action was more of a strike than a
mutiny, but in Calcutta jittery service chiefs had troops standing by.
The mutineers, however, received reassurance from a visiting Labour
member of parliament, and returned to work. But the red light had
gone on. Could an army consisting almost entirely of unwilling
conscripts be kept in India and used on riot and other demoralizing
duties? And could a Labour prime minister be prepared to extend the
military service of the sons of his principal supporters in order that they
might shoot down Indians?

The immediate effects, however, were of more consequence than
speculations about the future. The Royal Indian Air Force, imitating
the RAF, also became insubordinate and even went so far as to declare
its sympathy with the INA. But again there was no violence. That was
to be left to the Indian Navy. In Bombay, the principal naval base, a

number of ratings refused to eat or attend parade. The next day, three
thousand Indian sailors mutinied on board their ships and in barracks
ashore. They removed their officers—who were all white—attacked
British soldiers in the streets of Bombay and roamed the city in lorries
covered with slogans and the flags of Congress and the Muslim League.
They were, however, soon rounded up—significantly enough, by
Indian troops—without casualties on either side, and the mutineers
were confined to their barracks. The next day, however, they tried to
break out and the troops guarding them opened fire. Some ratings,
who had evaded capture, attacked the Indian soldiers with small arms
and grenades. The British called up aircraft but did not use them.
Those mutineers who had remained in ships in the harbour trained
their guns on the city and threatened to bombard it, and a broadcast
appeal by the admiral commanding was received with derision.

Congress leaders, including Patel who was in Bombay, urged the
mutineers to surrender, which they did. But four days of civil riots
and disorder followed in the city. The Navy also mutinied at Calcutta
and Madras and, rather more seriously, at Karachi, where the military
commander turned artillery on the mutineers causing considerable
casualties and loss of life. It was obvious that there had been organization behind the mutinies and some of it had undoubtedly originated
with left-wing elements in Congress. Though Congress condemned
the mutinies, for political reasons the mutineers were not punished with
the severity they deserved. Nehru and others were slowly beginning to
realize that it was *their* navy that was rebelling against authority,
that lawlessness, once encouraged, was very difficult to stop. Freedom
was at hand, and it needed only to be negotiated, not bought with
blood. But, in actual fact, neither Congress nor the Muslim League was
in a position to control events. There were others—political extremists,
religious fanatics, gangsters with friends in high places—whose fingers
were on the trigger. Any angry speech by a League or Congress leader
provided the excuse. The politicians might be genuinely horrified by
the consequences, but they seemed to think that it was not their responsibility. While they used the threat of violence as a political weapon,
there were others ready to give it reality. The politicians, with their
inflammatory speeches, had created a climate of horrified expectancy.
All over India, ordinary people were looking anxiously over their
shoulders, eyeing neighbours of a different religious persuasion and

wondering—sometimes not for long—whether they should strike first.

The conspirators—Hindu reactionaries of the Mahasabha, Sikhs sharpening their swords and their memories, princes addicted to bizarre 'eccentricities', left-wing agitators fresh from Moscow, and criminals with an eye to the main chance—were all waiting for some really big opportunity. Theirs was not a single conspiracy but a large number of separate, sometimes even personal, plans to create and take advantage of anarchy. The opportunity was soon to come.

In the meanwhile, the British, whose Intelligence had not yet altogether collapsed, were to some extent aware of what was going on. But they were hamstrung by the unprecedented political situation. It had finally been brought home to the administration that its days were numbered. Whatever it decided to do, however wise and good its actions, it was likely to be misinterpreted. And anyway, were the police and the army 'safe'? Could even British troops be trusted?

In the narrow world of the newspaper headline, everything seems clearcut. Great names are bandied about as if their bearers are the sole arbiters of events. But great happenings are always made up of more than the speeches and actions of the personalities who stalk the public stage. Behind the front men are the real deciders, who can influence events even by doing nothing. The British administration in India was winding down in the uncertainty of its members' future. Accustomed to act without fearing much more than departmental disapproval, officials were now not sure who they were ultimately responsible to. Men on the spot, who in the past would have assumed immediate responsibility and argued afterwards, were now more inclined to wait and consult higher authority, to debate what they should do before doing it. It was a perfectly understandable attitude for them to take. But for the men of violence, the signs were there to see. The British were weak, and they were unlikely to move decisively against disorder.

Back in the other world, in the rarefied field of the politicians, events were on the move. Out of them was soon to emerge the excuse the violent men were waiting for. Elections for the constituent assembly took place and Congress and the Muslim League surpassed even their triumphal showing at the last election. The League won 73 seats, all but five of those which had been reserved for Muslims, and Congress won

205. Ironically enough, the results gave satisfaction to both parties, although they did not mean that either side was prepared to breathe life into the assembly itself. Nehru had already stated, 'We [Congress] will remain in that assembly so long as we think it is good for India. . . . *We are not bound by a single thing.*' He had gone on to outline ideas for a much more powerful Centre than the one which had been suggested by the Cabinet Mission, and he also added that it was his belief that there would probably be no groupings of provinces at all. In effect, he was rejecting the whole basis of the mission's plan, so hopefully devised to placate Jinnah and the League; he seemed to think that there was no inconsistency in Congress accepting the plan and then going into the constituent assembly in order to change the only two provisions that might make it work. Of course, Nehru was under pressure from the representatives of provinces such as Assam, which had a Hindu majority but which would probably be forced to join a Muslim-majority group. He was also under pressure from the left wing of Congress, which seemed to think that nothing had changed since 1942 and that the real enemy was still the British. Nehru was simply re-stating his belief that the British were about to leave and that Congress would be able to push the Muslim League aside.

With Nehru's words echoing in Muslim ears, Jinnah met the council of the League. He had already demanded an assurance from the British government that the constituent assembly would be forced to follow the mission's plans for it, and had received some mild assurances in the House of Commons. Jinnah, however, was now ready for a showdown —no more talk of compromise, no more trust in the words of the 'treacherous' British. 'I feel we have exhausted all reason,' he said. 'It is no use looking to any other source for help or assistance. There is no other tribunal to which we can go. The only tribunal is the Muslim nation.'

The League withdrew its acceptance of the Cabinet Mission's plan for the constituent assembly. Jinnah spoke with feeling of his attempts to reach a compromise; the British had deceived him; they had backed down in face of Congress threats of another violent struggle; Congress was planning to dominate the assembly with its 'brute majority'. Henceforth, Muslims must fight their own battles.

'Are we alone,' he declaimed, 'to be guided by reason, justice, honesty and

fair play, when, on the other hand, there are perfidious dealings by Congress?
. . . Today Muslim India is stirred as never before, and has never felt so bitterly.
. . . Now there is no room left for compromise. Let us march on. . . . Never
have we in the whole history of the League done anything except by constitutional methods. . . . But now we are forced into this position. This day we bid
goodbye to constitutional methods.'

Jinnah was followed by others who seemed anxious to outdo him in
the warlike nature of their speeches. The council of the League called
upon Muslims to renounce all British titles and honours, 'in token of
their deep resentment of the attitude of the British', and the working
committee passed a resolution calling for Direct Action, 'to achieve
Pakistan . . . and get rid of the present slavery under the British and
the contemplated future of Centre Hindu domination'. 16 August was
to be Direct Action Day, though it was to be marked only by peaceful
meetings at which League leaders would explain why the Cabinet
Mission's plan had finally been rejected. Spokesmen of the League
maintained that the call for Direct Action was no incitement to communal violence. It was not a declaration of war, said Jinnah, 'it is
nothing but a statement about the steps we propose to take for our own
self-preservation and self-defence'. Congress, he alleged, was about to
launch another civil disobedience campaign. The British were getting
ready to suppress revolutionary activity. 'I also,' he said, 'am going to
make trouble'. The League's bellicose attitude was a further proof that
it had never had any real intention of working the Cabinet Mission's
plan.

Despite Jinnah's disclaimers, the threat of violence at least impressed
Congress—though not into any real attempt at conciliation. The
Congress Working Committee tried to explain away the ambiguities
in its declared policy. On 10 August it issued a statement declaring that,
while Congress did not approve all the Cabinet Mission's proposals,
it did accept the plan as a whole. Unfortunately, it could not leave well
alone and followed this statement with two paragraphs of explanation
which *seemed*, though the language was by no means clear, to bristle
with reservations. Six days later, after an appeal from Wavell, Nehru
went to Bombay to meet Jinnah.

In the meanwhile, negotiations had continued in an attempt to form
an interim government, but, in view of the League's rejection of the
mission plan, Wavell had sent Jinnah a letter on 8 August in which he

wrote, 'I have now decided to invite the Congress to make proposals
for an Interim Government'. Four days after this, the viceroy announced that Congress had accepted the invitation and that Nehru was
to visit Delhi to discuss details with Wavell. This was followed by a
letter from Nehru to Jinnah asking for his co-operation in a 'coalition
provisional government'. On the basis of this letter, Nehru and Jinnah
talked for over an hour. Nehru, still slightly suspicious of British intentions and afraid that Jinnah's intransigence might delay the independence he had fought for all his life, exerted his very considerable charm.
But mutual prejudices went too deep, and each man saw only the
image of the other which he had created in his own mind. There was
between them no respect, let alone trust. Jinnah saw 'an arrogant
Brahmin', Nehru a fascist demagogue. As Nehru drove away from
Jinnah's house, the black flags of the Muslim League seemed to flap in
his face—it was Direct Action Day. But this was Bombay, which had
only a small Muslim population, and all was quiet.

Away on the other side of India in Calcutta, however, Direct Action
had exploded into bloody madness. Bengal had a Muslim majority and
in Calcutta the provincial government was a Muslim League administration headed by H. S. Suhrawardy, a pleasure-loving and corrupt
politician who would have done well in the southern states of America.
During the war he had been minister in charge of food at the time of
the great Bengal famine of 1943, and it was authoritatively rumoured
that he had made a handsome profit out of the sufferings of his fellow-
countrymen. He had a well organized private army of thugs and was
not reluctant to use strong-arm tactics against political and business
opponents. His popularity with ordinary people was considerable, for
he had a high-coloured flamboyance which appealed to their drab
minds. Though a member of the Muslim League Working Committee,
he was really the president and sole beneficiary of the Suhrawardy
party. His political ideas were the product of personal ambitions and
he had no liking for Jinnah—a feeling which was heartily reciprocated. It was believed at the time that Suhrawardy hoped to make
Bengal an independent state after the departure of the British, but it is
unlikely that this shrewd voluptuary actually thought he could get
away with it. However, colour was given to this belief by a statement
he made in Delhi on 10 August. In it he declared that if Congress went
ahead and formed an interim government at the Centre, he would set

up his own interim government in Bengal. Nobody took much notice. Congress, in fact, did not believe that he could carry out his threat. Somewhat piqued, Suhrawardy decided that Direct Action Day might well be the best time to display his strength in the city of Calcutta. His bodyguard was in contact with the Muslim riffraff of the city—from which they had been recruited—and it would be easy enough for them to organize demonstrations of solidarity for their employer and, quite incidentally, for Pakistan. Calcutta has the worst slums in the world; crawling ant-heaps of terrifying poverty and disease. Out of them on the morning of 16 August marched the mobs—and they were not peaceful crowds off to a peaceful demonstration. Communal extremists and professional gangsters moved among them, spreading rumours that the Hindus were getting ready to kill all the Muslims in Bengal. 'Arm yourselves,' was the cry, 'and kill them before they kill you.' The gangsters had it all worked out. In Calcutta, Suhrawardy had declared a public holiday. Muslim shopkeepers were told to close their shops. Only Hindus would open theirs, and thus announce that they *were* Hindus. Then they could be killed and their shops could be looted. In the beginning, this was left to the professionals, but soon the scrawny, downtrodden slum-dwellers who followed behind began to take their part. Hindu men, women and children were waylaid, tormented, and then killed.

While all this was going on, Suhrawardy was addressing a mass meeting. He was in a jubilant mood and apparently did not notice the smoke rising from the many fires which had now been kindled in the city. Hindus and Sikhs—hardly needing encouragement from their own extremists—were now out for revenge, and soon found the innocent to wreak it on. There were no pitched battles, only sudden killing of the unarmed. The police, mainly Muslims, did their best, but they were naturally unwilling to attack their co-religionists. As soon as one street was cleared and the police had moved on, the mob moved up behind them. A crowd could disappear in a moment into the rabbit-warren of streets, only to emerge yelling for blood somewhere else.

The next day, as the author of this book entered Calcutta by the long road from the airfield, fires glowed on either side and the bodies of men, women and children, hideously mutilated, squelched under the wheels of the bus. The hot air smelt of fire and blood, and the mad yell-

ing of the mob echoed in the alleys. But the ordeal of Calcutta was by
no means over.

Sir Frederick Burrows, an ex-railwayman and trade union official
who had been appointed governor of Bengal by the Labour government as some sort of irrelevant proof that the old order in India (as
elsewhere) was changing, proved unequal to the demands of the crisis.
To his anxious inquiries, Suhrawardy replied that the police had everything under control. Burrows believed him. His British advisers
seemed paralysed. The army commander was away in Britain for a
conference, and his subordinates were not men of decision. Burrows
had toured the city on the first day, but the mobs had melted away in
front of his cavalacade and all he saw was empty streets. On the second
day, however, it became obvious even to Suhrawardy that the situation
was out of hand. The governor called in troops, and British and Gurkha
soldiers began to patrol the streets of what looked like a dead city. But
they could do no more than keep the gangs away from the main
thoroughfares. In the foetid alleys, the weak and the unprotected were
chopped to pieces or battered to death, and there was not very much
that could be done about it.

For four days this great city of over 2,500,000 inhabitants was a
stamping-ground for the underworld. Official figures gave 4,000 dead
and 10,000 injured—and that was probably on the conservative side.
Even then, the total in that terrible four days was greater than in all the
communal riots that had taken place throughout the whole history of
British rule. It seemed as if the civil war forecast by the politicians was at
hand, for the terror in Calcutta was a *civilian* terror created by ordinary
men and women incited to butchery and torture. No British were
assaulted; on the contrary, the few who were out in the streets received
only politeness from men whose fingers were still wet with blood.

Political leaders were horrified, but not horrified enough to go to
Calcutta. Only the viceroy, still clinging to his belief in Britain's
responsibility, went to the stricken city where he heard that all of the
picture was not dyed with blood. There had been attempts by Hindus
and Muslims working together to bring peace; decency and honest
human emotion had not been completely banished. Hindus had
sheltered Muslims and Muslims, Hindus, and many had died in an
attempt to protect those whom their leaders called enemies. But no
one except the viceroy really cared. The politicians condemned the

riots and hastened to deny responsibility for them, and the Calcutta riots at least gave Jinnah the satisfaction of overwhelming proof that Hindus and Muslims could not live together. The moral of the great Calcutta killings was that there must be Pakistan or civil war.

For the dead and the wounded, few had a moment to spare. Freedom was at hand and even if the purchase price included the blood of the innocent, what did it matter? Accusation, not action, was the order of the day. Jinnah accused Congress of fomenting the riots. Congress, with real justification, blamed the Muslim League government of Bengal.

But Congress's attention was really concentrated upon forming an interim government. Wavell, back from Calcutta, still believed that the only sure way to a stable India was for Hindus and Muslims to forget their differences and work together in the interests of India. While in Calcutta, he had had conversations with Kwaja Nazimuddin, a Muslim League leader who was known to be close to Jinnah, and had received a semi-assurance that, if Congress would accept the Cabinet Mission's plan in the way the mission itself interpreted it, the League might be willing to enter an interim government. Wavell, his conscience still raw from what he had seen in Calcutta, was only too willing to believe that Nazimuddin was expressing on behalf of the League a more reasonable and responsible attitude than it had hitherto taken. Perhaps by appealing to Congress, he could persuade them to a similar exercise of restraint and responsibility. Once again, Wavell deluded himself into believing that the nationalist leaders were concerned with moral issues and cared whether the people of India lived or died. They were not. At that time, they were concerned only with jockeying for power. Jinnah had begun to fear that Congress would form an interim government without League participation, thus getting a grip on the administrative machinery to the disadvantage of the League.

Wavell tried to persuade Nehru and Gandhi—who was once again being used by Congress as a figurehead—to agree to the Nazimuddin proposal. They would not, though Gandhi had said after the Calcutta rioting, 'We are not yet in the midst of civil war. But we are nearing it. At present we are playing at it.' Gandhi, however, was no longer in control of Congress policy, and Nehru was not prepared to co-operate. Why should he when control of an interim government, without Muslim League members, was in prospect? Wavell could not under-

stand how the apostle of non-violence and the Harrow-educated
socialist could be so indifferent to the sufferings of the people of India.
Wavell pointed out that if Congress alone formed a government the
Muslim League would retaliate with Direct Action. Did Nehru and
Gandhi view with equanimity the possibility of more Calcuttas? If
rioting were to spread, British troops would have to be used and they
would appear to be acting as instruments of a Congress government;
this could only lead to further violence, against the British as well as
against Congress. Gandhi's unhelpful suggestion was that British troops
should be withdrawn—this, at a time when other Congress leaders
were condemning the British for not doing more to preserve law and
order!

Wavell was emotionally unsuited to this sort of fencing. Arguments,
however wise, appeals to humanity, however justifiable, were totally
irrelevant. The viceroy and the political leaders were not even speaking
the same language. Congress still had a lurking suspicion that, though
the Labour government might mean what it said, there were powerful
interests in Britain and India using the League's demands as an excuse to
perpetuate British rule. There even seemed a possibility that the British
might arrest Congress leaders yet again. It was fairly obvious that
Congress did not have much faith in the Labour government's will or
in its power to control its representatives in India; the Labour government, they thought, was more concerned with reforms at home.

Now Congress began an underground campaign against the viceroy.
It was perfectly justified in doing so, for Wavell now appeared to be
trying to prevent Congress from joining the very government he had
specifically asked them to form. The British were famous—or infamous, according to the point of view—for their moral arguments.
Had they not always claimed to be trustees of the Indian people, and
had they not used that claim as an excuse to deny India self-government? Wavell's argument that something must be done to prevent
further bloodshed sounded like just another of Britain's moral excuses.
The modern bystander—especially the non-Indian able to judge by the
standards of his own experience—finds it easy to condemn Nehru and
Congress for pettiness, indifference, and general bloody-mindedness.
But these men had a heavy burden of experience, of oppression,
imprisonment, and broken promises. Suspicion, based upon the
evidence of the past, distorted their view of the present. 'Perhaps'

began to seem the most heavily-charged word in the language. The Labour party *had* supported India's claim for freedom, but perhaps it had done so only as part of the battle against its own political enemies. Was there really any reason to believe that, when in power, one Englishman was any different from another? The Labour government seemed genuinely about to grant India her freedom, but perhaps it was playing a double game. Perhaps, too, it might fall a victim to its own inexperience. Although it had appointed an ex-railwayman as governor of Bengal, it seemed otherwise to rely on the old rulers of India who were tainted with the guilt of the past.

The wisest move the new Labour government could have made after the war ended in 1945 would have been to replace Wavell, and the possibility had in fact been discussed. But who could they appoint instead? There were many in the Labour party who would have liked the appointment, who were as anxious as men of other political persuasions for the honours and awards of high office. The only really qualified candidates, however, were those most needed in the Labour cabinet at Westminster, a cabinet which was not conspicuous for its brilliance. But the primary reason for not appointing a new viceroy was India's very low priority in Labour thinking; the opportunity had come for great changes *in Britain*, and it was this that filled the minds of Labour leaders. Attlee, however, was soon made aware of how deeply Congress mistrusted Wavell.

The Labour party as a whole was pro Nehru-the-Fabian-socialist, and anti Jinnah and the religious fanaticism they thought was his only *raison d'être*. Attlee too despised Jinnah and underestimated his strength, believing that he would be forced to join an interim government in the end if only to protect his own interests. Attlee—who had come to the conclusion that the best way to bring this about was to go ahead and form a government without Jinnah—was therefore already conditioned to give a sympathetic hearing to Congress complaints about Wavell when they finally reached him. Gandhi sent a cable to Attlee suggesting that Wavell had been 'unnerved owing to the Bengal tragedy'; in public, he accused Wavell (though he later withdrew the accusation) of being pro Muslim. In fact, if there was one thing the British could not afford to be at this time, it was pro anybody, for the chances were that everybody would then become anti British. Attlee reasserted the authority of the British government, as was his right, by overruling the viceroy's attempts to bring about co-operation between Congress and the Muslim League. Some commentators have stigmatized this as an act of treachery, but it must be remembered that the viceroy—however great and good a man—was no more than a servant of the British parliament, and his sole function was to carry out the wishes of the government of the day.

Towards the end of August 1946, Attlee, in a personal telegram to Wavell, instructed him to go ahead and form an interim government without the Muslim League. Attlee's fear—and it was a well-founded one—was that, if procrastination continued, Congress would turn against the British government and once again break out in rebellion. Nehru admitted later that he would not have been prepared to go to jail again, but this 'revelation' is irrelevant, for even if Nehru had set his face against rebellion, he and the other leaders would probably have been swept aside by the right-wing Hindu elements who were still spoiling for a fight. The intellectuals of the Congress Socialist party were also belligerent, though it is doubtful if they really counted for much. However, the Labour government was not prepared to contemplate re-conquering India, especially with conscript soldiers. There was just a chance that the League might be frightened into joining an interim government. It was a long shot, but within a few weeks it seemed to have worked.

On 2 September, the interim government took office. Nehru, though he was called a vice-president (the viceroy was president), thought of himself as acting prime minister. He also held the portfolios of External Affairs and Commonwealth Relations. The rest of the portfolios were held by four Hindu members of Congress, including Patel and Rajagopalachari, one Congress member of the scheduled castes, three non-League Muslims—one of whom was a member of Congress—one Indian Christian and a Parsee. The commander-in-chief, Sir Claude Auchinleck, although he resigned his seat as 'War Member' to a Sikh, Baldev Singh, remained head of the army.

The Muslim League ordered every Muslim in India, from Jinnah himself 'to the smallest and most frightened little man in his hut, to fly a black flag from his house-top in silent contempt for the Hindu government'! But black flags could bring little comfort to Jinnah. The very thing he had been fighting tooth and nail to prevent, with every trick that his subtle mind could think of, had happened. There really was a Congress-dominated government at the Centre. And it might easily decide to move against the League and arrest its leaders. The League had its black flags and a few rifles—Congress now seemed to have both the Indian Army and part of the British army to carry out its policy.

This was, of course, an over-simplification, for the British could not have allowed the interim government to act against the League. Nevertheless, they had promised that an interim government would be able to act as if it were 'responsible', so how could they deny it the right to act against the League? If the viceroy were to interpose his veto, then the government's 'responsibility' would be diminished and Congress might easily withdraw. Fortunately, Jinnah came to Britain's assistance and they did not have to face what might have been a tragic dilemma. The Muslim League decided to join the interim government.

Throughout September and into the first week of October, consultations between the viceroy and Jinnah, and between Jinnah and Nehru, continued. The League tried to make conditions for entering the government but no agreement was reached. Congress would not give up its right to nominate a Muslim to one of its seats. At last, on 13 October, Jinnah replied to a letter from Wavell: 'It will be fatal to leave the entire administration of the Central Government in the hands of Congress,' he said, therefore 'we have decided to nominate five members of the interim government on behalf of the Muslim League.' The League nominees included only one of the party's leading figures, Liaquat Ali Khan, but, to everyone's surprise, one of the others was not a Muslim at all but a member of the Scheduled Castes Federation! The federation's leader, Dr Ambedkar, had vigorously denied Congress's right to speak for the Untouchables, so he accepted Jinnah's astute offer to give one of the League's seats to a member of the federation. But Jinnah's offer did not presage an extension of the Muslim League's activities into championing the cause of the Hindu minorities. It was simply a retaliation for Congress's choice of a Muslim for one of its own seats. Liaquat Ali made it quite clear that the League did not agree with Nehru's view that the interim government 'would function as a corporate whole, as a cabinet'. 'We have come into the government,' Liaquat said, 'with the intention of working in harmony with our colleagues—but you cannot clap with one hand.'

The conversations that led to the League's joining the government took place against a background of continuing communal violence which may well have contributed to the League decision, for it seemed that some sort of civil war was actually in progress and it was a civil war that the League could not control. Calcutta had remained uneasy after the great killing and there had been numerous outbreaks of violence in the city. In Dacca, a city in east Bengal infamous for its communal troubles, there had been numerous clashes between Hindu and Muslim. From about 10 October, there had been reports that, in the districts of Noakhali and Tippera, also in east Bengal, the Muslim majority was carrying out an organized war upon Hindus. Refugees escaping from these two districts brought with them lurid tales of murder, rape and arson. Hindu women, they said, were being kidnapped and forcibly married; conversions under the threat of death were taking place. Panic spread to the surrounding districts and many Hindus in places far away from the trouble spots fled from their homes in fear that their Muslim neighbours were about to attack them. Hindu newspapers were full of atrocity stories and the Muslim press retaliated with accusations that they were exaggerating and creating panic with the sole intention of discrediting the Muslim League government of Bengal.

The British this time acted swiftly, though Noakhali and Tippera were remote and communications were difficult. Troops and armed police quickly moved in. The RAF dropped leaflets, food and medical supplies, and refugee camps were established. By the end of the month the troubles had died down. The Bengal government's opinion was that there was no general rising of Muslims, but that, in the words of the governor, 'the disturbances have been caused by a body of hooligans who have exploited the existing communal feeling, and who, as they range the countryside are temporarily joined in each locality by belligerent Muslim toughs'. It was Calcutta all over again—the gangsters were the only true beneficiaries of Hindu-Muslim conflict.

The 'vernacular' politicians, who formed the vast majority of second-level leadership in both Congress and the League, joined with the leaders of the strictly communal parties in exploiting the troubles. Inflammatory speeches filled the air and native-language newspapers consisted of little but incitements to further violence. The leading figures of the two main parties publicly condemned the rioting and issued appeals for peace and, above all, avoidance of reprisals. They did very little, however, to discipline their lunatic fringes, nor did they suggest that censorship should be imposed on the press. Gandhi went to Calcutta and then to east Bengal on a personal mission of peace. At the beginning of November, Nehru, Patel, Liaquat Ali, and another League member of the interim government, Sardar Nishtar, visited Calcutta in a further attempt to calm the people. Shortly after their arrival, they were greeted with the news that massacres were taking place in the southern districts of Bihar. This time, it was Hindus, inflamed by tales from east Bengal, who were exacting terrible reprisals on a Muslim minority. Nehru and Nishtar hurried to the scene and made speeches vigorously condemning both their communities. Again the army had been called in, but by the time order was restored some 7,000 men, women and children had been murdered, usually under the most bestial circumstances. Congress, playing down Hindu responsibility, put the actual deaths at 2,000, the League at 30,000 killed and 150,000 refugees.

Bihar was not to be the last example of communal terror. It spread westwards in an obscene tide to the United Provinces. At Garhmuktesar, the site of an annual Hindu fair, a quarrel over admission to a sideshow was followed by a massacre of Muslims. In a nearby village where there was a majority of Muslim inhabitants, they retaliated by killing every Hindu. Counter-reprisals spread, resulting in several hundred deaths. Farther west, in the great city of Bombay, the back streets were seething with riot. Between 2 September, when the interim government had taken office, and 18 November, 622 people were killed.

To the soldiers—both British and Indian—fell the thankless and almost impossible task of keeping the public peace. Responsibility for law and order lay with the provincial governments, not with the Centre, and consequently, the army was often called in too late. If a provincial administration was Hindu its first reaction was to minimize the extent of Hindu reprisals; a Muslim administration was anxious to do the same when the offenders were Muslims. But the army, once called in, acted impartially against the rioters whatever their religion. One thing the bloodshed proved was that British fears that the army might be demoralized by having to fight its own countrymen and co-religionists were unfounded—at least so far. This must have given some satisfaction to the nationalist leaders. If it came to the worst, they

might even unite for self-protection behind the guns of the Indian
Army.

With their ultimate security reasonably assured, the nationalist
leaders could get back to their manoeuvres in what was undoubtedly
going to be a war of succession. But as they gathered together in the
interim government, the menacing shadows gathered too. Time was
running out and the British at least recognized that this was so, and
that they must negotiate not only with men but with the knowledge of
what lurked in the background. 'Fate,' in the words of André Malraux
in one of his early essays, stood 'behind each of these beings like death
in a ward of incurables.'

4 The Key to Indian Freedom

In a broadcast from Delhi on 25 October, Wavell declared that, with
the formation of a coalition government, 'India has taken another great
stride forward on the road to freedom', and that this was also the first
step towards the preparation of a new constitution 'which will enable
the British government to complete the transfer of power to India'. It
is not unreasonable to suppose that the viceroy's statement was meant
only to offer hopeful encouragement and reassurance, but it seems
likely that Wavell actually thought that, if Congress and the League
were brought together in the exercise of power, they would recognize
the advantages of continued co-operation. Again, with impeccable
logic, Wavell applied reason to an essentially unreasonable situation.
The proof of this was soon to be presented to him. The greatest
obstacle to co-operation, apart, that is, from Jinnah's fixed intention
to be obstructive, was the divergence between Congress' view of the
interim government's functions and the view of the League. Congress
regarded the government as a dominion government in all but name,
and, during the weeks in which it had functioned without League
participation, it had begun to act as if it was. In conjunction with the
minority members, the Congress bloc built up a system of joint
responsibility as if they were a fully independent cabinet in a liberal
democracy. This was done partly to disarm the viceroy who, in any
case of disagreement, could exercise his veto, and partly to reassure
left-wing critics of the Congress leadership that the ministers were not

tools of the British. This pretence of being a responsible cabinet—responsible to whom, is perhaps the obvious question—was certainly contrary to the mission's intention. The viceroy, however, seemed prepared to go along with the pretence, probably in the hope that it would encourage the Muslim League to change its mind and join the government.

The effect on the League, however, was rather different. Ironically enough, as soon as it did join the government it chose to make a stand on strict legality. As far as the League was concerned, its leaders said, this government was no more than the old Viceroy's Executive Council, and to call it a 'cabinet' was not only misleading but illegal. The vice-president—in this case, Nehru—had no justification for assuming himself to be the equivalent of a prime minister. Constitutionally, he had no specific functions except to preside at meetings from which the viceroy was absent. This interpretation—and it was the correct one—gave the League the excuse it required. It had decided to enter the government only to act as a check upon Congress and it was able to do so by pointing out that Congress was actually acting unconstitutionally. For this, Wavell was partly to blame. In his correspondence with Jinnah he had continually used the word 'cabinet', and he had gone out of his way to encourage Congress's belief that the interim government was to operate on the 'cabinet' principle. It now seemed that the League had not only self-interest but legality on its side, and, in order to avoid being outvoted by the Congress majority in the council, it could legitimately request the viceroy to use his veto.

This naturally angered Congress, and encouraged their growing suspicion that the British government—or at least the viceroy—hoped to perpetuate control by using the League to incapacitate the council so that it would become necessary for the viceroy to use his special powers. All along, Congress had maintained that there was an alliance between the League and the British, and there is no doubt that Jinnah was in fact receiving advice on tactics from pro-League British officials. There is certainly no evidence, however, for the suggestion that Wavell was engaged in some sinister plot of his own devising. His only fault—and it was a highly dangerous one—was that he was emotionally incapable of judging the complexity of the situation, and his honest blundering merely played into the hands of Jinnah and his friends.

Similar trouble also arose over the forthcoming meeting of the constituent assembly which, after postponement, was now planned for 9 December. Owing to the rather hasty way in which the Muslim League had entered the interim government, there had been no discussions over the League's decision to boycott the constituent assembly, and the day after the viceroy announced that the assembly would meet on 9 December, Jinnah issued a statement declaring that in his opinion this was 'one more blunder of a very grave and serious character' and that the viceroy was 'playing into the hands of Congress'. 'I want to make it clear,' he went on, 'that no representative of the Muslim League should attend the constituent assembly summoned to meet on the 9th of December 1946.' Wavell maintained that Jinnah had agreed that the League's entry into the interim government had been conditional on its willingness to take part in the constituent assembly, but Jinnah denied that he had given 'anything by way of assurances or otherwise'. Furthermore, after the 'mass-organized and planned ruthless massacres of Muslims in various parts of Bihar', he argued that there should be no question of holding the constituent assembly at all in such a 'highly-charged and explosive atmosphere'.

It was fairly obvious that the technique which had been used to persuade the League into joining the interim government would not succeed in getting it into the constituent assembly. The assembly meeting could not be postponed, however, because that would only add fuel to the Congress accusation that the British were using the League to hold up constitutional advance. Wavell was now so suspect by Congress that it became necessary for the next move to come from the British government itself, and the tactics would have to be spectacular, if they were going to work at all. The viceroy suggested to Attlee that he invite both Congress and League leaders to London and that Wavell himself should go with them. When the invitations were issued, Nehru replied that he did not feel that he and his colleagues should go to London, but that 'We would be agreeable to consultations with the representatives of the British government in India'. Congress in fact feared that there was to be an attempt to postpone the constituent assembly, for it was now 27 November and any discussions in London might easily be protracted to a date later than that fixed for the first meeting of the assembly. Pethick-Lawrence, informed of these doubts, told Nehru that the discussions had been suggested so as to ensure that the assembly *did* open on the date set, and that the British government had no intention of modifying the Cabinet Mission's plan. After some further haggling, Nehru agreed to go 'But we shall have to return by 9 December in time for the constituent assembly'. The British government agreed to this condition.

Jinnah, however, had been following this exchange of pleasantries with growing anger and trepidation. He was not prepared to go to London just for this. 'Unless,' he cabled Attlee, 'it is open for us to discuss the whole situation [i.e. the basis of the mission plan] it will be no use my going to London.' He received an ingenuous reply from Attlee, saying that his refusal to come 'must be based upon a misunderstanding of my telegrams to Nehru. There is nothing in it to prejudice full consideration of all points of view'. Jinnah had, of course, no intention of allowing Nehru to go to London without him, and he now decided he had played hard-to-get long enough. He telegraphed Attlee 'After your clarification and assurances, I have decided to leave for London tomorrow'! On 1 December, Wavell, Nehru, Jinnah, Liaquat Ali and Baldev Singh left for London by air.

The British government was not particularly hopeful about the outcome of the talks. All it really hoped to achieve was to persuade Jinnah into dropping the League's boycott of the constituent assembly. The discussions lasted only four days and, on 6 December, the British government issued a statement which made it quite clear that no settlement had been arrived at. It explained the absence of results by claiming that it had not expected any, 'since the Indian representatives must consult their colleagues before any final decision is reached.' The discussions had centred mainly on the interpretation of the Cabinet Mission's plan, and, in particular, the clause concerning grouping. The mission, though characteristically it had not actually said so, had intended that the constituent assembly would decide on groupings by a simple majority decision of the assembly, but that any province which might find itself forced by the majority vote into a group to which it did not wish to belong would be safeguarded by being allowed, after the first general election held under the new constitution, to withdraw from the group on the basis of a simple vote in the province's own legislature. This interpretation had not been acceptable to Congress, which wanted each province to decide independently whether to join a group. But Congress modified its view and said it would be prepared to abide by an Indian Federal Court ruling on the interpretation of the grouping clause. The British government, however, made it clear that as far as it was concerned, the British government's interpretation was the official interpretation, that the League had in fact been right all along, and that this interpretation must be accepted 'by all parties in the constituent assembly'. The government urged Congress to acknowledge this ruling in order to open the way for the League's reconsideration of its boycott. If it would not, then the matter should be referred to the Federal Court as soon as possible.

The League was naturally jubilant over the vindication of its views, but it was quick to condemn as a sop to Congress any suggestion of reference to the Federal Court. However, the League's main satisfaction was to be derived from the last paragraph in the British government's statement.

'There has never been any prospect of success for the constituent assembly, except upon the basis of an agreed procedure. Should a constitution come to be framed by a constituent assembly in which a large section of the Indian population had not been represented, His Majesty's Government could not of course contemplate—as the Congress have stated that they would not contemplate—forcing such a Constitution upon any unwilling parts of the country.'

It is in the last sentence that the significance lies, for it seemed to imply that the British government now considered it possible that they might have to implement the Pakistan solution in one form or another. The statement did not suggest that a constitution arrived at without League participation would be void; it said that it would not be forced upon 'unwilling parts of the country' by the British, nor would the British allow it to be imposed by Congress. This implication was bluntly put into words by Sir Stafford Cripps in the House of Commons, when he said 'If the Muslim League cannot be persuaded to come into the constituent assembly then the parts of the country where they are in a majority cannot be held to be bound by the results.' The statement, however, also implied that any 'unwilling' parts of such provinces as were claimed for Pakistan would not be forced into accepting a Pakistan constitution either.

The League claimed that the statement meant that a second constituent assembly—which they had been asking for all along—should now be set up. Nevertheless, the League's battle for Pakistan was by no means won. It was now up to Jinnah to prove to Congress—and the British—that he and he alone was the key to Indian freedom, and that without his agreement nothing could be done.

The British government, though it had implied the *possibility* of some sort of Pakistan solution, still hoped to be able to transfer power to a united India. In this it was supported by the Conservative opposition, although there too there was a division of opinion. The visit of the Indians to London had had its fringe effects. Nehru had deeply impressed the Labour leaders, while seeing Jinnah in the cold flesh had helped to confirm their antagonism to all he stood for. On the other hand, Jinnah had made some headway with Conservative politicians, and he remained in Britain after the conference was over to spread propaganda for Pakistan. In his conversations with members of the party of big business, he had emphasized the probability of civil war (and its effect on British business interests in India) if power was transferred to a Congress-dominated government. Winston Churchill still maintained in parliament that power should be handed over only to a united India and that Britain should stay in India until such time as agreement was reached between the two main parties, but he also suggested that there were in fact three choices before the British government. The first was 'Quit India regardless of what may happen there'; the second, 'Partition India between the two different races'; and the third, set up an 'impartial administration responsible to Parliament . . . to maintain the fundamental guarantees of life, liberty and the pursuit of happiness'. The 'fundamental guarantees' were presumably to be maintained by British bayonets.

Other Conservatives, however, after their talks with Jinnah, were not as sure as their leader that the third choice was the best. Sir John Anderson, in a speech in parliament on 13 December, put forward, as a 'broad truth to which I would subscribe', the proposition that 'one British community democratically organized and ruled could not in fact indefinitely hold in subjection another Indian community ripe for self-government'. This attitude reflected a growing opinion among some influential members of the Conservative party, and it finally led to grudging but genuine support for the Labour government's policies.

In the meantime, the constituent assembly had met in Delhi, as scheduled, on 9 December. Without the Muslim League it certainly had all the appearances of a Hindu and Congress-dominated body.

But it was not entirely an assemblage of party stalwarts, for Congress had nominated a number of men from outside its ranks who were distinguished in the law, scholarship and experience of public affairs. One Congress leader was conspicuous by his absence. Gandhi—the 'architect of this assembly', as Nehru put it—was still tramping through Bengal on his outstandingly successful mission of peace and reconciliation. Some members of the assembly, in particular the Liberal party leader and a representative of the Anglo-Indians, warned the assembly not to hurry decisions that might be resented by 'absent friends who might later decide to join the assembly', and the Indian princes, too—who had not as yet decided how to nominate their representatives, but who were beginning to realize that their own future position was in danger—publicly regretted the 'raising of any fundamental issues' in their absence. But the Congress majority was anxious to get on.

Neither of the major parties had as yet officially announced its views on the British government's statement of 6 December, but Jinnah returned to India with Liaquat Ali on 21 December and, at a press conference held at Karachi, declared that unless Congress accepted the statement the League saw no reason to modify its attitude to the constituent assembly. The next day, the Congress Working Committee itself issued a lengthy statement, the main gist of which was a tedious recapitulation of its old point of view. But the working committee refused to make the decision and passed the buck to the All-India Congress Committee which was due to meet early in January. The reason for this attitude was the only partly concealed divisions within Congress itself. Powerful elements, which had always considered Nehru a rather weak vessel, were now convinced that he was prepared to sacrifice Congress's dominating position in the assembly by giving the assurances demanded by the League. They thought—not wholly without reason—that the Congress leaders were more interested in personal power than in an undivided India. Partisans of such provinces as Assam, who thought that it would be forced under the mission plan to join a Muslim-majority group, were lobbying for some bold action by the Congress leaders, and even Gandhi now seemed to be working against Nehru, throwing his very considerable influence on to the side of those who thought too many concessions had been made already. Gandhi even advised the representatives of Assam and of the Sikhs to refuse to co-operate in the mission plan.

The British government was also exerting pressure. In its statement of 6 December, it had given the impression that it would permit problems of interpretation to be settled by the Federal Court. Now, during debates in the British parliament, government spokesmen asserted that the government would not be prepared to change its interpretation even if the matter *was* taken to the Federal Court. In consequence, at the January meeting of the All-India Congress Committee, Nehru pointed out that to refer problems of interpretation to the Federal Court for a decision had 'become purposeless and undesirable'. After considerable argument, mainly from the representatives of Assam and from the Congress socialists, a resolution was carried which, with some rather vague reservations designed to placate the minorities, finally accepted the British government's interpretation.

When the constituent assembly met for its second session on 20 January 1947, the League had still not reacted officially to this Congress resolution, and it was not until eleven days later that the League Working Committee met in Karachi. It issued a 3,000-word analysis of the constitutional problem, the gravamen of which was that the constituent assembly was illegal and should be dissolved, and that Congress's tardy acceptance of the British government's interpretation was merely a trick.

The constituent assembly went on with its business, dividing itself into committees and declaring that a chair would always be kept warm for representatives of the League. But the League had no intention of joining. It had now seen a weakening in the British government's determination to hand over to a united India and Jinnah hoped to capitalize on it. The League, if it had wanted to make the constituent assembly work, could have entered it and waited to see whether or not Congress had been genuine in its acceptance of the Cabinet Mission plan. But this was too big a risk for Jinnah to take. He could, too, have shown some public understanding of the fears that plagued Assam and the Sikhs of the Punjab, by giving them some assurance of fair treatment, but in all the words of the League's statement there was no glimmer of any such assurance.

Congress now demanded that the League should resign from the interim government and, on 15 February, Patel asked that the British government should force the League either to join the assembly or leave the 'cabinet'. The League claimed it had as much right to remain in the 'cabinet' as Congress had. Congress retaliated by itself threatening to resign if the British government did not act. The ball was now back in Attlee's court.

During all this controversy, communal violence had continued and there had been outbreaks of rioting in Lahore and Amritsar in the Punjab.

The British government had received from Wavell, when he was in London, a plan for the organized withdrawal of British civilians and troops from India to be used if the government should decide to quit without any further attempt to reconcile the two parties. This plan did not have the approval of General Auchinleck nor of some of the most experienced of Indian administrators. Wavell's idea was to arrange a phased withdrawal which would end with everyone being evacuated by sea from Karachi and Bombay. It was in fact highly desirable that a plan should be agreed for the protection in emergency of British nationals. Similar plans (without the final evacuation) had been in existence since the Mutiny of 1857, when the British had been caught off-balance by a civil and military uprising. Wavell, however, seemed to think that a phased withdrawal would fire Indians with the responsibility of making peace amongst themselves and carrying on the administration. Wavell's plan was intelligent, as an emergency plan. As anything else, it was dangerous rubbish. In the present state of the country, the British *could* not have withdrawn peacefully. If British troops could not keep the peace while they were deployed around the country, it was highly unlikely that they could keep it as they withdrew. It was only British troops and British-led Indian troops that were able to keep such peace as there was; withdraw them, and the gangsters and communal terrorists would have taken over the country. No British government could have sanctioned such a plan except in the direst circumstances.

There was no doubt, however, that if something was not done quickly such circumstances might yet arise. The British administration in India was even thinner on the ground than it had been in 1945. There had been no civil service recruitment during the war, and a scheme launched soon after it ended had been abandoned in the face of Indian opposition to any further recruitment of Europeans. Britain's control of the Indian Army was weakening rapidly as Indianization of the officer corps increased, and British Army troops in India were decreasing at a considerable rate as demobilization proceeded. Very soon there would be practically no one to withdraw. The only alternative to departure open to the British government would be, in the case of the civil service and the Indian Army, to re-open recruitment to Europeans, which would be unacceptable to Indians and not particularly appealing to British subjects looking for a secure career. As far as the British Army was concerned, the Labour government could certainly not extend the service of wartime conscripts. If it did, it would be faced with mutinous behaviour from the civilian-soldiers and heavy pressure from their parents at home, most of whom had voted the Labour government into office.

The only sensible solution was to do something which should have been done long before—fix a definite date for the British withdrawal from India and invite Indian leaders to work out some agreement for the transfer of power. Wavell had in fact asked many times for such a declaration and had envisaged 31 March 1948 as the date of the final stage in his plan for phased withdrawal.

The Wavell plan did at least force the Labour government to face the facts of a rapidly deteriorating situation. No longer could Attlee hide behind the Micawberish formula of hoping that something would turn up and solve the problem for him. On 20 February 1947, Attlee announced in the House of Commons that, despite lack of agreement on the Cabinet Mission's plan, he wished to make it clear that it was the government's 'definite intention to take the necessary steps to effect the transfer of power into responsible Indian hands by a date not later than June 1948'.

5 *Wars of Succession*

'I had come to the conclusion,' Attlee wrote later in his memoirs, 'that it was useless to try and get agreement by discussion between the leaders of the rival communities. Unless these men were faced with the urgency of a time limit, there would always be procrastination.' Here Attlee gives the impression that he, like Wavell, still clung to hopes of an agreement even if it was only brought about by shock tactics. But at the time, he killed even the faintest possibility of agreement—though while Jinnah remained alive, the possibility was in any case so faint as

to be non-existent—by providing in the House of Commons a rider
to his statement of 20 February.

'His Majesty's Government,' he said, 'will have to consider to whom the powers
of the Central Government of British India should be handed over, on the due
date, *whether as a whole to some form of Central Government for British India or in
some areas to the existing Provincial Governments,* or in such other way as may
seem most reasonable and in the best interests of the Indian people.'

At the same time, the prime minister also announced that Lord
Wavell's 'wartime appointment' as viceroy would be ended and that
he would be succeeded by Admiral Viscount Mountbatten of Burma.

The prime minister's statement was received with all the predictable
reactions. In India, Nehru welcomed the declaration as bringing 'reality
and a certain dynamic quality to the present situation'. . . . Congress
had been urging for years that the British withdrawal from India
should not be conditional upon agreement between Congress and the
League. . . . The British government had now accepted this. But all
Congress members did not take quite as sanguine a view as Nehru.
Many saw Attlee's statement in the House of Commons as an open
invitation for the League to continue to boycott the constituent assembly—to indulge, in fact, in a war for the succession. The Congress
Working Committee issued an invitation to the League to join in
discussions on the new situation. It also asked the British to give the
interim government the immediate status of a real cabinet, with full
executive control of the Services and of the administration.

The League, though welcoming Attlee's statement, criticized the
vagueness of the passage dealing with the manner of the transfer of
power. Nevertheless, its leaders felt that the principle of Pakistan had
now, however vaguely, been accepted by the British government. The
League therefore must intensify its efforts to ensure that the British
handed over power not to a united but to a divided India.

In Britain, the Conservative opposition, which generally speaking
had supported the Labour government's policy in broad principle,
now openly attacked the 20 February statement as far too radical. The
majority of Conservative members recognized the necessity of granting a form of self-government to India; after all, this was only an extension of a Tory policy consistently pursued over the previous twenty
years. They had also to some extent unwillingly recognized that

Britain's role in the world had been diminished by the late war. At the same time, the Conservative party had still not recovered from the tremendous shock of its defeat in 1945, which even Churchill's wartime popularity had been unable to avert. The blindest of Tory reactionaries could recognize the growing self-assurance of the 'working-classes', and their organic unwillingness to indulge in sacrifices for an empire which had in any case always been the preserve of the upper classes.

In the House of Commons debate on the prime minister's statement, it was significant that Tory members with some recent experience of India spoke in support of the government, and in the House of Lords, Lord Halifax—who as Lord Irwin had been viceroy at the time of the Round Table conferences—declared that he was not prepared to oppose the government's policy because he could not honestly recommend a better solution. The main criticism from other speakers was concerned with the shortness of the time allowed for framing a constitution either for a united India or a divided one. Churchill, Sir John Anderson, and R. A. Butler—the principal Conservative spokesmen in the Commons debate—pointed out that the prime minister's statement did not envisage protection of the minorities or of the rights of the princes, and was in essence a complete departure from the original Cabinet Mission offer. Anderson called it 'an unjustified gamble', and Churchill, with more rhetoric than foresight, declared that 'in handing over the Government of India to these so-called political elements we are handing over to men of straw, of whom, in a few years, no trace will remain'. He claimed that the nationalist leaders did not represent the mass of the Indian people, and although this argument was not unfounded it was hardly helpful. Who else could the British negotiate with? Churchill was so infuriated by Labour's 'treason' that this patriot of patriots even went so far as to suggest that the government should resort to the aid and advice of the United Nations. Butler was rather more in touch with reality, and he made it clear that he believed there would be more than one heir to the estate when the time came for Britain to hand over power. When it came to the vote, however, the opposition was helpless. A Conservative motion condemning the government's policy was defeated by 337 votes to 185.

While words rattled around the Houses of Parliament at Westminster, blood was flowing in India. The politicians, and their un-

acknowledged allies in the streets and byways, were already fighting
for the succession, each in his different way. The Muslim League, with
only fifteen months to establish its claim to take delivery of Pakistan,
was hard at work. And there was a great deal for it to do. There was a
League provincial government in only two—Bengal and Sind—of
the six 'Pakistan provinces'. Baluchistan had no elected government,
being administered by a British chief commissioner. In the North-
West Frontier Province (NWFP) and in Assam there were Congress
administrations, while the Punjab was governed by a coalition ministry
of the Unionist party (a party including Muslims, Hindus and Sikhs),
Congress, and the Sikhs' own political party.

The main League target was the last of these provinces, the Punjab.
Not only was it the largest and most fertile and prosperous of the
north-western provinces of India, but it held a strategic position and if
the League could gain control of it, they would cut the NWFP off
completely from the rest of Congress India. In the Punjab, 56 per cent
of the population was Muslim and the largest single party in the legislature was the Muslim League. The provincial League party believed
it had hitherto been kept out of office by the British governor, who had
encouraged a hastily-formed coalition to take office. But in fact, the
very existence of a government representing the principal communities had helped to maintain communal peace in the Punjab. The government alliance, however, was an uneasy one and the legislative
assembly was called only when absolutely necessary in order to pass
the provincial budget. Well before the 20 February statement, the
Muslim League executive had instructed the provincial League organization to launch, at the end of January 1947, an 'all-out non-violent
mass struggle against the reactionary Punjab regime' using as a
pretext the special powers which the coalition government had
assumed in order to reduce the risk of communal disorder. The provincial League had adopted Gandhian tactics, announced that it was
fighting for civil liberties, and invited Hindus and Sikhs to join it in the
struggle. It soon became clear that the League did have the support of
the Muslim masses, for thousands of demonstrators throughout the
Punjab began to defy the government's ban on public meetings and
processions. The authorities acted swiftly and with the minimum of
fuss. They arrested only the ringleaders and removed the remainder in
lorries to a considerable distance and left them to walk home! The

All-India Muslim League had now opened up its own attack on what it called 'persistent and widespread persecution', and League members of the central interim government had become vocal in their support of what was nothing other than a campaign to overthrow a legally-elected government.

Peaceful demonstrations had soon become larded with outbreaks of violence, and after the British prime minister's declaration of 20 February it became obvious that the coalition government in the Punjab no longer served any purpose. It had been formed in the belief that there was a distinction between problems of provincial administration and those affecting India's constitutional future, and that the negotiations with the British referred only to the central government. Now the whole business seemed to have been thrown open for discussion once again. The Punjab's chief minister decided it was necessary for all parties to confer upon the attitude the Punjab should take towards future events. His first step was to reach a settlement with the provincial League party, which, in return for the release of prisoners and the removal of the ban on public meetings, agreed to call off its civil disobedience campaign. Four days later the Unionist ministry resigned, and the following day the governor called upon the Muslim League leader in the legislative assembly to attempt to form a ministry.

But the various communities of the Punjab were now in a belligerent mood. For months, they had been collecting arms and drilling their private armies. This had been done quite openly although the Unionist ministry had chosen to close its eyes to it. One of the 'civil liberties' which the League was defending was the right to form private armies! On the same evening as the Muslim League was invited to form a ministry, the Master Tara Singh—a rabble-rouser of deceptively benign appearance, who was the political leader of the Sikh community—addressed a mass rally in words which had become sickeningly familiar in the oppressive atmosphere of India. Waving a large sword, he declaimed 'O Hindus and Sikhs! Be ready for self-destruction. . . . If we can snatch the government from the Britishers no one can stop us from snatching the government from the Muslims. . . . Disperse from here on the solemn affirmation that we shall not allow the League to exist. . . . We shall rule over them and will get the government, fighting. I have sounded the bugle. Finish the Muslim League.'

The provincial League was unable to convince the governor that it could form a stable ministry and on 5 March, under the constitutional authority vested in him, the governor himself took over the administration of the province. Communal disorder now began to spread with the aid of inflammatory speeches from so-called responsible leaders. Fierce battles took place between rival gangs, and whole streets were set ablaze by fire-raisers in the principal towns of the Punjab. Professional gangsters, of course, were doing their bit—and reaping the profits. By the end of March, strong measures had restored some order to the towns but in the villages the terror continued. Official figures gave two thousand as the number of lives lost but there were probably many more. The casualties in the wars of succession were beginning to mount up. Under the circumstances then reigning in the Punjab, there was no likelihood of any return to ministerial government. The Muslim League, in its endeavour to gain power, had not only ensured that power would be denied it but had brought the Punjab to the edge of civil war. Civil disobedience had once again inevitably led to bloodshed.

The politicians were now beginning to realize how bloody was the background against which they were playing their endless game. Nehru returned from a visit to the Punjab, sickened by what he had seen. 'I have seen ghastly sights,' he said on his return to Delhi, 'and I have heard of behaviour by human beings which would degrade brutes. All that has happened in the Punjab is intimately connected with political affairs. If there is a grain of intelligence in any person he must realize that whatever political objective he may aim at, this is not the way to attain it. Any such attempt must bring, as it has in a measure brought, ruin and destruction.'

One other thing, too, was becoming apparent. The British government's declaration of 20 February had *not* shocked the Indian leaders into co-operation. By fixing a date for the transfer of power, the British had done no more than intensify the fight for the succession. They had encouraged Indians to take the decision into their own hands, but those hands now held knives.

As the Punjab smouldered, the Congress Working Committee met to discuss the British government's declaration and to decide upon future strategy. In one of its resolutions it recommended partition of the Punjab into predominantly Muslim and predominantly Hindu and Sikh areas, a principle already suggested by the Hindus and Sikhs of the eastern part of the Punjab. This did not mean that Congress envisaged the possibility of dividing India itself; it was simply that, whatever happened in the future, one thing was now sure—there would be some sort of provincial autonomy, and it was obviously a good idea to set about creating new provinces which would not suffer from the basic communal problem. Even if division of India actually came, any Hindu areas which had already been cut away from the Muslim areas of the Punjab and Bengal would naturally opt for India. But this was only the long-term purpose of the resolution. Congress still believed that Jinnah was a rational politician, out—as they themselves were— for what he could get, and although he persisted in his demand for the six 'Pakistan provinces', they thought he would finally back down when faced with the certainty that two of these provinces—the Punjab and Bengal—would be divided. Since it also seemed very unlikely that either Assam or the NWFP would join a Pakistan grouping, Congress believed Jinnah would realize that Pakistan could not work, either administratively or economically. Again Congress misunderstood the nature of Jinnah's ambitions. The achievement of 'Pakistan' was only incidental to them; Jinnah was determined that Congress should *not* rule an undivided India; questions of viability were of no interest to him. Congress was not alone in holding this reasonable opinion of Jinnah. Many non-partisan observers at the time—including the author of this book—believed despite all appearances to the contrary that Jinnah might be persuaded that a federal India, with provincial autonomy, would be infinitely better than any tattered and truncated Pakistan. But all were wrong. And Jinnah was not prepared to wait for Congress to strike the first blow. He and his lieutenants were already at work organizing civil disobedience campaigns for the NWFP and Assam.

The situation in the North-West Frontier Province was unique in India. It had the largest Muslim majority—92 per cent of the population—of any in India, and the province was virtually free from communal rivalry just because the odds were so heavily weighted against non-Muslims. Early in nationalist history, when the League was still in the wilderness waiting for its Moses, Congress had claimed the allegiance of nationalists in the NWFP who had built up a strong movement known as the Red Shirts under the Khan brothers, Abdul Ghaffar and Dr Khan Sahib, the latter of whom was now chief minister.

The population of the province was mainly Pathan by race. Between the NWFP and the frontier of Afghanistan there were tribal areas, not directly administered by the NWFP government, whose tribes were also Pathan by race and semi-independent of government interference. Relations between the tribes and the British were handled by officers of the central department of external affairs. Muslim League propagandists had been active among the tribes, so that when Nehru visited tribal areas in October 1946, in his capacity as member for external affairs, he was received with hostility and even open violence wherever he went. The League used Nehru's visit for all it was worth, as a symbol of that Hindu domination it claimed was threatening the Pathans, and then, in the second half of February 1947, launched a civil disobedience campaign in the NWFP which soon followed the same sordid pattern as that in the Punjab. The League called for the resignation of Dr Khan Sahib, but he refused to be stampeded.

The situation in Assam differed both from that in the Punjab and that in the NWFP. In Assam the Muslims were in a minority, making up only about one third of the population, and the League's claim to Assam as one of the six 'Pakistan provinces' was based solely on its geographical position. Because of their comparatively small numbers, the Muslims in the province could not hope to achieve much success with a civil disobedience campaign, but this did not prevent them from trying. Conveniently for them, they could make use of an issue which had almost become traditional. Assam, fearing immigrants into its fertile lands from Bengal's poverty-stricken Muslim majority, had a history of evicting Muslim squatters. The British had done it, a coalition government headed by a Muslim League chief minister had done it, the current Congress ministry merely carried on the tradition. The League, however, nothing daunted, proceeded to organize mass invasions by Muslims from Bengal, and encouraged them to squat upon government-owned grazing land. As usual, the invasion began peacefully enough but soon degenerated into indiscriminate and bloody violence. At the beginning of April 1947, disorder had spread to such an extent that the government was compelled to call in the army.

Elsewhere in India violence also spluttered on, sometimes quiescent, sometimes erupting into bloodshed. Only the south remained reasonably silent. Agents of the extremists of all parties moved through the slums of the great cities, meeting on their missions of incitement communist agitators also intent upon spreading unease among the workers. Communist influence was growing amongst the peasants in certain districts, inciting them to violence against their landlords. In nine out of the eleven provinces of British India, such civil liberties as there had been were now pushed aside and the governments were ruling by ordinance, exercising wide powers of arrest and stringent control over demonstrations. And although the police and the army were still untouched by communal antipathies, it was feared that the canker might soon enter their minds too. India trembled with uneasiness and fear, fair game for the agitators, and every interested party was prepared to fish in the troubled waters, hoping to land some prize to their own advantage.

It was to this scene of blood and intrigue that the new viceroy came, landing at Delhi in the hot afternoon of 22 March 1947.

6 Leaping in the Dark

To anyone standing in the throne-room of Viceroy's House, New Delhi, on a day in late March 1947 and knowing nothing of what went on behind the scenes, it would have appeared that there was very little wrong with the Indian empire. The pomp and the splendour of a viceregal installation were at least superficially the same as they had always been. Covered with medals and decorations, the viceroy and vicereine stood at their gilded thrones surrounded by distinguished-looking Englishmen and the tributary princes of the king-emperor, gleaming like jewelled birds. Nevertheless, there were signs of the changing times. For one thing, there were motion-picture cameras and radio-microphones, and the audience was not quite what it would once have been. There were rather more Indians than usual, and many wore the homespun and peculiar white forage caps—the so-called Gandhi cap—which were the semi-official uniform of Congress. The viceroy, too, after the rich-sounding words of the oath and the equally impressive syllables of his august names had echoed away, broke a tradition—and made a speech. The phrases were crisp and decisive, like a battle order. He was there, he said bluntly, not to maintain British rule in India, but to pass it on.

Many in that room saw the viceroy only as the man they would have to persuade, trick if necessary, but above all make their friend. For despite the play-acting, the pomp and circumstance which they had just witnessed, this was not the noon-day of imperialism but its twilight. There was every reason for the viceroy to speak decisively. Unlike Wavell, he had received from the Labour government what seemed to be unambiguous instructions concerning his task.

These instructions are worth giving in full since, despite their apparent precision, they indicate that the Labour government—and in particular the prime minister—still wanted to believe that the 20 February announcement was going to shock the Indian leaders into some sort of co-operation among themselves; that the British cabinet was unwilling to face the unpalatable truths that Wavell had put to them; and that they still under-estimated, and in fact totally misunderstood, the nature and depth of Jinnah's demands. The government's instructions to Lord Mountbatten were contained in a letter from the prime minister:

Prime Minister to Admiral Mountbatten   March 1947

The statement which was issued at the time of the announcement of your appointment sets out the policy of the Government and the principles in accordance with which the transfer of power to Indian hands should be effected.

My colleagues of the Cabinet Mission and I have discussed with you the general lines of your approach to the problems which will confront you in India. It will, I think, be useful to you to have on record the salient points which you should have in mind in dealing with the situation. I have, therefore, set them down here.

It is the definite objective of His Majesty's Government to obtain a unitary Government for British India and the Indian States, if possible within the British Commonwealth, through the medium of a Constituent Assembly, set up and run in accordance with the Cabinet Mission's plan, and you should do the utmost in your power to persuade all Parties to work together to this end, and advise His Majesty's Government, in the light of developments, as to the steps that will have to be taken.

Since, however, this plan can only become operative in respect of British India by agreement between the major Parties, there can be no question of compelling either major Party to accept it.

If by October 1 you consider that there is no prospect of reaching a settlement on the basis of a unitary government for British India, either with or without the co-operation of the Indian [princely] States, you should report to His Majesty's Government on the steps which you consider should be taken for the handing over of power on the due date.

It is, of course, important that the Indian States should adjust their relations with the authorities to whom it is intended to hand over power in British India; but as was explicitly stated by the Cabinet Mission, His Majesty's Government do not intend to hand over their powers and obligations under paramountcy to any successor Government. It is not intended to bring paramountcy as a system to a conclusion earlier than the date of the final transfer of power, but you are authorized, at such time as you think appropriate, to enter into negotiations with individual States for adjusting their relations with the Crown.

You will do your best to persuade the rulers of any Indian States in which political progress has been slow to progress rapidly towards some form of more democratic government. You will also aid and assist the States in coming to fair and just arrangements with the leaders of British India as to their future relationships.

The date fixed for the transfer of power is a flexible one to within one month; but you should aim at 1 June 1948 as the effective date for the transfer of power.

In your relations with the Interim Government you will be guided by the general terms of the Viceroy's letter of 30 May 1946 to the President of the Congress Party, and of the statement made by the Secretary of State for India in the House of Lords on 13 March 1947. These statements made it clear that, while the Interim Government would not have the same powers as a Dominion Government, His Majesty's Government would treat the Interim Government with the same consultation and consideration as a Dominion Government, and give it the greatest possible freedom in the day-to-day exercise of the administration of the country.

It is essential that there should be the fullest co-operation with the Indian leaders in all steps that are taken as to the withdrawal of British power so that the process may go forward as smoothly as possible.

The keynote of your administration should therefore be the closest co-operation with the Indians and you should make it clear to the whole of the Secretary of State's Services that this is so, and that it is their duty to their countries to work to this end.

You should take every opportunity of stressing the importance of ensuring that the transfer of power is effected with full regard to the defence requirements of India. In the first place you will impress upon the Indian leaders the great importance of avoiding any breach in the continuity of the Indian Army and of maintaining the organization of defence upon an all-Indian basis. Secondly you will point out the need for continued collaboration in the security of the Indian Ocean area for which provision might be made in an agreement between the two countries. At a suitable date His Majesty's Government would be ready to send military and other experts to India in order to assist in discussing the terms of such an agreement.

You will no doubt inform Provincial Governors of the substance of this letter.

Armed with these instructions Mountbatten had made his preparations for perhaps the greatest challenge he had ever faced. He did so in a manner which had been proved under the stress of war. Two main factors had contributed to Mountbatten's success as Supreme Allied Commander in South-East Asia—his choice of subordinates, and his very lively sense of the uses of personal publicity. He had, of course, other qualities too, including immense charm. 'Charm' is often an empty word, but not in Mountbatten's case. With him, it managed to be simultaneously egalitarian and superior. Once, during the war Mountbatten arrived at a town in Burma a few hours after its capture. Everybody was very tired and rather grubby, but Mountbatten himself looked fresh and purposeful. Yet the impression he gave was not that he had just arrived from a comfortable base headquarters but that, somehow, he had managed to slough off the sweat and dirt to which everyone else had succumbed. He brushed aside the officers and the general 'bull' of a commander's parade, told the soldiers to break ranks, and began to confide his thoughts and hopes to them. It was a masterly performance, and at least one sceptical soldier—the author of this book —went away convinced that great events lay in the hollow of Mountbatten's hands and that there was no need to worry about their outcome. Wartime troops had been mellowed by the Mountbatten propaganda and personality, and in 1947 the time had come for Indian leaders to receive the same treatment.

The new viceroy had brought with him from England a special team of advisors—though 'advisors' perhaps is too large a definition. They were in fact part brains trust, part legmen, for the viceroy. Their role as advisors was mainly to consist of leaking suggestions, and 'appreciations' of the viceroy's point of view, to Indian political leaders. The men were very carefully chosen. The first was Field-Marshal Lord Ismay, whose authority as Churchill's wartime chief-of-staff made him acceptable to the Conservative party. Ismay had spent many years as a soldier in India and was on good terms with Auchinleck, the commander-in-chief. It was believed that he would be extremely valuable in the viceroy's probably delicate relations with the military and civil service hierarchy, who, on the whole, distrusted Mountbatten's Madison Avenue command techniques. Next was Sir Eric Mièville, who had been private secretary to Lord Willingdon when the latter was viceroy, and subsequently an Assistant Private Secretary to King George VI. Ismay had been brought out of a well-earned retirement by an appeal to his love for India, and Mièville came from the financial world of the City of London, to which many senior servants of the Crown seem to gravitate. The others who made up the team were Mountbatten's trusted and loyal wartime subordinates—Captain Ronald Brockman RN, Commander George Nicholls RN, Lieutenant-Colonel Vernon Erskine Crum, and Alan Campbell-Johnson, who had been in charge of Mountbatten's wartime publicity.

V. P. Menon, who was to play a significant part in the events of the next few months, later described the British government's deadline of June 1948 for the British withdrawal from India as 'a leap in the dark'. Mountbatten had intended to bring with him strong lights with which to brighten that dark, but it was often to happen that, when the 'lights' had passed, the darkness was even blacker than before. Mountbatten retained a number of Wavell's subordinates, too, in particular George Abell, who was believed by Congress to be pro-Muslim, and V. P. Menon, a Hindu who had been Reforms Commissioner and Constitutional Advisor to both Linlithgow and Wavell. Menon probably knew more about the princely states and the real problems involved in the transfer of power than anyone else in India. Since 1946, he had been a close friend and adviser of the Congress leader, Sardar Patel, and their association was to be of tremendous significance to independent India.

As soon as the charade of the installation was over, Mountbatten and his staff went to work on reconnaissance and intelligence. The effect of Lord Mountbatten's charm, and Lady Mountbatten's too, upon Nehru was profound. Where Nehru had distrusted the bluff, honest Wavell, he found the Mountbattens very much to his taste. This was not surprising, as the two men had much in common, and their attraction for each other was reinforced by one great dissimilarity. Nehru was introspective, questioning his ideas and actions in the lonely room of his own mind and rarely receiving clearcut answers. Mountbatten was extrovert, radiating self-confidence, and doing so with such an aura of certainty that it seemed also to flow into those who came in contact with him. Mountbatten supplied Nehru with the dimension missing from his own personality.

Gandhi, now relegated to the position of Congress's private saint, was also to receive the full blast of the Mountbatten charm, but there was really no point of contact between the two men. They might as well have been of different species. At the viceroy's invitation, Gandhi returned from a pilgrimage to the riot-torn areas of Bihar to meet him. When they met, Gandhi suggested a plan to the viceroy. There was in fact nothing new about the plan, for Rajagopalachari had first put it forward as long ago as 1940. Then, he had had Gandhi's secret approval. Now he had succeeded in persuading Gandhi to put it forward as his own. The viceroy, said Gandhi, should call upon Mr Jinnah to form a government, leaving it to Jinnah to decide whether there should be Hindu ministers or not; except for the viceregal veto, Gandhi added, the government should be given a free hand. The idea, though spectacular enough, had even less chance of being accepted by Congress in 1947—regardless of Gandhi's support—than it had seven years before. Inevitably, Congress threw out the suggestion, and Gandhi returned to Bihar.

One recent British commentator on the events leading up to the transfer of power has seen Congress's rejection of the plan as part of some Machiavellian plot by Mountbatten to eliminate Gandhi from future discussions because of his antagonism to partition. It was, however, hardly necessary for the viceroy to go to such lengths in order to dispose of Gandhi. The Mahatma no longer spoke for Congress and it is very doubtful whether he could have re-imposed his influence *even if he had wanted to*. At this stage, when India's freedom was in sight, Gandhi was no longer interested in it. He had returned to the role of Hindu reformer which he had, in fact, never discarded. Now he was concerned, as he had always been, only with reducing violence. He was slowly coming to the conclusion that partition might be the only way to do this, and he was later to throw such influence as he still possessed on the side of those who were prepared to accept Pakistan. Gandhi did have a sound sense of reality—although it was not always apparent—but he interpreted every event in terms of its effect on his own self-imposed mission of reform; even the partition of India was not now to be allowed to stand in his way. Unlike the other Congress leaders, Gandhi had never yearned for political power, only that those in power should be favourable to his ideas of reform. Now, in 1947, he was 77 years of age, and even saints do not live for ever. Before he died he wanted to put an end to the sufferings of the innocent. He returned to Bihar because, for him, the petty wrangling and intrigues at Delhi were of little importance in face of the greater menace which stalked India. And who, after a little thought, would deny that he was right?

With Jinnah, Mountbatten was also unable to establish any warm relationship, for Jinnah was just as self-confident as Mountbatten, and infinitely more rigid. Jinnah was partly convinced that Mountbatten was pro-Congress, and absolutely convinced that he was not to be trusted. It would have made no difference to Jinnah whoever had been sent out as viceroy. It was the British whom he distrusted, and Mountbatten's blandishments seemed only a variation on the old attempts to force him to accept a Congress-dominated central government. Jinnah was now as unapproachable—and as unamenable to reason—as Hitler at Berchtesgaden, and it was not long before Mountbatten realized that the chances of handing over power to a united India were remote, at least within the present time limit of June 1948. Mountbatten's instructions were precise, however—by that date or near it Britain must quit India, united or divided. For the first time, the actual strength of Jinnah seems to have been properly appreciated by someone in authority, and the conclusion was of overwhelming importance. Until then, practically everyone had deluded themselves into believing that the British could somehow hand over the inheritance intact, thus preserving a few shreds of justification for nearly two hundred years of British rule. The real truth was unpalatable, and no one in Britain had been prepared to swallow it even though their reluctance might imply that in fact they wanted to hold on to India. Whatever may be said of Mountbatten's handling of subsequent events, for one thing at least history should remember him—he refused to be sentimental about India's British past and was not afraid to face the awesome problems of her future.

But Mountbatten's discoveries were comparatively extraneous to the more immediate problem, which was how to hold up the drift to anarchy and civil war. On 15 April he invited Gandhi and Jinnah to issue a joint statement condemning the use of force for political ends and appealing to all communities to refrain from acts of violence. It was rather like telling a fire to stop burning. Jinnah in any case had no intention of calling off the agitation in the NWFP—according to him it was only 'non-violent civil disobedience'—and it was there that peace was most needed. Muslim League agitators were still working on the tribes, trying to arouse them. If they succeeded, the whole frontier might go up in flames, since the tribes were only too willing to accept any excuse for plunder and loot.

The interim government was utterly divided into two blocs who were scarcely on speaking terms, each pursuing policies designed to antagonize and humiliate the other. Nehru, in making diplomatic appointments abroad, for example, sent a Muslim member of Congress as ambassador to the United States, while the commerce minister—a member of the Muslim League—despatched trade representatives abroad who were more concerned with spreading propaganda for Pakistan than with doing business for India. The finance minister, Liaquat Ali, primed with advice from a Muslim finance-department civil servant who was pro-League, put forward a radical budget imposing a 25 per cent tax on business profits over £7,500 per annum. Since it was Congress which proclaimed a policy of socialism, the tax should have been welcomed by Congress, but the one snag was that most Congress funds came from Hindu big business. Liaquat's proposal was in fact a deliberate attempt to create a division between the business and socialist wings of Congress, but it caused so much trouble that the viceroy was compelled to intervene and the amount of the tax was reduced. The interim government stumbled on, managing somehow to keep its balance and waiting for someone to make a decision.

The manoeuvres of the interim government, however, were only a sideshow—the real game was being played out behind the scenes. Ismay and Abell were using all their powers of persuasion upon the Muslim League in an endeavour to convince its leaders that Mount-batten was not unfavourable to the solution of partition, and Nehru was undergoing one of those characteristic changes of attitude which had marked, like milestones, the road of his political life. The sufferings of the Indian people were now working upon his mind. So was the special type of despair to which he was a victim. Freedom was so near and he was impatient with the petty intrigues and falsities of lesser men. He, too, was getting old, and the hot furnace that is a Delhi summer seemed to burn away his vitality. Only one way out seemed to stare him in the face. 'By cutting off the head,' he was to say later, 'we shall get rid of the headache.' By the end of April 1947, Nehru's attitude to partition had been completely reversed. 'The Muslim League can have Pakistan,' he said. 'But on the condition that they do not take away other parts of India which do not wish to join Pakistan.' The decision, however, was not Nehru's alone. It was highly unlikely at this stage that, by himself, he could have carried Congress with him, and Gandhi apparently was still in favour of a united India—at least he had said nothing to the contrary.

There were more profound reasons for Congress to change its mind than Nehru's despair and the alleged influence of Lady Mountbatten over him. Sardar Patel had reported that the Congress machine was falling apart under the strain of communal disorder and the failure of its leaders to achieve independence quickly. Inside Congress, various groups were jockeying for power—jobs for the boys were in sight and they wanted the profits soon. There was a growing feeling inside Congress that even a divided India was preferable to no India at all. Business was declining, factories had been made idle by strikes, landlords were threatened by uprisings of their tenants. Powerful capitalist interests in Congress were now preparing for the possibility of disowning Nehru, just as they had disposed of Gandhi, and Patel was their spokesman. It was he who had first persuaded them to put up their money—now they were beginning to demand their dividends. It was also Patel who had put forward the resolution calling for the partition of the Punjab and Bengal. Now he was to put forward the partition of India, not to satisfy Jinnah but to save Congress from collapse. The socialists did not count—had never counted for much—in Congress, and they could safely be ignored.

Through V. P. Menon, Patel had already had it suggested to the viceroy that he might be prepared to be talked into partition if Mountbatten would set about persuading him. Mountbatten, using all his very considerable arts of persuasion, did manage to convince Patel. The viceroy thought that he had won another victory. But with Patel, Mountbatten was really out of his depth.

There is no doubt that Jinnah now had powerful allies in Congress.

However, the public had to be kept in the dark; Congress must seem to yield to the logic of the situation, to accept the Pakistan solution reluctantly but in the interests of *the Indian people*, so that there might be an end to the murder of the innocents. There was, of course, always a possibility that communal violence might die out of its own accord, through the inertia of the Indian people, as had tended to be the experience of the past; an Indian mob would grow tired of violence with almost the same speed as it could be incited to it, and the hot weather, too, though encouraging quick tempers, also produced a lassitude which inhibited prolonged activity. There was, however, little real possibility of violence subsiding altogether, for agitators were still at work among the people, and Congress did its share in maintaining the atmosphere of unease. The department of information and broadcasting in Delhi, of which Patel was in charge, issued news stories which led inevitably to further violence. Many of these stories appear to have been either misrepresentations, criminal errors, or downright lies. One example will suffice. A newspaper report, later traced to the department, disclosed that the police had discovered three hundred and three rifles in a Muslim village. In fact, only one rifle had been found, and this was the standard British weapon officially called, after the size of its bore, 'a ·303'. Stories such as this undermined the work Gandhi and others were doing in the troubled areas and kept communal fears simmering.

The Muslim League, of course, was not idle either. Apart from its campaign in the NWFP, it was also engaged in a more subtle war on the interim government. Partition was not merely a question of drawing lines upon a map; the assets of British India also had to be divided. The most important of these assets was the Indian Army. On this issue, Liaquat Ali emerged as one of the principal architects of Pakistan. While Jinnah remained remote, Liaquat Ali acted. Liaquat was the very opposite of Jinnah. He was short and jolly, where Jinnah was thin and withdrawn. Liaquat, who had been educated in India, was a considerable orator, while Jinnah delivered his tedious speeches in the manner of a pedantic schoolmaster. Liaquat breathed warmth and earthy assurance, while his leader gave the impression that he had just returned from Mount Sinai. As early as 8 April 1947, Liaquat had put forward to Mountbatten a suggestion that the armed forces should be reorganized so that they could be easily divided when the time came for partition. This, of course, pre-judged the outcome of the political settlement and Mountbatten was not prepared to consider it. 'The mechanics won't permit it,' he said, 'and I won't.' But Liaquat was not going to give up the initiative. Instead, he produced a remarkably detailed plan, blandly remarking that the preparation for such a plan would take time, but 'if taken in hand immediately it should be ready about the time that a decision on the main constitutional issue is reached'. He also pointed out that the British government's deadline for the transfer of power was so near that the viceroy ought to have some plan ready just in case it became necessary. This was obviously an occasion when Congress—if it had really been prepared to fight partition—should have resisted any suggestion of dividing the armed forces, for it was clear to everybody that Liaquat's proposal was loaded. If the army could be divided, the greatest obstacle to political partition would have been overcome.

But the only real resistance to Liaquat's plan came from General Auchinleck, the commander-in-chief, who bluntly replied that: 'The Armed Forces of India, as they now stand, cannot be split up into two parts each of which will form a self-contained Armed Force,' and he buttressed his opinion with facts and cogent argument, the gist of which was that there was not enough time for reorganization before June 1948. Auchinleck further warned that rumours of a plan to divide the army should not be allowed to reach the general public. 'I wish to stress,' he wrote, 'that in the present state of communal unrest in India any publication of such discussions might well be disastrous to the continued morale and efficiency of the Armed Forces.' Auchinleck was supported in this opinion by the defence minister, Baldev Singh.

While the stone that Liaquat had thrown was spreading its ripples, Mountbatten and his staff had been at work preparing a draft plan for the transfer of power. As early as 11 April, Ismay had handed V. P. Menon 'the bare bones of a possible plan for the transfer of power', and asked him for his comments on how, for example, to divide the Punjab, Bengal and Assam. Menon's reply included a number of suggestions for dealing with most of the problems that might possibly arise.

The draft plan was also submitted to the governors of the provinces, who had been summoned to Delhi for a conference with the viceroy, and some of the plan's details were leaked to various interested parties.

By the time, therefore, that the constituent assembly met for its third session on 28 April, it had become obvious that partition of some sort was inevitable. The assembly nevertheless continued to pass resolutions, all of them seeming to indicate that the assembly supported the idea of one strong, central, government. Its discussions, however, were by no means all abstract exercises, for much of what it decided later formed the foundation of the Indian constitution. One of the most spectacular of its decisions was that Untouchability should be abolished and discrimination made an indictable offence. At the time, however, the assembly's activity seemed to be irrelevant, and, realizing this, its members adjourned on 2 May.

Though there was now general belief among the higher echelons that partition was in sight, Gandhi suddenly came out strongly against partition of the Punjab and Bengal. After a brief talk with Jinnah, which had been arranged by the viceroy, Gandhi declared that he did not 'accept the principle of division', and began to preach the gospel of unity—without, however, much of his old conviction. This was partly because he was becoming conscious of his inability to influence Congress as he had done in the past. Gandhi had sought to use Congress for his own narrow purpose, but Congress had used him in the struggle against the British. Now, when the prizes of freedom were within grasp, he was no longer needed at the helm. Saints are out of place when there is hard bargaining to be done between businessmen.

Jinnah was as hostile as Gandhi to the division of the Punjab and Bengal. He denounced as a 'sinister move' the proposal to divide the provinces. If such a division was logical, why, he asked, should not the same principle be applied in other provinces? That, too, was logical, however ridiculous it might sound. Perhaps, he suggested, the problem of Hindu minorities in Pakistan and Muslim minorities in Hindu India could be solved by an exchange of population. The answer to this, of course, was that it would be much easier to exchange populations *after* Bengal and the Punjab had been divided, because then the numbers involved would be smaller.

But was Jinnah's point, about division taken to its logical conclusion, as ridiculous as he made it out to be? In fact, looking around India at that time, it seemed that fragmentation was inevitable. Some of the larger princely states pointed out that, when British paramountcy lapsed, they would legally be completely independent and they might choose to remain so. The Sikhs were claiming a state of their own, to be carved out of the Punjab. In the NWFP, the Pathans were suggesting 'Pathanistan' as a solution to their 'national' aims. In Bengal, Suhrawardy was still dreaming of empire, and he declared that rather than submit to vivisection he would create a 'sovereign, independent, and undivided Bengal in a divided India'. Jinnah, naturally, denounced Suhrawardy's intention; but certain Congressmen, after being reassured by Suhrawardy that both Hindus and Muslims would share in the government of the new state, gave him their support.

With all these rival claims in the air, violence was growing just when the administration was becoming progressively weaker. Calcutta had a daily toll of dead and was always on the edge of new massacres; in the Punjab, fire-raising and assassination continued; the Red Shirts, the Congress movement in the NWFP, abandoned its lip-service to non-violence and began arming volunteers. In retaliation, the League was smuggling arms, many of them of Russian origin, from Afghanistan, while at least one European arms manufacturer was offering special terms to emissaries of the League.

Large-scale migration from 'unsafe' areas was already taking place, and many refugees flooded into Delhi and the surrounding countryside. The administration's grasp was obviously weakening. Rumours of division *had* reached the army. The police were not above suspicion, as everyone had thought; in fact they were riddled by communal divisions. One thing became apparent—even June 1948 was too far away, and it was more than possible that the existing machinery of government would not last that long.

Mountbatten's handling of this situation has received much criticism. It has even been suggested that the date of June 1948 was fixed to suit his convenience, because he wanted to return to the Navy as soon as possible. This is unfair to Attlee as well as to Mountbatten. June 1948 had already been planted in Attlee's mind by the Wavell plan for phased withdrawal. It was also roughly the date at which experts thought the administrative services in India would have become so short of British staff as to be unable to continue. Naturally enough, Mountbatten had been anxious to set some sort of time limit to his appointment; his future lay in the Navy, and it was highly unlikely that having been the last viceroy of India would count very much towards promotion. He had, in fact, asked for and received an assurance that he would not lose in seniority by his appointment in India. The experts' estimate to Attlee coincided with the time Mountbatten thought he could safely spare from his career in the Navy.

After a few weeks in India, however, Mountbatten came to the correct conclusion that June 1948 was not too soon but too late. Wavell's estimate had been far too hopeful—the British administration was dying on its feet. Mountbatten was faced with two simple alternatives. He could wait until the administration collapsed—and, with it, such law and order as still prevailed—facing, in the interim, growing hostility from both the major political parties. Or, as rapidly as possible, he could make the best possible arrangements for handing over power to a divided India. Both alternatives were hedged with the threat of tragedy. The only possible aim was to try and minimize its extent.

Critics, with the past laid out before them like a comic strip, can weigh cause and effect in the context of a complete episode. The makers of events do not have that privilege. Because partition led to the deaths of hundreds of thousands of innocent people in the Punjab, that is no criterion by which to judge partition itself. In April and May 1947, the author of this book saw not only the actual trouble spots of northern India but also some of those places which were as yet untouched by the disease of communal violence. He listened to men who were not only talking of war but actively preparing for it. He saw armouries of weapons, some stolen, some bought, some manufactured in secret workshops. In one place, he even saw light artillery, mortars and a small tank. Some of the princes were engaged in increasing the strength of their state forces, and not only for the purpose of defending themselves. In one mind at least, there was no doubt that partition meant fewer might die. There was no alternative which would have guaranteed peace, and Jinnah, Nehru and the viceroy were not the final arbiters. If partition were agreed, it would however be in the interests of both parties to clamp down on the extremists in their own areas, because it would give them a vested interest in keeping the peace. Mountbatten made his choice, and history will remember him for the speed and decision with which he pursued its fulfilment. He made mistakes, pushed the wheel of history at times a little too forcefully, but few men could have done better and most would have done worse.

India had already entered the valley of the shadow, and her only hope was to be hurried through it as quickly as possible.

Although Mountbatten now seemed convinced that partition was inevitable, however, he did not believe that it would be wise for the British to do the dividing. What he felt should be done, in fact, was to take Gandhi's old advice to the British, and get out and leave India to it. He did not seem to realize that neither Congress nor the League would ever agree upon the mechanics. Both sides preferred that the viceroy and the British government should make the decisions for them. Having consented to an amputation, they did not want to think of the knife—all they hoped to have to do was chloroform their consciences and, if anything went wrong, blame the surgeons.

Events now began to move with the speed of a landslide. On 2 May, Ismay flew to London with the viceroy's appreciation of the situation and his proposals for action. It was for just this kind of job that Ismay had been asked to accompany Mountbatten. He had a deep affection for India, and his general leaning was towards a conservative approach to the problem of the transfer of power. But he was also extremely shrewd and intelligent, and he seldom allowed sentiment to obscure his appreciation of the facts. He had been deeply shocked by the communal antipathies in India. 'It tore at you,' he said later, 'all the time. . . . We British had all the responsibility and none of the power. The police force was undermined and the Civil Service was frustrated and madly anxious. They were blamed by both Nehru and Jinnah for everything that went wrong.' Ismay was soon convinced that to delay partition was to invite the most terrible disaster. He and George Abell were instructed to secure cabinet approval of Mountbatten's draft plan, 'to hammer it out clause by clause with the Government and officials concerned'.

Before Ismay left, there had been a continuous round of discussion and argument. The viceroy's brains trust thought they now had the situation taped. Auchinleck, too, had become convinced that there was no alternative to partition, and he had left for London on 29 April to explain to the government just what strategical problems would be created by dividing the Indian Army. But one question of considerable importance, or so it seemed to Mountbatten, was discussed the day before Ismay and Abell left for London. This was whether India, after independence, would remain in the British Commonwealth. On the surface, this may have seemed irrelevant to the great issues then facing Mountbatten and the British government. It may have appeared as an attempt to salve British pride. But that was not the first consideration.

Suppose that, after partition, one of the new states wanted to join the Commonwealth while the other did not? Britain might then find herself siding in world affairs with one part of the old India against the other. If past speeches by Congress leaders were anything to go on, they did not want to remain in the Commonwealth, because membership would imply the dominion status which they had rejected long before. But at the meeting before Ismay left for London, Mièville casually disclosed that V. P. Menon had told him Patel *might* be willing to accept dominion status, at least for some period after independence. Menon had in fact managed to convince Patel that, as the situation now stood, Britain favoured the Muslim League, but partition, 'with both India and Pakistan as dominions, would eliminate the League's preferred status with the British' and 'facilitate the parliamentary approval of the transfer of power'. Patel had yielded to this argument. But Nehru was not told of it; it was now becoming fairly obvious that Patel was the most important figure among Congress leaders.

Menon was soon, with the viceroy's approval, to put a dominion status plan to Nehru, and the time was approaching when Congress leaders would jettison all the beliefs to which they had stuck so tenaciously before it became obvious that the British were leaving. Menon was 'asked to prepare a paper setting out the procedure whereby a form of dominion status under the alternative plans of Partition and Demission' might be agreed, a simple-sounding request, but one of considerable future importance for India and the Commonwealth. Its final effect was to change the form of the Commonwealth and even allow a republic to remain inside it.

The plan Ismay and Abell took with them to London on 2 May was highly ingenious, but it had been worked upon in a closed and private room by Mountbatten's brains trust. Before he had left for India, Mountbatten had received from Attlee a number of skeleton plans, prepared by the prime minister's advisors, for settling the Indian problem. But no Indian had been involved in putting the flesh around this one, and the comments which V. P. Menon attached to a draft given him by Ismay were ignored; Menon insists that he told Ismay the plan would not function. It had in fact been an original draft that was sent to Menon, in the hope that he would leak the gist of it to Patel, and the plan Ismay actually took to London was an altered and amended version.

In considering the plan, Mountbatten was guided by his conviction that the Labour government would be most unwilling to accept the onerous task of actually dividing India into two new states. His own view of the government's attitude was that it wished to be rid of India as soon as possible and at almost any price. Here he misjudged the Labour prime minister, though probably not some of his colleagues. Attlee was certainly anxious to dispose of the Indian problem, which was taking up too much of the government's time, but he was also conscious that his government needed a boost to its status and prestige. A Conservative administration could have handed India over to anarchy and chaos, for imperialists were expected to be callous, but the 'party of the people' could not. Furthermore, the disposal of India— one of the great imperial assets—must not appear to be a unilateral act by the ideologues of the Labour party. Attlee wanted to achieve at least some measure of bi-partisan responsibility. The Conservatives were already condemning him for rushing independence. If India were to dissolve into a blood bath, criticism would become really virulent, and the prime minister would also have to face attacks from the 'do-gooders' in his own party, who would be quick to censure him on those abstract grounds of humanity which are so difficult to counter. Mountbatten, however, thought that if he adapted the original Cabinet Mission plan to suit the new situation, he would be offering Attlee the sort of solution that would appeal to him, especially as the prime minister had already said that it might be necessary to hand over power to the provinces themselves. The viceroy also mistakenly believed that he held the Indian leaders in the hollow of his hand, so Ismay took with him to London the viceroy's assurance that the plan would be accepted by both parties in India. Disillusionment was not long in coming.

The plan sent to London was deceptively simple—to transfer power to the provinces, leaving only a weak federal administration at the centre. Any polarization into groups would then be a matter for the individual provinces to decide, *after the British had left*. Mountbatten thought that the only likely resistance to this plan would come from Jinnah. As no one other than Mountbatten and his staff had actually seen the plan in its final form—only a few highlights had been disclosed verbally—the viceroy should have had every reason for feeling uneasy. But it was not from Jinnah that Mountbatten was to receive the first signs of criticism. This came first from V. P. Menon, who had accompanied the viceroy to Simla on 7 May and was at last able to put forward his—and Patel's—view on the subject.

On 8 May, at the invitation of the viceroy, Nehru arrived at Viceregal Lodge, Simla. He was accompanied by a newcomer, V. K. Krishna Menon. V.K.K., as he was known to distinguish him from the many other Menons, was no relation to V.P. Most of his political life had been spent in London, where he had been a socialist member of the St Pancras Borough Council and an active propagandist for Indian freedom. V.K.K. had returned to India to claim his just reward when the jobs were being distributed, and he was now very close to Nehru who had become somewhat isolated from the rest of Congress. V.K.K. was rather out of touch with Indian realities and he still believed that it would be possible for the British to hand over to a united, and of course Congress-dominated, India. If this was to be achieved, he knew the splitting of the Indian Army must be avoided at all costs, and he had told Nehru so. But the advice came too late. The idea of splitting the army had been accepted, at least in principle, even if Mountbatten still seemed to believe that it might be possible to hand over an undivided army to the proposed federal government if the British government was prepared to back his new plan.

When Nehru arrived, Mountbatten gave V. P. Menon permission to talk to him about dominion status—to which Patel had already agreed—but not about the plan which Ismay had taken to London. The next day, 9 May, there was a general discussion at which the viceroy encouraged Menon to outline to Nehru his own scheme for the transfer of power to two central governments, one for Pakistan and one for Hindustan, each with an interim constitution based upon the old India Act of 1935. Nehru found the scheme appealing, though he made a show of not altogether liking the idea of dominion status on the grounds that it still retained overtones of dependence. But he was by now determined that even dominion status should not stand in the way of India's freedom, and in any case, after independence, a free India could easily decide to leave the Commonwealth if she wanted to. Such questions, though important perhaps to the British government, did not carry the same weight with Nehru or Patel. Having accepted

partition it was not difficult to swallow dominion status, especially as
it could be regurgitated later on.

Mountbatten, however, seemed to have been hypnotized by dominion status into underestimating the value of Menon's opinion on the
other plan that Ismay was now persuading the British government in
London to accept. After the 9 May discussion with Nehru, Mountbatten had it announced that there would be a meeting on 17 May of
all the important Indian leaders—Nehru, Patel, Jinnah, Liaquat Ali,
and Baldev Singh—in order that the viceroy might present to them a
new plan for the transfer of power. This plan, the one Ismay had taken
to London, had now been accepted by the British government, though
with some modifications and misgivings and only on the strength of
Mountbatten's assurance that the plan would be acceptable to the Indian
leaders.

On 10 May, however, Mountbatten suddenly decided to see what
effect the draft plan would have on Nehru, to try a dummy run before
the meeting planned for the following week. Within half an hour,
Mountbatten was forced to face the fact that he had completely misjudged the reaction his plan might bring from Indian leaders. Nehru
was blunt—the draft was totally unacceptable. It would, he wrote next
morning in a memorandum to the viceroy, 'invite the Balkanization
of India' and 'provoke certain civil conflict'. He also condemned the
plan as likely to 'endanger relations between Britain and India'. This
was undoubtedly serious—for the viceroy. Ismay in London had convinced Attlee that the plan he had brought with him was workable
because it would be acceptable to the Indian Leaders. Now one of them
had shown that it was not.

Fortunately, there was at least one thing on the credit side—the plan
had not yet been made public. If it had been, the trust Mountbatten
had so carefully built up would have dissolved in rancour and suspicion. Mountbatten had been saved from an error which would not
only have been catastrophic for him personally but also for India.
Nehru was in fact right; the plan *was* an open invitation to the princes,
the private armies, and the Suhrawardys to go ahead with their own
private plans. The Mountbatten scheme of federation would not have
led to simple division but to dangerous and chaotic fragmentation. All
that had really emerged from the careful planning of Mountbatten
and his staff was the fact that fundamentally none of them understood

the situation in India any better than their predecessors or the politicians back in Britain.

Mountbatten fortunately had one great quality—his resilience. He was like a rubber ball that, sharply kicked, only bounces higher, and he was not the man to waste time over analysing his mistakes. Being entirely empirical in his approach, he was able after only a short pause to begin searching for a way out of what might well have been a disastrous situation. Luckily, an alternative scheme was already in existence. He had encouraged V. P. Menon to explain it to Nehru only the day before. Nehru was called back and asked if Congress would accept a new draft plan based on the Menon scheme and incorporating Nehru's own criticisms. Nehru replied—rightly, for he was not in any position to do so—that he could not speak for Congress. Not, he added, without first seeing a revised draft. Since Nehru was leaving that evening for Delhi, it did not seem possible to produce anything for him before he left; but with only a few days to go before the much publicized meeting at which the viceroy was supposed to present a new plan to the Indian leaders, the utmost speed was necessary. Menon was instructed to get his scheme in writing before Nehru left Simla.

Meanwhile, the viceroy instructed his PRO, Alan Campbell-Johnson, to cook up some reasonable-sounding excuse and issue a communiqué announcing that the meeting had been postponed. Mountbatten then cabled Attlee that the plan the government had accepted would have to be abandoned and another one, now, in preparation, substituted for it.

Menon produced his draft on time, and has since been praised for, as one writer put it, taking 'exactly four hours to draw up a plan which was to change the face of India and the world'. This is by no means the case, of course, for Menon had had his plan ready to produce ever since he received from Ismay the draft of what was later to form the basis of Mountbatten's scheme, and he had even discussed it in outline with Patel. He already knew that his scheme was acceptable to Patel and if there were to be any opposition from Nehru, Patel could soon overcome it. As it happened, Nehru was in any case prepared to accept partition and, though he might quibble on details, he would certainly not object to the broad principle.

Campbell-Johnson meanwhile issued an unconvincing communiqué: 'Owing to the imminence of the Parliamentary recess in London,' it said, the meeting of 17 May was postponed until 2 June. No one was deceived by this specious excuse.

Mountbatten was now faced with a mystified and angry Attlee. Cables came from London demanding explanations. Ismay, too, who had used all his powers of persuasion to get the original plan accepted, complained that he had not the remotest idea what was going on. One cable from Attlee demanded the viceroy's immediate presence in London so that he could explain his behaviour in person. For a while, Mountbatten was not sure whether to go or whether to stand on his dignity and threaten to resign if he did not receive what would be in effect a vote of confidence. On reflection, however, he realized his responsibilities to the government which had appointed him, and on 14 May he cabled Attlee that he would fly to London on the 18th. When he left Delhi, Mountbatten took Menon with him. It was a wise move. Menon was a solid and experienced civil servant—a wise man in a den of not particularly daring Daniels. His sober and intelligent approach was just what was needed to convince Attlee. It succeeded, though Attlee's confidence in Mountbatten's judgement was somewhat eroded. But Mountbatten was able to convince the prime minister that the new plan represented, reasonably accurately, the views of the nationalist leaders and that it actually could be carried out despite the shortness of time. On Mountbatten's instructions, Ismay had already suggested that the date for the transfer of power should be moved forward, and Attlee had also been advised by other sources that the June 1948 date was unsatisfactory on purely administrative grounds. As far as the problems of the Indian Army were concerned, Auchinleck had been unmanned by the instructions given to him to prepare for its division and his advice was of little value; in actual fact, he was almost completely ignored by both the British government and the viceroy. He plodded on with the thankless and valuable task of preparing for the operation, but though as a good soldier his mind was in his task, his heart was not, and he seemed mainly worried over the difficulty of protecting British lives—which were not in fact in danger.

During the discussions in London, one date now seemed to meet with general if somewhat dismayed agreement—15 August, barely two-and-a-half months ahead. Such momentous and unparalleled haste appeared to savour of panic, and panic certainly played its part. But it was not the panic of men unhinged by fear. A large body of evidence had now reached the government's hands from all manner of sources, including the Intelligence services which had been producing valuable information on the attitudes of Indian leaders outside Congress and the League. The foundations of British India had been built upon sand, the sand of a people's consent. That consent was now trickling away, and the walls of the imperial edifice—so solid-seeming in the past—were crumbling. The British, however, who had neither the strength nor the inclination to bolster them up, seemed in danger of being crushed when they fell. Perhaps, the government thought once again, shock tactics might inspire the Indians themselves to carry out repairs.

7 Moments of Truth

Between the viceroy's return from London on 31 May and his meeting with the Indian leaders two days later, contradictory statements and blustering appeals from all sides set up a smokescreen which concealed the fact that Congress and the League had actually accepted the inevitable partition of the country.

Jinnah declared that he was immovably opposed to the partition of Bengal and the Punjab, though in fact Muslim League leaders had already acknowledged to themselves that if Pakistan were to be achieved at all this concession would probably have to be made, and Jinnah had already said 'better a moth-eaten Pakistan' than no Pakistan at all. But the League felt that pressure must be kept up, just in case the viceroy was to return from London with some other plan. Jinnah had to preserve an unyielding façade until the very last moment, and, to show Congress that he was still belligerent, he put forward an entirely new demand for a corridor through Hindu India, connecting what would be the two halves of Pakistan. No one, least of all Jinnah, took the demand seriously—but it helped to keep the pot boiling.

Gandhi, too, was still pretending that Congress would resist partition even at the risk of that very violence he was working so hard—and with considerable local success—to restrain. 'Even if the whole of India burns,' he said at his prayer-meeting on 31 May, 'we shall not concede Pakistan, even if the Muslims demanded it at the point of the sword.' Why did Gandhi utter such inflammatory sentiments at such a late

date, especially when he had already in fact agreed to partition at a
meeting of the Congress Working Committee when Patel and Nehru
announced their own acceptance? At that meeting, Gandhi, who had
returned from Noakhali in order to attend, complained that no one
had told him of the changed attitude of the Congress leadership towards
partition. Nehru replied that Gandhi had been kept constantly in the
picture about what was going on. Gandhi denied this, and Nehru then
remarked that Noakhali was far away and, though he may not have
sent Gandhi full details, at least he had informed him of the broad
outlines. It seems clear that Gandhi really had been kept in the dark, in
case he might still try to persuade Congress not to accept their leaders'
decision. But he was not in fact prepared for a showdown and con-
tented himself with saying that Congress must honour decisions and
commitments made by its leaders. Why then did Gandhi later insist,
in public that partition was unacceptable, even at the risk of civil war?

There is no simple, clear-cut answer. Gandhi was an extremely
complicated personality and his thoughts and actions displayed the
emotional characteristics of the fanatic mind. He was mild, yet ruthless when he thought it necessary to attain his ends. Like so many religious reformers, he loved Mankind but was not above hating men who
stood in his way. He could move through the countryside preaching
peace when surrounded by violence, but when he was away from the
sight of violence, he could incite men to fight. Was he now hoping in
some way to discredit those Congress leaders who had rejected him in
their hour of triumph? Or was he attempting to dissociate himself in
advance from any responsibility for Congress's decision to accept partition, a decision which would certainly come as a shock when it was
made public? Gandhi had a very astute and agile mind although he
disguised it as much as possible behind contradictions of thought and
action. It seems probable that, at this time, he had come to recognize
that the Indian National Congress might no longer be the ideal instrument for his plan of a Hindu reformation, and that he was slowly
moving towards the possibility of some new political alignment. There
is no doubt that he had had a number of discussions with orthodox
Hindu politicians, one of whom—after Gandhi had been assassinated—
told the author of this book that the Mahatma had said that, though he
was against partition in principle, it might well be the only way of
lessening communal tensions to such a level as would permit him to get

on with his work of reform, but that nevertheless he would still fight
it as hard as he could. After independence, the orthodox Hindu political
parties were to attack Gandhi violently for having played a double game,
and it was such attacks which led finally, though indirectly, to his
assassination by a Hindu extremist in January 1948. It now seems sure
that Gandhi *was* playing some sort of double game, but it has proved
impossible to find out with any certainty just what the game was.
Gandhi is dead, and so is the Hindu leader who, a year before his death,
'revealed' his version of the story to the author. Such 'evidence' as has
emerged since the event has come from untrustworthy sources. But it
does seem that, if Congress had moved away from Gandhi, Gandhi
was also moving away from Congress as the pettiness of its leaders'
ambitions came to light and they fought over India for what they could
get out of it. If Gandhi had lived, it is possible that he would completely
and irrevocably have broken with Congress and formed a new political
party which would more accurately have expressed his peculiar views.
Such speculation, however, is not of much profit except to his heirs.
But there is no question that, by June 1947, Gandhi's position was to
say the least equivocal.

The position of the minority leaders, however, was not. The Sikhs
in particular were spoiling for a fight and were letting the whole world
know it—the whole world, that is, except the viceroy and the leaders
of Congress and the League. Jinnah probably did not care, while Nehru
and Patel were not particularly interested.

As the viceroy's meeting with the Indian leaders approached,
Mountbatten for some reason remained worried that Gandhi might
upset any arrangement arrived at for partition. There was, however,
really nothing to worry about on that score. On 2 June, the meeting
convened. It was an odd meeting, devoid of drama or any sense of the
magnitude of the occasion. Those present were Nehru, Patel, Kripalani
(the Congress president), Jinnah, Liaquat Ali, Sardar Nishtar, and
Baldev Singh. Mountbatten made a last appeal for acceptance of the
Cabinet Mission plan in its original form, but this was only a formality
and was treated as such. Then the viceroy announced the British
government's new proposals. For the first time, everyone was in agreement. Perhaps there might have been a quibble or two about details,
but the viceroy was able to handle them. The only danger was that, on
reflection, Congress or the League might decide to stand out for

impossible concessions. But even Jinnah's refusal to commit himself without consulting his working committee was merely a gesture. When the viceroy saw Jinnah again at 11 p.m. the same evening, the League leader expressed a general agreement, tempered with only one or two points of argument. 'His [Jinnah's] delight,' Mountbatten reported to London, 'was unconcealed.' And why not? The long campaign was virtually over. There would be no Hindu government of an undivided India. Jinnah could afford to relax his rigidity for a moment and show 'delight'.

Next day, the plan was officially published. It was mainly concerned with the way in which inhabitants of the so-called 'Pakistan provinces' could express their opinion on whether they wanted a new constituent assembly or were content with the present one. This was a roundabout way of saying that the provinces were to be asked whether they wished to join Pakistan or not. The method of tapping opinion was to vary in the different provinces. In Sind, Bengal, and the Punjab, the choice was to be made by the members of the provincial legislative assemblies, but in the two latter provinces the assemblies were to meet in two separate parts—one representing the Muslim-majority districts and the other the rest of the province—and to vote separately. If each part then decided that it wished to remain united with the other, the assembly as a whole was to be asked to vote upon whether it wished to join Pakistan or India. If, however, either part voted in favour of division from the other, then it would be assumed that division should for the time being be drawn between the Muslim and non Muslim-majority districts. The viceroy would thereafter appoint a boundary commission to arrive at a final decision.

If Bengal decided in favour of dividing itself, a referendum would then have to be held in the Sylhet district of the province of Assam— the only Muslim-majority district in that province—to find out whether its inhabitants wanted to join their Muslim brethren in what would be East Bengal. A method also had to be devised for voting in British Baluchistan, which had never had an elected government, and in which there were no electoral registers.

The North-West Frontier Province, where a Congress government still held office, presented a different problem. There, a legislative assembly vote would be unlikely to reflect the real views of the electorate, and it was therefore decided that there should be a referendum of the whole electorate (which did not, incidentally, mean the whole adult population).

The plan concluded with a statement that the British government was prepared to hand over power before June 1948, and that it intended to introduce legislation during the current session of the British parliament to transfer power to one or two successor states at some date in 1947. At a press conference on 4 June, the viceroy indicated—though not officially—that the date the government had in mind was 15 August.

The actual significance of the earlier date took some time to penetrate the preoccupied minds of the nationalist leaders. Congress, in its official response to the new proposals, tried to extract an assurance from the viceroy that, if the new India were to decide to leave the Commonwealth, Pakistan would automatically be expelled. Under private pressures this demand was dropped. Another Congress suggestion was that the referendum in the NWFP should offer a third choice—for the province to become independent as 'Pathanistan'. This was not acceptable to the viceroy, nor was it in fact seriously meant by Congress which had only put it forward as a sop to Dr Khan Sahib.

Jinnah, under pressure from Suhrawardy, suggested that if a referendum were to be taken in Bengal, it also should include the choice of independence. Then Bengal would afterwards presumably choose to join Pakistan in one piece. Jinnah was not serious about his proposal either, for he distrusted Suhrawardy and was pretty sure that an independent Bengal, once in existence, would be unwilling to give up its independent status.

On the whole, these demands were gestures, meaningless left-overs from past tactics. In reality, everyone had been thrown off balance by the fact that partition was now inevitable. Jinnah was overwhelmed by his success. Congress, on the other hand, was crestfallen and rather ashamed at having lost its fight for an undivided India. The 'Sikh Representative', Baldev Singh, whose community perhaps had most to lose by partition, did not seem to realize what was happening. Not that he counted for much, even in his own community; the real, influential Sikh leaders were preparing to resist partition with guns and knives, far more decisive weapons than words, they thought, especially when no one seemed to care very much what happened to minorities as long as Congress and the League were satisfied.

But what about the physical problems of partition? The administration, the public services, above all, the army? The nationalist leaders, preoccupied with the struggle to satisfy their varying ambitions, had not thought about it, but assumed that the British no doubt had another plan up their sleeves. They did. Each of the Indian leaders was soon presented with a document headed 'The Administrative Consequences of Partition'.

The nationalist leaders now faced a moment of truth, a point in their careers when words and threats had to give way to facts. The problem that confronted them—of dividing in just seventy-two days the people, the assets, and the liabilities of British India, of dissecting something that had grown up slowly over more than a century—came as a shock. In a hot, crowded little studio at the Delhi station of All-India Radio, the viceroy, Nehru, Jinnah, and Baldev Singh went to the microphone to speak to the Indian people, the majority of whom were not listening and would not have understood even if they had been. The consequences of the message, however, were soon to be brought home to them with fire and sword. But at that moment, no one cared, just as no one had really cared before—except Gandhi, still on his mission of peace. At least one minority had won everything it had hoped for. The leaders of the Muslim League and the leaders of Congress had won, in one case not all they had hoped for, but in the final analysis more than either had expected. Now they were prepared to be magnanimous towards the innocent. Jinnah, in his broadcast, asked the NWFP League to call off its 'civil disobedience movement', and it was abandoned immediately as was the similar campaign in Assam. Baldev Singh's speech was as colourless as his personality. Only Nehru tried to rise to the immensity of the occasion, to the terrible grandeur of the end of an empire and the beginning of a new era for India and her people. 'We are little men,' he said, 'serving great causes, but because that cause is great something of that greatness falls upon us.' There remained only a few weeks in which to show whether he was right or wrong.

Certainly it seemed for a while that some of the greatness *had* rubbed off on the nationalist leaders. Jinnah refused to countenance the extremism of some League members who demanded that he should not accept partition of the Punjab and Bengal, and in this he had the majority of the League behind him. Like Congress, they saw that this

was not the time for outrageous demands. For them, too, the perquisites of power were within reach. By 400 votes to 8, the Council of the
Muslim League authorized Jinnah 'to accept the fundamental principles
of the plan as a compromise'.

The All-India Congress Committee passed a resolution of acceptance, too—free for once from ambiguous qualifications—by 157 votes
to 29, with 32 abstentions mainly by orthodox Hindus. The committee
did, of course, reassert its faith in Indian unity, and several speakers
prophesied that partition would only be temporary and in a short while
India would be once again united. Gandhi recommended, despite all
his public objections, that the committee accept the plan, though he
too hinted that he thought Pakistan could not last and would soon want
to rejoin India.

In other quarters, there was opposition to the plan, but it came from
men who were not in a position to alter any political decision. Their day
was yet to come, and they would try to prove their point with blood.
The orthodox Hindu parties condemned the plan. So too did 'nationalist' Muslim members of Congress, headed by Maulana Azad. The
communists reserved their attacks for the British. Following a lead from
Moscow, they condemned partition as an extension of the old British
policy of 'divide and rule' and claimed that dominion status was a
sinister device for carrying it out—though they did not explain how.
But they were right in thinking that dominion status was important.
It was now becoming clear why so much effort has been expended by
the viceroy on persuading both Congress and the League (though
Jinnah was already convinced) that they must accept dominion status.
It was only, Mountbatten insisted to the Indian leaders, a device for
ensuring the smooth transfer of power. Outside India, it was not viewed
in that way at all, but rather as a triumph of British statesmanship and
a proof that, as the British were still clever enough to transform a
dependent empire into an interdependent commonwealth, they could
by no means be written off the world stage. However, the real reason
for Britain's insistence that both the new successor states should be
dominions had nothing at all to do with India, or with the Commonwealth for that matter. It was not so much designed to ensure the
smooth transfer of power to India as to guarantee the approval of all
political parties *in Britain*. Instead of liquidating an empire—a negative
achievement—the Labour government appeared to be creating a new

dynamic Commonwealth, admirably adjusted to a changed world. There was also a rather more pertinent virtue, for the new plan appeared to fulfil two of the main conditions enshrined in the Cripps offer of 1942 *to which all parties had given their pledge of support*; that there should be agreement between the major Indian political groups, and that there should be a period of dominion status. This was confirmed, though with great caution and many reservations, by Winston Churchill in a statement on behalf of the Conservative opposition.

There was another proposal also designed to neutralize opposition in Britain. This was that both the new dominions should have the same governor-general, who would act as a sort of super, though constitutional, ruler. In theory, the idea was brilliant, and it was felt that it would certainly appeal to those who still believed the Labour party was forcing Britain to leave India in an undignified and panic-stricken shuffle. It is not quite clear just where the idea originated, although it was certainly not with the viceroy, but the suggestion was included in the draft that Ismay had taken to London on 18 May. Congress, which at this stage was prepared to agree to anything as long as it got independence, had agreed to have Mountbatten as the first governor-general of the Hindu part of India as well as to the principle of sharing the governor-general with Pakistan. It would not really have mattered who held this high office, since, under the new dispensation, he would have nothing like the power that had been wielded by the viceroy of British India. There is no doubt that the invitation to Mountbatten was made almost entirely as a piece of not too costly flattery, but if Mountbatten were to become governor-general of both the new dominions Congress believed that his impartiality would be weighted against Jinnah.

The idea was immediately appealing to Mountbatten, as it would have been to anyone with a sense of romance. To be last viceroy *and* first governor-general was quite a distinction. The Attlee government in London had also welcomed the possibility, not only for its propaganda value at home but for the fact that, if there was one authority common to the two new dominions, it would probably make the actual transfer of power easier. But the plan was no more than an exercise in abstraction, made possible only because neither Mountbatten, his 'advisers', nor the British government, seemed yet to understand what they were actually doing. They were not involved in

some theoretical staff course, but concerned with a real and tremend-
ously complex situation. It looked as if no one had learned from experience. Every action seemed to be played off the cuff, and if one thing
failed, there was no time—or even inclination—to find out why; there
was time only to substitute something else from an apparently inex-
haustible supply of alternatives. Any proper appreciation, for example,
of Jinnah's character—and there was plenty of evidence from which to
deduce it—would have shown that the odds against his accepting anyone other than himself, and in particular Mountbatten whom he
neither trusted nor liked, for the office of governor-general of Pakistan
were overwhelming. Even if Jinnah had been forced by expediency to
accept some super-governor-general, it is unlikely that he could have
stomached Mountbatten. In fact, if a super-governor-general had been
appointed for the two dominions, the British would still have been
subject to criticism and abuse, and the suggestion which the communists had already been spreading that it was a British trick to retain
power, would have gained weight. The idea was, in fact, only supported out of a mixture of political self-interest, ignorance, and personal
ambition.

When the question had been put to Jinnah, he had played for time.
Under pressure, however, he said that he would prefer two governors-
general to one, but that he felt the British should appoint a supreme
arbitrator to divide the assets between the two new dominions. He
went so far as to grant that he would be happy to see Mountbatten in
that appointment. But he refused to put his proposal in writing, and
when Mountbatten tried to bully him into doing so he immediately
closed up. When the viceroy went to London, he was informed that in
any case such an appointment as Supreme Arbitrator would not only
be unworkable but would need special and complicated legislation
which the government was not prepared to indulge in.

On the viceroy's return to India, efforts were made to convince
Jinnah that it would be in Pakistan's interests to share a governor-
general with 'Hindustan', as it was then called. But Jinnah would not
respond. The viceroy's charm was ineffective, and it was not until
2 July that Jinnah finally informed the viceroy that the first governor-
general of Pakistan would be—Jinnah. Mountbatten, who thought it
was only Jinnah's vanity that was at stake, still would not give up,
partly because he himself wanted to be the super-governor-general,

but more particularly because he had once again assured Attlee that Congress and the League would agree to such an appointment. But all attempts, including intervention by the Nawab of Bhopal, a close friend of Jinnah, were unsuccessful, and on 5 July, Liaquat Ali asked the viceroy to make an official recommendation to the king that Jinnah should be first governor-general of Pakistan. In the same letter as contained this request, Liaquat said he hoped that Mountbatten would stay on as governor-general of India (as Congress had now insisted their dominion should be called). This hope, which was almost immediately reiterated by Congress, was on the surface a peculiar one to come from Liaquat Ali. It was, however, smart tactics from the League's point of view, because, though the Muslim leaders were not sure that Mountbatten was trustworthy, they were absolutely convinced that any Congress member who became governor-general would not be. On the whole, they expected to be better off with a British governor-general in India.

Jinnah's refusal to accept a joint governor-general came as a shock both to Mountbatten and the British government. It also presented a new problem—should Mountbatten accept the appointment as governor-general of India alone? His staff argued fluently that he should, in the interests of stability; in order to persuade British officials and Service personnel to stay on and help the new dominion; in order to smooth the division of the Indian Army. His being there, they added, would also help to prevent communal disorder, which had 'improved out of all measure in the past three months as a result of His Excellency's presence'. This was a total and irresponsible misreading of the facts. The only really worthwhile point made by the viceroy's staff was that if there were to be two native governors-general, the Tory opposition at home might use it as an excuse to delay the passage of the transfer of power Bill until after 15 August. There was little foundation for thinking this, but it was in fact just possible that the opposition might try and delay the Bill, although their strength in the House of Commons was small and the government, if it had wished, could simply have forced a vote and defeated them. As it happened, the Tories at this stage—it was now 4 July and the Bill had already been introduced—were unwilling to resist the passage of the necessary legislation.

Mountbatten decided to accept the Congress leaders' invitation and, on 7 July, Ismay was sent to London in order to convince the government and the opposition that the decision was right. The arguments he put forward sounded sensible to people so ignorant of the real situation in India, and he was successful. Even Winston Churchill agreed, in the belief that the appointment of a British governor-general would ease communal tensions and 'strengthen the ties of sentiment between India and the rest of the Commonwealth'! He also thought the appointment would help in preserving the interests of the princes. In two out of these three beliefs he was to be terribly wrong.

The questions of dominion status and the appointment of a new governor-general took up far more time and energy than their real importance warranted, and there were many other questions of singular pettiness which also diverted the viceroy from the major tasks that faced him. Much-needed time was given to the problems involved in designing the flags of the two new dominions and the etiquette of addressing Indian leaders as 'esquire'. In fact, there was an inescapably surrealist air about the preoccupations of the viceroy, his staff, and the nationalist leaders, as 15 August loomed nearer and nearer. The viceroy had been advised by more than one responsible person that there would be massacres in the border regions of the new dominions when partition took place. Lieutenant-General Tuker, the military commander who was C-in-C of Eastern Command—an area which included Calcutta and the districts that were to be divided in Bengal—had submitted a plan for the division of the army and its redisposition into areas which were likely to need it, as early as the spring of 1946. His was a detailed and practicable plan, but it was pigeon-holed by Auchinleck who was then still trying to keep the army undivided. As late as June 1947, it was again rejected, apparently on the grounds that the nationalist leaders would find it unacceptable. Mountbatten did not seem to be worried by the possibility of trouble in the Punjab and Bengal. He was convinced that at the first sign of disorder, he would be able to crush it by using aircraft and tanks. According to the posthumously published and very carefully edited memoirs of Maulana Azad, the viceroy assured him that he would take the sternest measures to suppress communal violence as soon as it appeared. Unfortunately, Azad's memoirs are not trustworthy, though there is evidence from other sources which seems to confirm that the viceroy thought he could cope with any disturbances which might take place.

If Azad's statement is true, then Mountbatten gave his assurance of stern measures *at the first sign of trouble* at a time when it was already comparatively common knowledge that a number of people—quite apart from the Sikhs, who were openly drilling and practising with weapons—were planning violence. Can it reasonably be assumed that this was not, however, common knowledge as far as the viceroy was concerned? There is some evidence that the Criminal Intelligence Department and other Intelligence agencies of the government of India were in a state of collapse. Many agents were now worried about what would happen to them when the new governments took office, and feared that they might soon suffer for having spied on the nationalists; they had not received any assurance that their names and the Intelligence files would not be handed over to Britain's successors. There was, of course, no likelihood of this happening, but it is in the nature of things that a spy should be suspicious even of his employers.

Fairly detailed information about possible trouble *was* reaching Delhi, but it seems that no proper evaluation was being made and the viceroy consequently was not fully aware of the potential explosiveness of the situation. At the same time, Mountbatten does not seem to have treated the possibilities with great seriousness. His idea of using aircraft to break up crowds of rioters was all very well in the countryside, but not of much use in the rabbit-warrens of the towns. In any case, there were not enough aircraft in India to handle a serious outbreak, and no real attempt was made to reinforce fighter squadrons on the off chance that they might be needed.

Basically, however, the attitude of both the viceroy and the major Indian political leaders was the same. None of them believed that major violence would break out. They wanted to believe that partition would solve the communal problem and that, once it took place, reason would prevail. In the case of the Congress leaders, this was the sole public justification for accepting partition at all; it was supposed to settle the communal problem and remove the root cause of disorder. All sides, then, turned away from the possibility of violence and chose to ignore it. The only adequate precautions that could have been taken —redisposition of the army into known trouble spots before the date of partition—were not taken for purely political reasons. But these reasons were reinforced by a basic unwillingness to believe, in spite of all the evidence, that there would be major disorders in the Punjab and probably in Bengal as well, when partition came.

The main trouble was that there was no time to think of everything. No time to explore every angle of a frightening and complex situation. Consequently, some things had to be ignored. Unfortunately, one of these was the risk of violence. Why, in fact, *was* so little time allowed, and who decided to bring the date of the transfer of power forward by nearly a year? It has been suggested that the decision was made by Lord Mountbatten himself and forced upon the British government by his public announcement on 4 June. But this suggestion once again overrates his authority. The viceroy, however dynamic and powerful a figure, was still the agent of the British government and his area of independent decision was circumscribed. Once the cabinet in London had accepted the thesis that June 1948 was too late a date—because the administrative services would be unable to function long before then— the idea of getting the job over as quickly as possible had an immediate appeal. All the more so because Attlee was firmly convinced that the only way to arrive at a workable solution without having to contend with the organic procrastination of Indian politicians, was to keep them in a state of shock. Only in this way, he and many others believed, could the Indian leaders be forced to face reality. Above all, the government had decided that India must have no grounds for complaints against the British. The aim now was to make friends of the two new dominions, keep them in the Commonwealth, and protect British investments and business undertakings in both India and Pakistan. Every action henceforth was to be subject to the criteria of political expediency; under the circumstances there was really no alternative. There seems little doubt that the date of 15 August had been discussed during the viceroy's visit to London. All were agreed that June 1948 was now out of the question and that even December 1947 was probably too late, and some date had to be announced publicly.

The transfer of power was not a simple legislative act, arrived at and put into practice in normal circumstances. It had to be carried out like a military operation. No commander fights without the risk of casualties; he only tries to minimize them. Mountbatten's instructions were to succeed—at the least cost. The hundreds of thousands killed later in the Punjab can only partly be blamed on faulty Intelligence and tactical errors. They were the legacy, not of Mountbatten, but of the nature and the shortcomings of nearly a hundred years of British rule and of opposition to British rule.

There is no doubt that Mountbatten tackled the awesome problems of dividing the assets of the Indian empire with a speed and brilliance which it is difficult to believe would have been exercised by any other man. Mountbatten defined his own part as that of 'the mechanic who keeps the car running but I do not actually sit in the driving seat and turn the wheel'. In fact he did, though there were also any number of back-seat drivers, and his journey was not on smooth, well-known roads but over difficult and broken terrain. He was the force behind the organization of partition, maintaining the sense of urgency and the need for decision. A calendar with the days in enormous red and black letters reminded his staff of the passing of time as the deadline moved towards them. Mountbatten's was a tremendous achievement, and the tragedy that hedged it should not be allowed to diminish its reality. The tragedy could have been worse, and if the transfer had been de-layed—as some critics think it should have been—it would hardly have been less.

The machinery set up to prepare for partition was basically simple. At the apex there was a Partition Committee with Lord Mountbatten as chairman, Patel and Rajendra Prasad (later India's first president) representing Congress, and Liaquat Ali and Sardar Nishtar, the League. Baldev Singh was excluded after Jinnah had objected that he would be too pro-Congress. The committee's function was to co-ordinate—through a steering committee of two high officials, Chaudri Muhammad Ali, a Muslim, and H. M. Patel, a Hindu—the work of a large number of expert committees and sub-committees dealing with every-thing from the division of the armed forces, through railways and telegraphs, to the duplication of files.

The Armed Forces Committee included a British chairman and a number of British officers. Their task was both dangerous and difficult, for there was no easy way to divide army units. Until shortly after the Mutiny of 1857, entire regiments had been either Hindu or Muslim, but units were then mixed to strike a balance between the two religions, so that each might act as a restraint upon the other. Because of this, units would now have to be broken up completely and then re-assembled, although while this was being done it was arranged that some central administrative control would remain. At the same time, commanders-in-chief of the two new dominions' armies were to be appointed so that they and their headquarters administration would be ready to take over. In the interim, the supreme commander was to be the then C-in-C of undivided India, Field-Marshal Auchinleck, who was to be subordinate to a Joint Defence Council. He was to have no operational control over the new armies, except in the case of units in transit between the two dominions, and his only function was to oversee the proper division of men and materials. It was hoped that joint control would come to an end after 1 April 1948.

The division of the armed forces was to take place in two stages. The first was to consist of a rather rough-and-ready separation on a purely communal basis, followed by the immediate concentration of Muslim-majority units in what was to be Pakistan and of other units in the rest of the country. The second stage was to cover the voluntary transfer of individuals who wished to join units in either Pakistan or India. The first stage was carried through with unexpected smoothness. Before the end of June 1947, final decisions had been reached on the Navy and on some units of the Army.

The Civil Services also had to be divided, and both European and Indian members were asked to stay on and help with necessary reconstruction after the transfer of power. The British government guaranteed compensation and pensions, graded according to length of service, to British officers who would be deprived of their careers.

By the end of June, both Bengal and the Punjab had decided in favour of internal partition. In Bengal, the decision was reached in an atmosphere comparatively free from communal disorder, though tension was only just concealed below the surface. In the Punjab, however, there was a daily quota of bomb explosions, fire-raising and murders in Lahore, the provincial capital, and Amritsar, the sacred city of the Sikhs. The Muslim-majority areas had voted against the division of the Punjab, as was to be expected, but the non-Muslim areas voted in favour. The consequence of these votes was that the central Partition Committee was replaced by a Partition Council, the only change being that Jinnah took over from Sardar Nishtar. Partition Councils were also set up in the Punjab and Bengal and, in the latter, the Muslim League government was enlarged to include Hindu ministers from the western districts. In Sind, the legislative assembly voted to join Pakistan, a foregone conclusion, and in Baluchistan a council of tribal chiefs unanimously voted to do the same. In the Sylhet district of Assam, the referendum resulted in a majority vote in favour of Pakistan. From an organizational point of view, everything seemed to be running smoothly.

But there still remained the North-West Frontier Province where a Congress ministry was still in office. The referendum was very carefully organized by a team of forty British officers with experience of the Frontier, under a Referendum Commissioner who was also English. The choice before the electors was either to join Pakistan or India; but actually there was no choice. For simple geographical reasons, the province could not join Congress India, and for religious reasons, the people would not join Hindu India. The verdict was a foregone conclusion, and the population would obviously vote for Pakistan. Nevertheless, the Red Shirt movement was still angling for the alternatives to be changed to Pakistan or Pathanistan. Even Gandhi thought this a good idea. Abdul Ghaffar Khan had asked Jinnah to agree to the NWFP declaring itself independent on the understanding that it would join Pakistan if the new Pakistani constitution was acceptable; he told Jinnah that he and his followers would even be prepared to send delegates to the Pakistan constituent assembly, on condition that they would be able to withdraw if they wanted to. To this 'insidious and spurious' demand, Jinnah would not listen, especially as he knew that Muslim League influence had grown immensely in the NWFP after the partition plan had been announced. The referendum passed off peacefully in the presence of some 15,000 troops moved in for the occasion. The result was 289,224 votes in favour of joining Pakistan and 2,874 in favour of India. The Red Shirts, who had called on their followers to boycott the referendum, had failed, as had the Afghan government which, in the hope of gaining territory for itself, had strongly supported—and still does today—the Pathanistan movement. It had even sent an official Note to the British government in which it claimed that all inhabitants of India west of the river Indus were really Afghans and should be allowed to decide whether they wanted to join Afghanistan. The Note was not even acknowledged.

While this and many more activities in preparation for independence were taking their sometimes smooth, sometimes difficult course, the Labour government in London was busy piloting the Indian Independence Bill through the British parliament. The Bill's twenty clauses passed their Third Reading without a division on 15 July, and on the same day the Bill was introduced in the House of Lords. Three days later, in the company of such other measures as the South Metropolitan Gas Bill and the Felixstowe Pier Bill, it received the royal assent. 'Never before,' said *The Times* leader-writer, 'in the long annals of the Parliament of Westminster, has a measure of this profound significance been afforded a passage at once so rapid and so smooth.'

The occasion had been embellished with much empty rhetoric, but there was real irony behind prime minister Attlee's somewhat ingenuous claim that the Bill was 'not the abdication but the fulfilment of Britain's mission in India, a sign of strength, and the vitality of the British Commonwealth'.

8 A Crucible for Chaplets

Among the problems that faced the British as the day of the transfer of power came nearer was one of which they seem to have expressly washed their hands; that of the princely states. It had been made quite clear that when British rule ended, paramountcy would lapse too and all the princely states would consequently be at least legally independent. Most of them were small, some only a few acres, and completely surrounded by British India, and the Congress attitude towards them had been hardening since 1937 when popular governments had taken office in the provinces. In 1938, Gandhi himself had made Congress policy plain and had warned the princes that they would be wise 'to cultivate friendly relations with an organization [Congress] that bids fair in the future, not very distant, to replace the Paramount Power— let us hope, by friendly arrangement'. Congress had established an All-India States Peoples' Conference and had carried out campaigns in some of the states, but they had found themselves roughly handled, and attacked the states, even such well-run ones as Mysore, as 'sinks of reaction and incompetence . . . propped up and artificially maintained by British Imperialism'.

In 1947, the princes no doubt remembered Pandit Nehru's words of 1939: 'We recognize no such treaties [between the states and the Crown] and we shall in no event accept them. . . . The only paramount power that we recognize is the will of the people.' It was unlikely that even the larger states could now manage to retain their independence, save perhaps those who for reasons of geography might be able to form an alliance amongst themselves. The states had survived because the British had seen them as the only partners, however junior, that they could really trust. The British had pledged themselves, in the words of Queen Victoria in 1858, to 'respect the rights, dignity and honour of the native Princes as our own'. As long as the British remained in power, princely self-interest drew them together, but now the rights and the dignity if not the honour of the British were passing from India and the future of the princes was being returned to their own rather inexperienced keeping. The British could not legally help them, except in refusing to transfer paramountcy, because by the various treaties between the Crown and the individual princely states, no British or British-Indian authority could make laws for them. The British parliament had in fact no right whatsoever to decide the future of the states, for their inhabitants were not British subjects.

Nevertheless, the government of India had become more complex since 1858 as the mechanics of the modern world came to India through railways, currency, post and telegraph, and so on. The states had become much more bound up with British India. The Government of India Act of 1935 had sought to bring them politically into the government of the whole of India by establishing a federal form of administration, but negotiations for bringing this about had been interrupted by the outbreak of war in 1939. Because of this, the only official relationship between the government of India and the princely states was through the viceroy as Crown Representative, and it was handled by the Political Department in New Delhi. In 1921, under British pressure, the princes had formed themselves into a Chamber of Princes where it was hoped they would evolve common policies for all the states. But many of them, including the largest, Hyderabad, had refused to join and the chamber became in fact almost entirely a mouthpiece for the medium-sized states, the mass of the smaller ones having very little representation; 127 of them had only twelve members in the chamber. This had not been of much consequence while the British were still in power, but now that independence was at hand, the states presented a serious problem to Britain's successors. One thing was certain—no popular government could tolerate islands of mediaevalism in its midst.

From 1937 onwards, the Political Department had tried to induce the princes to reform their administrations and to allow at least some measure of popular government, not too unlike that introduced into British India. If the princes agreed, it was pointed out, their position would be much stronger when they came to negotiate with the successors of the British. For two reasons this advice was not taken. Firstly, the British stuck to the legal letter of their treaties with the states and refused to 'coerce' the princes into carrying out their suggestions. Secondly, the princes received the advice as an affront to their dignity, even the rulers of the smaller states being unwilling to give up any of their autocratic power. There is no doubt that, despite the treaties, the British could easily have forced the princes to make changes in their administration, but it can only be assumed that they did not really wish to. At one time during the war, the princes had begun to consider some sort of alliance amongst themselves, but this was geographically impossible except in the case of a few of the larger states. In 1942, the chancellor of the Chamber of Princes had asked for an assurance from the Cripps Mission that 'they [the princes] should have the right to form a union of their own, with full sovereign status'. He was not given an official assurance, though privately he was told that such a scheme might be considered by the British government. A glance at a map of India will instantly show that such a union would not have worked because of the large tracts of non-state territory separating the lands of the members of any union that might have been formed.

Various plans had been suggested while independence was under discussion, including one that Britain should retain paramountcy over certain states after the transfer of power. This, however, was quite impossible, if only on the grounds that it would appear as if Britain was trying to hang on to a foothold in India, hoping to keep her weak and divided. Such a solution would only have led to friction and possibly even to war between the British-protected states and the successor governments of India and Pakistan. All that Britain could do was strengthen the position of the states when the time came for them to negotiate with her successors, and give them some protection by not transferring paramountcy automatically to the successor governments. Congress, in whose dominion the majority of the princely states would lie, thought this attitude was wrong and that it would inevitably lead to the Balkanization of the country. Congress maintained, with perfect justice, that Britain's relations with the states were a corollary of her occupation of the rest of India, and that they had no *raison d'être* when this ended. Therefore, Congress insisted, the states were part of the structure of British rule in India and paramountcy over them should revert to the successor authorities.

In 1945, when it became reasonably clear that the British intended to transfer power at some not too distant date, the princes finally woke up to the danger that the Political Department had been warning them about for years. In January 1946, the then chancellor of the Chamber of Princes, the Nawab of Bhopal, listed the objectives at which the states should aim. These included 'popular institutions with elected majorities to ensure the close and effective association with the governance of the States'—without, of course, 'impairing the continuance of the ruling dynasty'. But by then it was too late, though it is doubtful whether any time after 1940 would have been early enough.

During the negotiations over independence, the British had not really had the time, or the inclination, to discuss in any detail how the princes should act when power was finally transferred. All the British government was explicit about was its refusal to hand over paramountcy to its successors, though the Cabinet Mission of 1946 had made it clear that they hoped and expected that the states would join the proposed Indian Union. The states had then been invited to nominate representatives to the new constituent assembly when it met. But what the British thought did not really count any more. They, in the politest way, had washed their hands of the future. It was the attitude of Congress that mattered, and the states got a very dusty answer from Nehru in July 1946. 'It is inconceivable to me,' he said, 'that any state will be independent and outside the limits of the Union.' This was taken as a hint that the states would be forced to join, if not by popular pressure from inside then by the central government itself. In fact, Congress was already trying to bypass the princes. It demanded that any states' representatives to the constituent assembly should *not* be nominated by the princes but elected by their peoples.

The Muslim League's attitude to the princely states was rather different to Congress's. The League could afford to be friendly, since very few of the states lay within the proposed borders of Pakistan.

Jinnah had been very careful in his pronouncements on the subject and apart from occasionally criticizing the Hindu Maharaja of Kashmir had indicated that, while the states would always be welcome to join Pakistan, there would be no coercion. It is possible that Jinnah was trying to convince the princes that they would have everything to gain by siding with the League against their common enemy, Congress. As the majority of the princes and their subjects were Hindu, however, an alliance with the League did not particularly appeal to them, especially as the threat of civil war between the two communities loomed larger. It seemed likely to the princes that they might be over- thrown by their own subjects if they openly supported the Muslim League. The majority of the princes, in fact, never seriously considered the possibility of an alliance with Jinnah, and some of them were con- spicuous in attempts to promote communal harmony. What, however, were they to do when Congress leaders went on uttering threats against them?

But as independence approached, Congress became more accom- modating, and a meeting took place early in February 1947 at which it was agreed that proposals would be worked out for states representa- tion in the constituent assembly. Unfortunately, the princes were not in agreement among themselves. One of them, Baroda, made his own separate arrangement to send three representatives elected by the State legislature, but finally, after some argument, the representatives of eight states—Baroda, Cochin, Udaipur, Jodhpur, Jaipur, Bikaner, Rewa and Patiala—took their seats in the constituent asembly on 28 April 1947. By July, another 37 states, including Mysore and Gwalior, had sent representatives to the assembly.

A large number of states, however, preferred to wait until para- mountcy had lapsed before they negotiated their position with the successor governments. One of these was Bhopal, whose ruler had resigned as chancellor of the Chamber of Princes after complaining to Mountbatten that the British were deliberately evading their responsi- bilities. As the Muslim prince of a Hindu state which was surrounded by Hindu India, Bhopal felt that his personal future was to say the least insecure, and he immediately set about trying to form in Central India a federation of states which would have some chance of independent existence.

The princes were not without allies amongst the British. Their 'kingdoms of yesterday' had considerable appeal to the romantic notions of the many middle-class Englishmen who had been associated with them. A nostalgia for the past glories, a weakness for the pompous flummery of the princes' mediaeval courts, had blinded them to the mediaeval irresponsibility that too often reigned behind the Arabian Nights façade. At least one Englishman was to put up a fight on behalf of these atavistic remnants of a bygone age. Fortunately, he did not succeed; if he had, the massacres in the Punjab might not have been the end of the sufferings of the innocent. This man was Sir Conrad Corfield, head of the Political Department of the government of India. He was determined that at least some of the princely states should be saved from the grasping hands of Congress.

Corfield had the advantage of knowing practically everything there was to know about the states and their relations with the Crown, whereas Mountbatten knew little and cared less. The viceroy had no sympathy for mediaeval autocrats and was much more concerned about the major problems of partition. This gave Corfield his opportunity. He was determined to do everything in his power to make things awkward for Congress when the time came for them to negotiate with the princely states. In London in May 1947, when he had conversations with the secretary of state—of which he did not inform the viceroy either before or after—Corfield insisted that paramountcy should not be allowed to lapse until the actual day on which power was transferred. This would give the states an immediate advantage, for it would allow of no agreement to accede to either of the new dominions before they had come into existence. To this proposition the secretary of state agreed, and Corfield returned to India in the plane that was going out to collect Mountbatten and take him back to London on 31 May. The viceroy did not know of Corfield's return, and Corfield kept out of his way until Mountbatten left. As soon as he had gone, Corfield gave orders that the files on the princes—which contained the fullest details of their private and public scandals—should be destroyed, and that all arrangements currently in existence between the states and the government of India—concerning military stations, railways, postal services and the like—should be cancelled immediately.

On 13 June, after the viceroy's return to India, the matter blew up. Congress had got wind of what was going on, since it was impossible for the cancellation of service agreements between the states and the government of India to be kept quiet. At a special meeting, Nehru demanded an explanation from the viceroy and an inquiry into Corfield's actions, which he described as irresponsible.

Corfield's defence was simple. His actions, he said, had the approval of the secretary of state; this was true. But he had acted without the knowledge or the approval of the viceroy. Mountbatten made no criticism at the meeting itself, but relations between the two men became extremely cold. Corfield, however, had succeeded in destroying documents that might have been of assistance to Congress, and had obtained the British government's assurance that paramountcy would not lapse until 15 August. But he had not been completely victorious, for both Congress and the League decided to set up a States Department to deal with the princes, and the first shots in the struggle were soon fired. Both the League and Congress now had a powerful ally in the viceroy, who had been particularly offended by Corfield's actions, and between them, they were able to defeat Corfield's scheme. He and his associates, however, continued to advise the princes to hold out for independence. Some, in particular Travancore and Hyderabad, took this advice and declared publicly that they would not join either of the new dominions. Travancore, at the very southern tip of India, hundreds of miles away from Pakistan, even announced that it would appoint a trade agent in the new dominion. Within the state of Hyderabad, there was an important Indian Army base, at Secundrabad near the capital, and some seven or eight thousand Indian troops with armour were still stationed there. Corfield had hoped that his cancellation of agreements would force these troops out before 15 August, when, under Congress control, they might become a powerful argument against Hyderabad's decision to remain independent. The ruler's constitutional adviser, Sir Walter Monckton, had in fact transmitted a request from the Nizam that the troops be removed.

Corfield, with all his experience, was still not wily enough to defeat Congress opposition when it came. Patel, perhaps the most intelligent and cunning of the Congress leaders, took over responsibility for the new States Department and asked V. P. Menon to be its first secretary when independence came. Menon accepted and immediately put forward a plan of campaign. This, and his actions at the time of the Mountbatten Plan, give Menon every right to take his place in history as one of the principal architects of independent India, but it is only very recently that his true influence on events has come to be properly appreciated.

Menon's plan of campaign was deceptively simple—negotiate immediately with the princes, but only on the three subjects, of defence, external affairs, and communications. Of these, the most important was defence. Most of the princes would be incapable of preserving order in their states if there were any large-scale rioting, and a discreet reminder of the threat of civil disorder should make them amenable. If the rulers accepted protection as they had accepted it from the British, this would be the first step towards a new relationship, a new paramountcy exercised by Britain's successors. The next stage was to get Mountbatten's co-operation. The groundwork had already been laid by Corfield. But Mountbatten's approach was not merely the result of pique at being by-passed by the Political Department.

Mountbatten now knew a great deal more about the problem of the princely states than he had done before. They had been just as much an instrument of British rule in India as had the army and the civil service. It was in relations with the states that the principle of 'divide and rule' had actually been practised. These enclaves of reactionary government had initially been preserved as a breakwater against rebellion in those parts of India directly controlled by the British, and the general backwardness, irresponsibility, and outrageous behaviour of their rulers had been quite deliberately overlooked as a reward for their loyalty. If the princes were left the right to independence, it would mean that the partition of British India between Muslim and Hindu would be aggravated by an infinitely more dangerous partition of the rest of the country. Such partition would have no reasonable basis whatsoever. Over three hundred of the states which were to become independent on 15 August had an average area of less than twenty square miles each. It was rather as if some of the suburbs of a great city were suddenly to become sovereign states which could and would interrupt transport services, drains and telephone wires, if they felt like it. The consequences would not only be ludicrous but fraught with danger. Mountbatten's view, now that he had come to think about it, was that the British had created the position of the princes and it was up to them to see that it was not a burden to their successors. In fact he realized that the question of the princes might easily destroy the delicate balance that had finally been reached between the claims of the Muslim League and those of Congress. The problems that faced independent India were already frightening enough. The princes might make them worse—and, incidentally, it was more than likely that it would be the British who would be blamed.

Mountbatten cabled the secretary of state in London, suggesting that a clause should be inserted into the Independence Bill limiting the powers of the princely states and automatically transferring paramountcy over the smaller ones to the two new dominions. The secretary of state replied that this could not be done without altering the government's publicly declared policy towards the princes. Again it was perfectly obvious that the government in London did not understand the nature of the problem. Corfield had been successful in his persuasion. The government's attitude was partly the result of the deference paid in Britain to 'Law'. In the history of her connexion with India, Britain had always sought to protect herself with treaties, even if the other party to the treaty was only a puppet. The British had always been reluctant to break treaties, even bad ones, and the Labour government—trying desperately to appear respectable—was only too willing to cling to the letter of some outdated legal agreement.

However, there was one saving 'legality' that would allow Mountbatten to minimize the danger of states independence; this was the Cabinet Mission's hope in 1946 that the states would join the then-proposed Indian Union. There was now to be no Indian Union, but two dominions instead; this, however, did not really invalidate anything. Furthermore, the princes had declared to the Cabinet Mission that they would be willing 'to co-operate in the new development of India'.

Congress leaders continued to make threats against the princes. Nehru bluntly stated that if any foreign power recognized the independence of any state it would be taken as a hostile act. Even Gandhi spoke up and warned the princes that if they declared independence it would be 'tantamount to a declaration of war against the free millions of India'. Congress, however, did not intend to leave the matter at speeches by its leaders. The leaders of the various Congress organizations in the princely states made it abundantly clear that they intended to raise the people against their rulers, and they suggested at the same time that the only way in which the princes might retain their wealth would be to negotiate with Congress as rapidly as possible.

The Muslim League, which had so much less to lose, still radiated sweet reasonableness.

So in fact did Sardar Patel. When the Congress States Department was established, he publicly assured the princes that all that need be agreed upon were the three subjects of defence, external affairs, and communications:

'In other matters,' he said, 'we would scrupulously respect their autonomous existence. . . . I should like to make it clear that it is not the desire of Congress to interfere in any manner whatever with the domestic affairs of the States. They [Congress] are no enemies of the Princely order but on the other hand wish them and their people under their aegis all prosperity, contentment, and happiness. Nor would it be my policy to conduct relations of the new Department with the States in any manner which savours of domination of one over the other; if there would be any domination it would be that of our mutual interests and welfare.'

This was an invitation for the princes to join with Congress as equal partners in the new dispensation. What was offered, Patel implied, was something better than the subordinate status of the old paramountcy.

On two levels—local threats and central reasonableness—the princes were slowly being jockeyed into a decision. Nothing, however, could be done without the approval of the Crown Representative, because legally the princes had no relations with the Indian interim government or with the new States Department. It was now time for Mountbatten to exercise the right he still maintained of advising the princes. But as long as the princes thought there was a possibility that the British government might agree to some new form of relationship, they would listen to Corfield's advice and not heed the honeyed words of Sardar Patel. Patel, however, was well aware, through informants in the Political Department, that Corfield was doing all he could to persuade certain of the states to form alliances and declare themselves independent.

On 25 July, as time was running out, the viceroy called the princes to Delhi to their last meeting with the representative of the king-emperor —although it was in fact the first time Mountbatten had addressed the princes in that capacity. His persuasiveness was at its height. The weather was unusually hot even for a summer in Delhi, but the viceroy, arrayed in full viceregal splendour, seemed only to draw strength from the heat like a salamander. The princes sweated and dozed, some angry, most resigned, as Mountbatten outlined his devastating case. Technically and legally, he said, they would all be independent after the British had gone, but in fact they had always been a part of India, economically and administratively. If they tried to break away altogether, the structure would dissolve in chaos, and they, he reminded them, would be the first victims. He then produced a draft instrument of accession which had been circulated prior to the meeting. This document called for cession only in the three fields of defence, external affairs, and communications. There would be no financial liabilities and no encroachments upon the individual autonomy or the sovereignty of the states. He pointed out that, of course, this document applied only to India, in which most of the states would lie. Jinnah had already agreed to negotiate separately with those few states which would lie within the borders of Pakistan. 'My scheme,' said the viceroy, 'leaves you with all practical independence you can possibly use, and makes you free of all those subjects which you cannot possibly manage on your own. You cannot run away from the Dominion Government which is your neighbour any more than you can run away from subjects for whose welfare you are responsible.' The princes had now been apprised of the Crown's opinion as to what they should do. For years they had looked to the British for advice—and here was the last they were likely to get.

Behind the scenes, Congress pressure continued. For many of the princes, the choice lay between saving their palaces, their jewels and their dancing girls, or running the risk of being overthrown after independence. The safeguards offered by the viceroy were in reality rather flimsy. The British could not effectively guarantee them, and an independent India would be able to brush them aside whenever it chose. To accede was a gamble; not to accede would mean the certainty of removal from their thrones. In their dilemma, the princes had nowhere else to turn. Corfield had been packed off to England by the viceroy, and others who remained behind were too preoccupied in intriguing with Bhopal and the Rajput states to bother with the rest. The princes now appointed a committee to examine both the draft instrument and a standstill agreement which would perpetuate existing relations between the states and the rest of India. The committee included among its members the Nawab of Bhopal and the prime ministers of Hyderabad and Travancore, both of which had declared their intention of remaining independent after 15 August.

Under Mountbatten's patient persuasion, the princes began to sign the instrument of accession until, by the time of the transfer of power, the majority had acceded. Bhopal had been forced to give up his attempt to form a federation of Central Indian states, primarily because of disagreements amongst the rulers themselves, and partly by the fact that Congress agents had repeatedly reminded him of his own dangerous position as the Muslim ruler of a predominantly Hindu state. The Rajput states, who had hoped to attract the Rajput soldiers of the Indian Army to join their armed forces, also at last saw reason. There was just not enough time to prepare themselves.

But some of the princely states were determined not to accede to Congress India if they could help it. Even after Corfield had left India, certain members of the Political Department were still active in the attempt to make things as difficult as possible for Congress. Legally, of course, they had every right to advise the princes in what they thought were their best interests. But their actions were contrary in spirit to the intentions of the British government which, in its ignorance, had not seen the dangers implicit in the lapse of paramountcy. The men of the Political Department had been allowed to act as they did because of the haste in which the British government decided to transfer power; there was not time to think of everything. Fortunately, when Mountbatten finally became aware of what was going on, his immense energy and determination were too much for them. It is a sad comment on that responsibility which was so often claimed as the keystone of Britain's mission in India that, at the end, some Englishmen—through what might be charitably described as a mistaken sense of duty—should have run the risk of multiplying chaos and suffering.

The viceroy had made it plain at the meeting on 25 July that states whose frontiers marched with those of both dominions could choose which one they wanted to accede to, and some of the Rajput states were in this position. After the failure of the scheme for an independent grouping of Rajput states, members of the Political Department quickly suggested that some of them should accede to Pakistan. One of these was the state of Jodhpur.

The Maharaja of Jodhpur was a high-living young man with expensive tastes in women and aeroplanes. He and the ruler of another of the states, Jaisalmer, paid a secret visit to Jinnah, who received them with great warmth and offered to accept whatever terms they cared to make. But Jodhpur was not altogether a fool. For the Hindu ruler of a Hindu state—and one proud of its long history of martial defiance to the old Mughal emperors—to accede to a Muslim dominion was to invite trouble. After a few days, he gave in to Congress.

To all the princes' furtive attempts to save themselves, Patel responded publicly with sweet words. He welcomed Bhopal into the fold with the statement that 'During the last few months it had been a matter of great disappointment to me that your undoubted talents and abilities were not at the country's disposal during the critical times through which we were passing, and I therefore particularly value [your] assurance of co-operation and friendship.'

The Maharaja of Travancore, in the face of demonstrations arranged by the local Congress organization, also gave in. On the whole, it looked as if the campaign so nearly lost had now been won. Unfortunately, the exceptions were to cause trouble, and in one case at least to go on causing it right up to the present day. Only three states were to be awkward—Junagadh, Hyderabad, and Kashmir—but the consequences of their awkwardness more than outweighed the success with the others.

The trouble with Junagadh did not break out until after 15 August, when it became known that the Muslim Nawab had decided to accede to Pakistan and that Pakistan had accepted the accession. The Nawab of Junagadh was not untypical of many of the princes. The 'eccentricity' of his tastes had been discreetly overlooked by the British in payment for the loyalty of him and his like. There were so many wicked princes in India that the record of their lives is more like an additional volume by the Brothers Grimm than a glossary of the sort of people one would expect to be allies of such a moral people as the British. But as in so many things, India provided the exceptions. The king-emperor needed tributary kings in order to enhance his glory. He got some very queer ones, and just a few who were good and reasonably decent rulers. On the whole, the preservation of the princes in the amber of British power is one of the less pleasant aspects of British rule in India. The true conditions in the states were too often concealed behind the romantic novelists' view of jewelled elephants, gorgeous turbans, and 'age-old magic'. The princes encouraged this view, and got on with enjoying their 'age-old' vices.

The ruler of Junagadh was no exception. He loved to watch deliberately wounded animals torn to pieces by deliberately starved hounds. Surrounding his palace were rooms, pleasantly furnished—and each with a servant and a telephone—for every one of his hundred or so dogs. In fact, a dog's life in Junagadh was infinitely superior to that of the majority of the people. This comparatively small state of four thousand square miles lay on the south-western coast of the Kathiawar peninsula north of Bombay, an area of great beauty and scenic grandeur. Its chief seaport was some 350 miles away from Karachi, the new capital of Pakistan, and it was surrounded on all sides except the sea by states which had acceded to India. The complex of states in Kathiawar was like some demented jigsaw. Most were tiny fragments scattered over the peninsula. There were even bits of Junagadh embedded as enclaves inside other states, and enclaves of other states' territories remained inside Junagadh. At the meeting on 25 July, the Nawab of Junagadh had given the impression that, though he himself was a Muslim, he would accede to India as most of the other states in Kathiawar had already decided to do. It was a most sensible decision, since over 80 per cent of the 816,000 inhabitants of Junagadh were Hindu. But the Nawab postponed the actual signing of the instrument of accession—and then plumped for Pakistan. He even went further and occupied two tiny states, Mangrol and Babariawad, which had decided to accede to India in an attempt to assert their independence of him and the overlordship he claimed over them.

The Nawab's change of attitude between 25 July and 15 August had been brought about by Muslim League tactics similar to those which Congress was pursuing in other states. A Muslim League agent simply obtained the ear of the Nawab by assuring him that Congress would kill his dogs, stop him hunting, and, generally speaking, prevent him from enjoying his traditional pleasures, while Pakistan on the other hand would be happy to allow him to continue in his innocuous pursuits and would even be prepared to help him against his own subjects should that ever be necessary.

The other Kathiawar states, led by Nawanagar, regarding this as a threat to peace, appealed to the new government of India and began to mass their own state troops on the Junagadh borders. The Indian government had not been officially informed of the Nawab's accession to Pakistan—in fact, they only learned of it from the newspapers. The government complained to Pakistan, but got no reply. It was perfectly obvious that Pakistan must know very well that Junagadh, for geographical reasons alone, could not actually join Pakistan, but the Muslim League's old policy of creating as much trouble as possible for Congress had not been abandoned when independence came. Apart from sending a few men to help the Nawab's depleted police force, the Pakistanis did nothing except sit back and enjoy the situation. The Indian government was reluctant to walk into what was so obviously a trap. Soft words had been issuing from Sardar Patel's lips. The princes, though still slightly uneasy, had been on the verge of breathing again, and a delicate relationship might very easily be upset if one of their number was 'coerced'. There was also a possibility that Pakistan might object. A request to Liaquat Ali Khan to allow the people of Junagadh to decide for themselves received no reply.

While continually repeating its desire for an amicable solution, the Indian government was finally forced to act. If it had not done so, the rest of the Kathiawar states might have gained the impression that India was unable or unwilling to protect them. Indian Army troops were sent to the Junagadh borders and all communications with the state, as well as supplies of coal and petrol, were cut off. A body of Congress supporters from Junagadh itself was encouraged to set up a government-in-exile, in accordance with the best European precedent.

The Pakistan government did not react officially until 7 October 1947, when it claimed that, since Junagadh had legally acceded to Pakistan, no one else had any right to intervene. It said it was obvious nonsense to suggest that Junagadh was a threat to the other Kathiawar states. The Pakistanis, however, were willing 'to discuss conditions and circumstances wherein a plebiscite should be taken by any state or states'; but India should first withdraw her troops from the borders of Junagadh. The phrasing of this Pakistani offer was deliberate. The sting was in the word 'any'. The Pakistanis really hoped for a plebiscite in Kashmir, a Muslim state with a Hindu ruler who was still dithering over which dominion he should accede to, but the government of India refused the idea of a plebiscite unless they received a firm assurance that Pakistan would agree to deal with the case of Junagadh and Junagadh alone.

Indian troops in Kathiawar were now reinforced to a strength of 1,400 men, a troop of light tanks, and a squadron of aircraft. In addition to these, there were 2,000 states' troops. On 26 October, seeing the red light, the Nawab left Junagadh in his private aircraft, with the state jewels, as many dogs as he could get aboard, and three of his four wives, for the safety of Karachi. The chief minister, faced with disorders organized by Congress workers, soon appealed to the government of India to take over the administration of the state. The government agreed, and Indian troops crossed the state frontier. Pandit Nehru, in telegrams to Liaquat Ali, explained that the occupation of Junagadh was merely temporary and would only last until such time as a plebiscite could be held. He invited the Pakistan government to send representatives to discuss the procedure. Pakistan, however, preferred to stick to the letter of the law; Junagadh's ruler had acceded the state to Pakistan as he had every right to do; the Indian occupation was therefore a violation of Pakistani territory, and until India withdrew there was no purpose in holding discussions. There the matter rested until February 1948 when a plebiscite resulted in the not unexpected decision to join India.

The situation in Hyderabad had one thing in common with that in Junagadh. Over 80 per cent of the population was Hindu but the ruler, known as the Nizam, was a Muslim. The army, the police, and the government, were all in the hands of the Muslims, who formed a ruling minority. There the similarity ended. Hyderabad was considerably larger in area—some 82,000 square miles—and had a population of sixteen millions. The state, positioned roughly in the centre of the Indian peninsula, had no outlet to the sea and after partition would be completely surrounded by Indian territory. Consequently, it was not practicable for the Nizam to accede to Pakistan with which his only possible communication would be by air. The only choice other than state independence was that he should accede to Congress-dominated India, but such a choice was abhorrent to the Nizam, who had always considered himself superior to all the other princes, and had been allowed by the British to act with considerable independence. If he were to accede to India, he would be giving in to his Hindu subjects, who, under Congress instigation, were now becoming vocal. In addition to his natural dislike of Congress, the Nizam was influenced by the fact that his own personal position was largely dependent on Hyderabad's ruling Muslim minority. This minority was backed by a kind of political party, called the Ittehad-ul-Muslimin, which was fanatically pro-Islam. Without their support, the Nizam could not have continued to rule. Since they demanded independence, so must he, and, as we have seen, he demanded it publicly in June 1947. Despite pressure from the Ittehad, however, the Nizam was not prepared to act foolishly. He realized that it would be wise not to antagonize India, so he dispatched to Delhi a negotiating committee whose principal members were the chief minister of the state, the Nawab of Chhatari, and Sir Walter Monckton, his constitutional advisor.

It seemed from this negotiating committee's attitude that the Nizam was willing to give up most of the powers demanded by the instrument of accession, but that he wanted to do so by treaty, as if he were an equal. Also, he insisted on the right to remain neutral if there should be a quarrel between India and Pakistan, and he reserved the right to send his own representatives to Britain and elsewhere. Earlier, the Nizam had asked the British government for dominion status for Hyderabad, and this had naturally been rejected. But the Nizam still wanted to retain some sort of relationship with the British Crown, although what he hoped to gain from it is not clear. Mountbatten's advice to the Nizam, however, was direct—forget about the past, sign the instrument of accession, *then* negotiate with Congress. The advice was sound; India could hardly grant concessions to Hyderabad without inviting the risk of demands from other states. Even the biggest of the states would have to agree to the same terms as everyone else. It seems very likely that the Nizam would have accepted Mountbatten's advice if it had not been for the pressure put upon him and the advice given to him by the Iagos of the Political Department. By 15 August, no accession had been made. The Muslim press in Hyderabad was referring to the Nizam as 'His Majesty', and Muslim mobs were celebrating Hyderabad's independence.

A standstill agreement had been arrived at to fill the vacuum when paramountcy lapsed, so that the various services could continue, but the life of the agreement was only two months. During these two months, the Hyderabad army was enlarged to about 25,000 men, and armament purchases were made abroad and flown in by air, some in aircraft loaned by Pakistan. The Ittehad was arming a force of terrorists known as the Razakhars. At the same time, however, the Nawab of

Chhatari and Monckton were spending most of their time in fruitless journeys back and forth to Delhi. The Indian government, with the massacres in the Punjab to demonstrate what could happen when communal violence got completely out of hand, was unwilling to make concessions to the Nizam. Meanwhile, the Hyderabad state Congress, with powerful support from outside, began a civil disobedience campaign demanding accession to India and popular government in Hyderabad. It did not suggest deposing the Nizam, for it was obviously hopeful of driving a wedge between him and his more fanatical Muslim supporters. By the end of September, however, more than 1,300 local Congress leaders had been arrested. Under the circumstances both Chhatari and Monckton tendered their resignations to the Nizam, but he refused to let them go, partly because he was not a free agent and wanted to keep the negotiations going in the hope that some agreement might emerge which he could reasonably accept.

Lord Mountbatten, now governor-general of independent India, was permitted by the Congress leaders to see whether he could succeed by personal negotiation. It was assumed that he, as the cousin of the former king-emperor, might have some influence with the Nizam, though that influence had not been much use before. By 21 October, Mountbatten had at least managed to extend the standstill agreement by one year, during which time it was hoped that some wider agreement might be arrived at. When Chhatari and Monckton returned to Hyderabad to obtain the Nizam's ratification of the agreement, however, news had reached there that Kashmir had acceded to India. Muslim mobs demonstrated outside Chhatari's house demanding that Hyderabad should make no concessions to India, and the Ittehad threatened 'Direct Action' against the Nizam, if he should give in to India. Under this pressure, he refused to ratify the agreement and publicly announced that he did not contemplate acceding to India. Chhatari and Monckton again offered their resignations and this time they were accepted. A new negotiating committee was appointed which included a representative of the Ittehad.

Congress was now becoming impatient, and Sardar Patel made a number of speeches pointing out that what had happened to Junagadh might well happen elsewhere. Despite everything, negotiations continued, and the standstill agreement was finally ratified in November.

The Nizam claimed that the agreement in no way permanently prejudiced 'my rights as an independent sovereign', but the answer was
not encouraging. 'Placed as Hyderabad is,' wrote Lord Mountbatten,
'its interests are inextricably bound up with those of India, and my
Government hope that before the present agreement expires, it will be
possible for Hyderabad to accede to the Dominion of India.'

The internal situation in Hyderabad did not improve. The Razakhars took over control of the government and started raiding villages
in Indian territory. With charming good manners, Sardar Patel waited
until Mountbatten had left for England at the end of his tour of office,
before he began a propaganda campaign alleging that Hyderabad was
in a state of internal disorder. In September 1948, in what was euphem-
istically called a 'police action', Indian troops entered Hyderabad to
'restore order'. The Hyderabad army and the Razakhars put up very
little resistance, and the Nizam, claiming that he had been misled by
his advisors, acceded to India. He was allowed to remain as constitutional head of the state, to keep his great wealth, and to receive a privy
purse of £750,000 a year. Apart from the nationalization of his vast
estates, he was not much worse off than he would have been if he had
acceded at the very beginning.

Junagadh and Hyderabad had been settled without too much trouble.
Pakistan could only protest and take both cases to the United Nations,
where they were not even discussed. But Kashmir was, and still is, a
very different matter. The state—77 per cent of whose inhabitants
were Muslims—had common frontiers with both Pakistan and India.
The frontier with Pakistan was long, and the only all-weather roads
into Kashmir, by which supplies were transported, ran to Pakistan. To
India there was only a fair-weather highway, closed by snow in the
winter. In Kashmir, too, were the head-waters of Pakistan's most
important rivers, the Indus, the Jhelum, and the Chenab, essential for
irrigation of the thirsty land. The situation of the Maharaja of Kashmir
was a mirror-image of that in Junagadh and Hyderabad, for he was a
Hindu ruling a Muslim state. After the Sikh wars in the 1840's, the
Maharaja's grandfather had been allowed to buy Kashmir from the
British, who had inherited it from the Sikh kingdom of the Punjab,
for nearly a million pounds sterling. Kashmir is very beautiful, full of
lakes and mountains, rather like an Indian Switzerland. It is also of
considerable strategic importance, lying as it does across the routes

followed by most of the historic conquerors of India, except the British.

At the time, it did not seem unreasonable to assume that even such a stupid ruler as the Maharaja Hari Singh would feel that he must accede to Pakistan, but the political situation in Kashmir, rather like that in the North-West Frontier Province, was not straightforward. There was indeed a Muslim party in the state, closely tied to the All-India Muslim League, but the most important figure in state politics was Sheikh Abdullah, who, though a Muslim, was president of the National Conference party which was equally closely tied to Congress. In June 1946, the Sheikh had been imprisoned for demanding the Maharaja's abdication, and in August 1947 he was still in jail. As in Hyderabad, only in reverse, the mainly Muslim state was governed by a Hindu Maharaja with Hindu officials and mainly Hindu troops.

The choice before the Maharaja was not particularly heart-warming. If he acceded to Pakistan it would probably mean that he himself would have to abdicate. If he joined India he would be going against Kashmir's geographic, religious and economic affinities, which all lay with Pakistan. Complete independence was out of the question, because the state could not exist without supplies from outside. He was under considerable pressure from Congress not to make a hasty decision, for haste would probably have meant accession to Pakistan. Kashmir held considerable personal interest for Nehru, whose ancestors had come from there. But, more realistically, because Nehru hated the thought of an India divided by religion, the state's accession to India was important. If Kashmir went to Pakistan for religious reasons alone, it might result in public demonstrations which would imperil the lives of Muslims still left in India. As a result, the Maharaja was advised not to make up his mind at least until he had been able to talk to Nehru. Gandhi, off on another mission of peace, said the same thing, and even offered to go to Kashmir to talk to the Maharaja. Mountbatten, however, decided he must go himself. He did not succeed in persuading the Maharaja to accede to India—or to Pakistan. Mountbatten *could* probably have forced him to make a decision, but that decision would in the circumstances almost inevitably have been in favour of India. Mountbatten felt that he could not run the risk of the British government being accused, through his actions, of such obvious partiality. He would have been wise to have allowed someone else, preferably

V. P. Menon, to go in his place. By 15 August, all that had been achieved was a standstill agreement between Kashmir and Pakistan, and negotiations were in progress for a similar agreement with India.

Congress had hoped that the Maharaja would release Sheikh Abdullah and that he and his followers could arrange popular pressure in favour of accession to India. But the decision was taken out of the Maharaja's hands. The Muslim inhabitants of the district of Poonch were a martial people who had supplied thousands of hardy soldiers to the old British Indian Army. After partition, former soldiers in Poonch demonstrated in favour of Kashmir's acceding to Pakistan. When these demonstrations were fired upon by the Maharaja's Hindu troops, the demonstrators rose in rebellion and put the state forces to flight. The rebellion sparked off further disorder, for the rule of the Maharaja had not been pleasant. The Kashmiri peasant was extremely poor; state taxes were crushing; many Kashmiri homes were without windows because of a special window tax; there was even a tax on hearthstones, wives, animals, on practically everything, in fact. The money went to support a profligate and bigoted ruler and a small minority of Hindu officials.

Strictly speaking, the state was known as Kashmir and Jammu, the latter being a Hindu-majority area. Into Jammu, which bordered the Punjab, had fled many Hindu and Sikh refugees from the massacres in the Punjab, lusting for revenge against Muslims. They attacked the Muslim minority in Jammu with fire and sword.

While all this was taking place, the tribes of the Frontier areas were responding to the cry of 'Islam in danger!' And on 22 October thousands of tribesmen invaded Kashmir, bent upon Hindu women, loot and murder. Though the Pakistan government denied any responsibility for the tribal invasion, it undoubtedly supplied the tribes with transport, machine-guns, mortars and light artillery, while Pakistani army officers, ostensibly on leave, led the contingents. The tribes swept across Kashmir like a forest fire, killing and burning as they went. When they were only twenty-five miles from the state capital, Srinagar, they paused to quarrel over the division of the loot. On 24 October, the Maharaja decided to accede to India and appealed for India's help against the tribes. He also informed Mountbatten that he was about to set up an interim government under Sheikh Abdullah, who had recently been released from detention. Indian troops were flown in and, after a fortnight, they beat back the invaders. Open war between the two new dominions was only narrowly averted, for Jinnah's immediate reaction to the flying in of Indian troops was to order the Pakistan army to move into Kashmir. The commander-in-chief, however, was an Englishman who refused to act without reference to the supreme commander, Sir Claude Auchinleck. Otherwise there might have been the prospect of two armies, each commanded by British officers, each fighting the other. Auchinleck flew to Lahore and saw Jinnah. He pointed out that to dispatch Pakistani troops into Kashmir would be an act of war and that he, if Jinnah insisted on this course of action, would order all British officers, including the commanders-in-chief of both the Pakistani and Indian forces, to resign immediately. Jinnah, impressed by this straight talking, decided to invite Nehru and Mountbatten to Lahore to discuss the frontier problem. It is still unresolved today, and as explosive as it ever was.

Pakistan's attitude to Kashmir was motivated by rather different forces from those which influenced their view of Junagadh and Hyderabad. In the latter two, it was simply a case of the normal bloody-mindedness of the Muslim League's traditional policy towards Congress. But Kashmir was another matter. The Muslim League leaders, having thrived by exacerbating the rivalry between Muslim and Hindu, were by now the victims of their own propaganda. They had cried 'Wolf' so many times that they believed the animal was real. They were firmly convinced that Congress was merely biding its time, waiting for the British to get out of the way, and that it would then reoccupy Pakistan. Many responsible Congress leaders, including Gandhi, had prophesied that Pakistan would only be short-lived. Some of these men even believed what they said. Jinnah believed they did too, and Kashmir looked like the first step towards reconquest. The leaders of Pakistan thought that they were surrounded by enemies planning their destruction. Indian territory already enclosed Pakistan from the east and now, with the accession of Kashmir, it appeared that India was trying to close in from the north. This Pakistani feeling of encirclement has vitiated Indo-Pakistan relations ever since that time.

Apart from the cases of these three states, however, the problem of the princes had at least temporarily been solved by the date of the transfer of power. It was perhaps the greatest single achievement of the

last weeks of British rule. The princes could have caused chaos throughout the length and breadth of India, and the consequences would have
made the tragedy of the Punjab almost a minor episode in the bloodshed that would have resulted. As 15 August came and went, the
princes seemed to have gained a reprieve. In actual fact, it was only a
stay of execution.

The states could not be allowed to survive, since anachronisms—
especially anachronisms of evil memory—had no place in the modern
world that was soon to burst in upon India. The States Ministry, as the
Congress States Department became after independence, headed by
Sardar Patel but actually the responsibility of V. P. Menon, soon set
to work to rationalize the situation. Menon was particularly well
suited to the task. He was an excellent administrator, fertile with workable ideas, but he was also very conscious of the evils of princely rule.
'When I came up here years ago, a poor boy from Malabar,' he related to an American newspaper correspondent in his Delhi office, 'I
went into a shop one day and watched a Maharani buy a hundred
expensive saris. Another time I was present when a Maharaja walked
into a sporting goods shop and casually ordered 100,000 rupees' worth
of hunting rifles. And one day, on one of my civil service assignments,
I was stopped at fifteen different state customs posts on a thirty-mile
drive through Kathiawar. I thought it was time this sort of nonsense
was stopped.'

Menon set to with a will to consolidate the states into groups, ab-
sorbing some into the provinces that surrounded them. In the end, only
six princely states remained as separate political units; Mysore and
Hyderabad, because of their size, Manipur, Tripura, and Kutch,
because their strategic position on the frontiers made it desirable that
they should be directly administered by the central government, and
Bhopal, because of a special arrangement with the Nawab. The
possessions of the princes were whittled down. In time, some of them
were to set themselves up as tourist attractions for foreign visitors, to
turn their palaces into hotels. Recently, however, some have re-entered
politics, standing for seats in their former dominions, usually for parties
opposed to Congress. But their power, exercised so arrogantly for so
long, is at an end and India is all the better for it.

In 1946, a Congress leader, Asaf Ali, had warned the princes: 'Chaos
will prove a powerful crucible for chaplets and bejewelled tiaras.' But

it was not chaos that did the work; it was Lord Mountbatten, Sardar
Patel, and above all the ubiquitous V. P. Menon.

9 The Peace Treaty without a War

As the Indian Independence Bill passed through the British House of
Lords in the middle of 1947, the Liberal Peer, Lord Samuel, hailed it as
'the peace treaty without a war'. In one sense he was right. It looked
very unlikely, as India neared independence, that the British would
suffer. But his phrase overlooked the evidence of history. The Bill was,
in fact, to end a war that had been going on for over thirty years, and
it brought peace only between India and Britain. The last battles were
still to come between Hindu and Muslim, and Britain could not shirk
part of the responsibility for them.

The passing of the Bill itself was not the end of Britain's liability. It
was easy enough to declare, in somewhat turgid parliamentary language, that the great adventure was over and that two heirs would
inherit the estate. But first that estate had to be divided in such a way
that the heirs would not quarrel and come to blows over the will. Part
of that task was comparatively simple and could be settled without
complaint. But the British were obliged, in the Punjab and Bengal, to
establish the actual frontiers between the two new dominions. It had
originally been suggested that the decision might be left to the United
Nations, but that organization was too new and untried for such a
formidable task. As the parties in India were unwilling to settle it themselves, the British had to do it for them. It is more than likely that, with
its characteristic ignorance of the tremendous difficulties involved, the
British government did not realize how difficult the task would be.
The Muslim League and Congress had finally agreed upon policy, and
the partition lines had been roughly decided. It seemed that all that was
necessary was to tidy up a few details on the spot. An obviously impartial arbitrator ought therefore to be appointed, and the British
government put forward the name of Sir Cyril Radcliffe (now Lord
Radcliffe), a distinguished lawyer with absolutely no knowledge of
India whatever. Radcliffe had in fact been asked in June 1947 to head a
joint Indo-Pakistan commission, which would decide upon the division of assets as well as upon the frontier lines. But with the rapid

approach of the date for the transfer of power, it was decided to separate the two functions and appoint a separate committee to deal with the assets.

Radcliffe arrived in India on 8 July 1947. Before he left London, he had been told very little of what would be expected from him. It is of course possible that the prime minister had not been prepared to risk frightening him off, but it is much more likely that he was not aware of the problems involved. Radcliffe knew that the transfer of power was fixed for 15 August, but he was under the impression that the temporary division of Bengal and the Punjab was to continue after that date. He was soon to be disillusioned. The viceroy explained that the matter had to be settled in five weeks—earlier if Radcliffe could manage it! It was originally intended that Radcliffe should act only as the impartial chairman of two committees—one for Bengal and one for the Punjab—each consisting of four Indian judges. In each of the committees, two of the judges would represent Congress and two the Muslim League.

The unfortunate Sir Cyril now began to realize just what his sense of public duty and the British prime minister's curious reticence had let him in for. It was obvious that the Indian judges, who were supposed to make the decisions, were subject to powerful outside pressures. Everything was fine for Radcliffe—he could go back to Britain. But the judges would have to live and work in the new dominions. They soon made it clear to Radcliffe that they could not risk the responsibility and that the decision would have to be his alone. In the circumstances, it is difficult to blame them, and in fact they should not have been asked to carry such responsibility. They had not really been *asked* to join the committees at all; they had been ordered to do so, to protect their country's interests against the evil machinations of their colleagues.

Surprisingly enough, Bengal—in spite of Suhrawardy's attempts to gain independence, or at least the status of a free city for Calcutta—presented Radcliffe with a comparatively easy task although he was inundated with schemes and suggestions. He observed that the province had 'few, if any, satisfactory natural boundaries'. It was just not possible simply to draw a line on a map which would smoothly divide the Hindu from the Muslim areas, nor could he avoid severing the railway system and the rivers on which so much of the transport of the province moved. In the end, he decided on a line running north to south, from

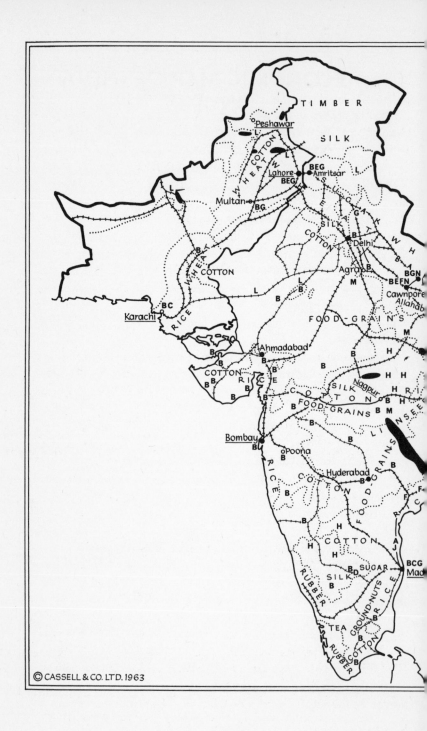

ECONOMIC MAP OF INDIA IN 1947

Showing the railway system and the
boundaries of the Indian Union.

++++++ Broad Gauge ········ Narrow Gauge
lesser lines not shown

———	Partition lines between India & Pakistan 1947	**G**	Machinery & Engineering (including railway works)
········	Provincial boundaries	**H**	Manganese
	10 largest cities of India 1941	**J**	Mica
Madras	Capitals of Provinces underlined	**K**	Petroleum
	Coal mining areas	**L**	Salt
	Copper	**M**	Iron Ore
	Cotton Mills	**N**	Sugar refining
	Docks		
	Gold		English miles
	Iron & Steel		
	Jute Mills		0 50 100 200 300 400 500

the Himalayan foothills east of Darjeeling, to the Bay of Bengal east of Calcutta. Calcutta, the largest city in the country, therefore went to the new dominion of India. In any except religious terms, the partition was highly unsatisfactory. For example, Pakistan was allotted an area which grew about 85 per cent of the world's jute production, but there were no mills for processing it. On the Indian side of the frontier, there was very little jute, but at least one hundred mills, as well as the principal port from which jute products were exported. Economically, the partition was completely mad. But once the division of India on religious lines had been established, no other criterion was possible.

Radcliffe awarded most of Sylhet, the Muslim-majority district of Assam which had voted to join Pakistan, to East Bengal, along with some bits of the adjoining districts which also had a majority of Muslim inhabitants. Though the 'award', as Radcliffe's decisions came to be known, satisfied no one, the prime ministers of East and West Bengal appealed to their people after the partition to accept it as the best possible solution, at least for the time being. Adjustments are still going on to this day.

In the Punjab, however, Radcliffe was not so lucky. Whatever his decision, one party was sure to be aggrieved, and it was to be the party ready and willing to cause the most trouble. When Radcliffe arrived in the Punjab, he found it seething with partly-suppressed violence. The Sikhs, who stood to lose everything they valued to Pakistan, descended on him with plans, arguments, threats, and even bribes.

Lahore, where Radcliffe was trying to arrive at his decision, was caught in the grip of the Indian hot weather. (Kipling, that sadly misjudged laureate of the Indian scene, has caught all its horror in a story about Lahore, which he called 'The City of Dreadful Night'.) In the Indian hot weather, even the air seems malevolent and grips one by the throat. In 1947, the rains were late and there was very little difference between the burning day and the stifling night. Tempers are easily frayed at such a season, and the edge between utter lassitude and sudden violence is as thin as a knife-blade. In this sort of atmosphere, Radcliffe found the weather and the politicians equally hostile. He knew nothing of the country. He did not even know what it actually looked like, and there was no time for him to go and see the land he was dividing. The maps that were presented to him by various interested parties had all been cooked up the better to support their claims.

He had, in fact, great difficulty in finding a decent large-scale map which actually showed the contours of the land, the canals, and the exact positions of the rivers. When he did find one, he immediately realized that the problem which faced him was not so much that of the people's religion as of the water which irrigated their fields.

The Punjab had been the showplace of British India. In it, some of Britain's greatest colonial administrators had played out their parts. There they had built up a vast and complicated irrigation scheme, based upon the five rivers which give the Punjab its name. Because of these canals, the Punjab had become the garden and the granary of India. The irrigation system must necessarily be disrupted by partition, since the rivers that fed the canals and ditches that watered the fields were in the eastern part of the area, which was destined to go to India. Radcliffe suggested that, before he announced his award, some agreement should be reached between the two sides for joint control of the waters. He was brusquely told to mind his own business and get back to drawing lines on the map. The religion of the people, and nothing else —however important—was the only factor that was supposed to concern him. Food, and the possibility of famine, were the politicians' burdens, not his. Exhausted by the heat, horrified at the sheer impossibility of producing a plan that would not cause suffering or tragedy of one sort of another, Radcliffe did what he was told and drew his lines upon the map. The Bengal award was ready by 9 August, and the Punjab award two days later. On independence day, Radcliffe flew back to Britain. The public announcement of his awards was delayed until 17 August to avoid marring the rejoicings on the day of freedom. When the Punjab award was declared, it aroused the most bitter criticism, especially from Pakistan. Ministers attacked it as 'disgusting', 'abominable' and 'one-sided', and the Muslim League newspaper *Dawn* threatened that 'even if the Government accepts the territorial murder of Pakistan, the people will not'.

As the day of independence came, the signs of chaos rose to the surface. The public services slowly collapsed as the engine-drivers, the engineers, the soldiers and the civil servants began to move from one part of the country to the other. To add to man-made troubles, the overdue monsoon threatened a shortage of food. This would have been bad enough in normal times, but when transport was dislocated by the division of rolling-stock, serious famine was far from improbable. The transfer of police officers—Muslims to Pakistan, Hindus to India—had demoralized a service which was not particularly trustworthy at the best of times. The Sikhs, whose homeland was to be arbitrarily divided between Pakistan and India, whose holy places would be on both sides of the border, and whose people—nearly a million of them—were about to be left to the mercy of the Muslims of Pakistan, had already begun to battle for their faith and their possessions. Extremists on both sides were inciting the mobs to revenge. Criminals who hoped to benefit from the breakdown of public order were patiently at work.

The last British governor of the Punjab, Sir Evan Jenkins—a brave and intelligent man of long experience—bombarded the viceroy with assurances that if something drastic was not done soon the whole of the Punjab would go up in flames. Sikh leaders had told him openly and frankly that they intended to fight. They now admitted that when they had agreed to partition, they had not really understood all the implications and that they had not expected that their homelands would be divided. The British had let the Sikhs down, they said, and unless the British government did something about it the Sikhs would make the Punjab a desert of burning villages. Congress, they believed, had let them down too, in its desire to grasp power for itself. Congress thought it could ignore the Sikhs; the Sikhs, however, were not weak Hindus but a nation that had once ruled the whole of the Punjab before the British conquered them.

For some reason—and without any justification whatsoever—the Sikhs had thought that, since in all previous constitutional negotiations they had received a consideration entirely out of proportion to their numbers, no final settlement would be reached which did not make their interests its primary concern. They *had* put forward a claim for a Sikh state, but there was no homogeneous mass of Sikhs in the Punjab and they did not constitute a majority in any of the districts. The Muslim League had made no attempt to give them any assurances of protection should they find themselves handed over to Pakistan. Accept Pakistan, Jinnah had told them, and then we will give you justice. Because of this far from encouraging attitude, the Sikhs had preferred that the Punjab be divided rather than that the whole province should go to Pakistan. But they had managed to persuade themselves that, at partition, the whole of their community would go to India. They claimed that the boundary ought to lie upon the river

Chenab, which was in fact some 80 to 140 miles west of the frontier that was finally fixed by Sir Cyril Radcliffe. Though the Radcliffe award was not announced until after 15 August, before then it became fairly obvious to the Sikhs that their interests were being ignored and that the province was being divided purely upon a religious-majority basis. Baldev Singh had obviously so convinced himself that no decision would be finalized which did not make Sikh interests the first consideration, that he had not really followed what was being done *with* his approval and consent. But, as the date for the announcement of the award approached, even he began to have doubts, and he told a meeting of Sikhs in Delhi that they should prepare for a struggle, 'without looking for help from any quarter'.

Mountbatten and his advisers, however, were more worried about the effects of partition in Bengal than in the Punjab; in Bengal, they had the precedent of the great Calcutta killings. Everyone, presumably on the strength of Baldev Singh's agreement to the partition plan, had expected the Sikhs to accept the division of the Punjab quietly. But at last the viceroy began to realize that the Punjab was potentially even more explosive than Bengal. On 15 July, he called a meeting of his immediate advisers to discuss the Punjab situation, and four days later he himself visited Lahore for talks with Jenkins. Mountbatten saw enough to convince him that something had to be done. At a meeting of the Partition Council held soon after his return to Delhi, it was decided to establish a Punjab Boundary Force to maintain law and order in the province under the direct control of the supreme commander, Field Marshal Auchinleck, and the Joint Defence Council. This was to be another example of the terrible effects of ignorance reinforced by haste. Unfortunately, the decision to establish an independent military force for use in the Punjab came too late and, though it did magnificent work with great resolution, the Force was tragically unsuccessful.

It was decided, mainly on the strength of Sir Evan Jenkins' warnings, that the Force must be in operation by 1 August. The commander was to be Major-General Rees, a veteran of the Burma campaign against the Japanese. The Force was composed of both Muslims and non-Muslims and Rees was to have as advisers Brigadier Ayub Khan (later to become president of Pakistan) and a Sikh, Brigadier Brar. Later, two additional advisers were appointed. Altogether, the Force numbered about 50,000 men and there was a high proportion of British officers to command them. This super police force was to operate in an area of some 37,500 square miles, where the population consisted of over fourteen million Hindus, Muslims and, above all, Sikhs. Everybody was confident that such a force would easily preserve the peace, but they were to be proved horribly wrong; Rees, a small and rather self-opinionated man, was sure that his force could handle a few ill-armed peasants, which was all he and everyone else expected he would be up against; Mountbatten expected the mobs to come out into the open and be crushed by superior fire power and military expertise. On the whole, it seems that Sir Evan Jenkins' reports were not treated with the seriousness they deserved. This was perhaps partly because of the collapse of the Intelligence service in the Punjab. Very little 'reliable' information was getting through to the viceroy, and Rees, too, was fated to suffer from an absence of Intelligence. Furthermore, he was not to have aircraft for aerial reconnaissance.

Satisfied that there was no longer anything to worry about in the Punjab, Mountbatten flew to Calcutta on 30 July to find out whether Bengal also would need a boundary force. There he was assured by General Tuker that he would guarantee the preservation of order. Mountbatten returned to Delhi with the feeling that everything that could be done had been done.

It has been suggested by some commentators that the Sikhs could have been mollified by last-minute concessions from Congress and the Muslim League. Jenkins proposed that such concessions should be offered, and V. P. Menon had put forward a scheme for turning the great Sikh shrine some twelve miles north of Lahore into a 'sort of Vatican'. Mountbatten, however, did not act on these suggestions. Many reasons have been put forward for this inaction, including personal fatigue, unwillingness to be snubbed by Jinnah, and others with as little foundation in fact. It is most unlikely that anyone at that time seriously believed that Jinnah would be willing to make concessions to the Sikhs, for, to him, concessions to the Sikhs would have seemed to be concessions to Congress. Jinnah was only just in control of his followers, and he was under heavy pressure from Muslim extremists. He would almost certainly not have been able to convince them that concessions were either necessary or wise. Furthermore, it is unlikely that the Sikhs themselves, determined on war, would have been content with minor adjustments of territory, or Vatican status for their shrines. Whatever the reasons, no concessions were asked for, and none were made.

The Sikhs made no attempt to conceal their warlike preparations. Master Tara Singh, like some Old Testament prophet, was exhorting his followers to go out and smite the Amalekites, inflammatory leaflets were being distributed, and instructions sent to the various Sikh communities to prepare themselves for action. Trains were to be attacked, the headworks of canals dynamited, refugees ambushed, Muslims driven from their homes, and there was even a plot to assassinate Jinnah in Karachi on 14 August. This information came into Jenkins' possession from such Intelligence agents as were still operating, but it did not really need Intelligence agents to find out that the Sikhs were organizing themselves for battle. The author if this book was in the Punjab at the time, and, when he was passing through a village a few miles from Amritsar, he was actually invited to watch a body of about three hundred Sikhs drilling with rifles and tommy-guns. He was even asked to adjudicate at a hastily-arranged rifle contest, in which the targets were dummies of Muslim men, women, and children. There would not be a Muslim throat or a Muslim maidenhead unripped in the Punjab, he was told, and he was left in little doubt of the men's willingness and ability to carry out the threat.

The information collected by Jenkins had now become a sizeable dossier against the Sikh leaders, and it was taken to Delhi and placed before a meeting of the Partition Council on 5 August. Jinnah and Liaquat Ali demanded that the Sikh leaders be arrested but this would have done little more than inflame their followers to an even higher pitch of excitement. To stop the Sikhs now, it would have been necessary to arrest the entire community. In any case, the most vocal leaders were not the real organizers of rebellion. Patel advised against the arrest of Tara Singh; Nehru did not commit himself either way. The viceroy, in whose hands final authority still lay, hesitated to come down on either side without first consulting Jenkins and the new governors-designate of East and West Punjab, Sir Francis Mudie, a consistent supporter of the Muslim League, and C. R. Trivedi, a distinguished Indian who had been a governor under the British. All advised that the Sikh leaders should be left alone, and they were probably right. Each gave the advice for different reasons; Jenkins thought that it was now too late for arrest to have any effect, Mudie did not care, and Trivedi reflected the opinions of Sardar Patel.

By 14 August, the edge of independence, thousands of innocent people had already been killed in the streets of Lahore and Amritsar and in the villages of the Punjab. Refugees were beginning their sad journeys out of the Punjab, Muslims to Pakistan, Hindus to India. Many were attacked and butchered on the way. About 80,000 Hindus and Sikhs had collected in Delhi alone. Hindu extremists, too, were at work in the border regions, inciting the people to murder and arson.

Gandhi again did his best to reduce violence, moving through the riot-torn areas with his customary disregard for personal safety. But he did not spend much time in the Punjab; he too believed that the worst trouble would be in Bengal. There, he was to be outstandingly successful. There he showed his real greatness. Not Gandhi the reformer, not Gandhi the Hindu politician, but the Gandhi behind them both, the man who hated suffering and violence. Though, through his past actions, he had contributed as much as anyone to the communal divisions which now resulted in bloodshed, he went out to face that bloodshed when it came, and by doing so saved thousands of lives. The Sikhs, however, were not particularly impressed by the Mahatma, holding him to be as responsible for betraying them as anyone else in Congress. But by this time there was nothing anyone could do in the Punjab, neither a saint on the march nor a Boundary Force of 50,000 men.

Lord Samuel's heart-warming comment can now be seen for what it was—just another of the politicians' empty phrases. A peace treaty there undoubtedly was, but it was starting a war as well as ending one.

10 *The Tryst with Destiny*

On 14 August three men, two soldiers and a civilian, met on the airfield at Lahore in the Punjab. They were Field-Marshal Auchinleck, Major-General Rees, and Sir Evan Jenkins. The aircraft that had brought Auchinleck from Delhi had passed over burning villages and streams of refugees trudging east and west, and the news Jenkins had to report was not reassuring. The police force was virtually non-existent; most of the men had deserted, and over 10 per cent of the city of Lahore had been burned by fire-raisers. There was very little the three men could do about it. The civil administration, as Jenkins had so often warned, was near collapse. Rees had insufficient men to allow him to police the whole city and still keep enough men for all the other trouble spots, and he was also becoming doubtful about the trustworthiness of his own troops as they watched their co-religionists —whether Muslim, Hindu or Sikh—murdering and being murdered. British troops might have saved the day but, for political reasons, they could not be used even if they had been available in sufficient numbers. All that could be done was to try and save as many lives as possible. To do more was out of the question. This was no longer rioting; it was war, purposefully organized and fought by trained soldiers, many of them ex-members of the British Indian Army. Rees, for all his experience, did not have a chance.

In the Punjab, the Sikhs were not so much inflamed by the threat to their religion as fighting with cold calculation to save their very considerable material possessions. There, only superior force could stop them. In Bengal, violence threatened too, but it was not so well organized nor so well armed. It was still the mad violence of religion, irrational and emotional, and it could still be halted by an emotional counter-appeal that would have been useless in the Punjab. Gandhi, having left the Punjab, had begun to make his way to Noakhali, where he felt his presence was once again needed. On the journey he was approached by a delegation of Muslims from Calcutta and by the British governor of Bengal, Sir Frederick Burrows. Most Muslim officials had already left Calcutta and the police force was now almost entirely Hindu. Burrows felt that the Hindu population would now take revenge on the remaining Muslims for the horrors of the great killing of the previous year. All the delegates pleaded with Gandhi to use his influence to prevent another and perhaps even more terrible outbreak. For Gandhi, this presented a real dilemma. He could not be in two places at once. However, using that moral blackmail at which he was so adept, Gandhi agreed to stay in Calcutta only if the Muslims would guarantee peace in Noakhali. This they agreed to do. Messages were sent to the Muslim leader in Noakhali ordering him to control his followers. The fact that he obeyed these orders and that there were no more than minor outbreaks of communal violence at Noakhali, supplies evidence that, on certain levels, the Muslim League was still in a position to control its members' activities. By the same token, it is difficult to avoid the conclusion that the League, despite the denials of its national leaders, was in fact *organizing* violence.

There is, however, considerable evidence that at this time the national leaders of both Congress and the Muslim League were no longer in absolute control of their more militant followers. Now that it was no longer necessary to fight the British, the homogeneity of purpose which the freedom struggle had imposed upon Congress and the League had disappeared. Men like Jinnah and Liaquat Ali, Nehru and Patel, were aware of this, and it partly explains their reluctance during the crisis to do more than make speeches. It is very probable that, if they had given orders, those orders would not have been obeyed.

Gandhi, however, could still exert his peculiar powers over the people and, in Calcutta, he was to have a most improbable ally in his crusade for peace. That ally was Suhrawardy, former prime minister of Bengal. All Suhrawardy's attempts to keep Bengal free and undivided had failed and his own future was not particularly bright. Jinnah had had his revenge; there was to be no place for Suhrawardy in the new dispensation. Jinnah had appointed someone else to be governor of East Bengal and, when Suhrawardy visited Karachi, it was made quite clear to him that as long as Jinnah was alive there would be none of the plums of office for the ex-prime minister. Suhrawardy returned to Calcutta and immediately went to see Gandhi, who, with the shrewdness which so rarely deserted him at times of real crisis, asked Suhrawardy to join him. Suhrawardy agreed and the two of them took up residence in the Calcutta slum of Beliaghata. This was a Muslim area surrounded by Hindu slums, evil-smelling cesspools of disease, poverty and crime of a desperate, grinding, and bloody kind almost unknown in the West.

When Suhrawardy arrived to join Gandhi, who had already moved into a decaying mansion, he was met by a large crowd of militant Hindus organized by the Hindu Mahasabha, a party strongly opposed to Congress and to Gandhi, who it believed had betrayed them by agreeing to partition. Suhrawardy, for all his deficiencies, was no coward and he refused to show fear. Gandhi finally persuaded the mob to let him through and, together, Suhrawardy's courage and the presence of Gandhi began to have their effect. The two men, so oddly dissimilar, jointly addressed large crowds of Muslims and Hindus, while students and many middle-class Indians also played a part in soothing the people. On 15 August, mixed parties of Hindus and Muslims moved through the city shouting a welcome to independence and proclaiming their belief in the brotherhood of Hindus and Muslims.

Gandhi took no part in the ceremonies of celebration. In Delhi and Karachi, the politicians hailed their triumph, but Gandhi spent the day in a Calcutta slum, fasting, spinning, and praying. At 8.30 a.m. that morning, to the sound of a 31-gun salute and the raising of the new national flag, the last viceroy of India had been sworn in as the first governor-general of the Dominion of India. Mountbatten read out a message from King George VI, now no longer Emperor of India:

'On this historic day when India takes her place as a free and independent Dominion in the British Commonwealth of Nations I send you all my greeting and heartfelt wishes. With this transfer of power by consent comes the fulfil-ment of a great democratic ideal, to which the British and Indian peoples alike are firmly dedicated.'

In Karachi, Jinnah was also installed and read out a similar message from the king.

But the sound of the ceremonial guns was being echoed by real guns in the Punjab. Rees's force, upon which so much faith had been pinned, was already beginning to break up under the strain. The men were worried about the safety of their families, and the Sikhs and Hindus amongst them were being urged to desert or at least look the other way when violence took place against Muslims. The British officers were well aware of these strains, but there was little they could do about them. The only real chance of controlling the situation would have been for the forces of both new dominions to act decisively in their own territories. But this was not possible, since both sides had agreed to leave control to the Boundary Force. The setting up of this force was a major error. It removed responsibility from where it should have lain —with the armies of the new dominions. But the British government, Mountbatten, and the nationalist leaders had allowed the political considerations of the transfer of power to inhibit proper appreciation of its likely effect.

The principal blame, however, must be carried by Britain's Labour government. When, in 1945, it found that for the first time the opportunity to remake Britain in its own image was actually within its grasp, other considerations took second place. Labour's victory in the elections had only been one battle in the long war of the class struggle. The citadels of privilege were falling, but many still remained. Labour politicians were incredibly ignorant about India but they were not prepared to listen to men who knew. Caught in the web of their own propaganda, they could scarcely accept advice from the only experts they could have turned to—the rulers of India, that privileged class of British administrators who represented everything the party despised. But, as time passed and the decision was made to transfer power, the government was at last forced to ask the opinions of the generals and the civil servants. It only accepted their advice, however, when that advice seemed to support their own preconceptions. When Labour ministers were informed that the British administration in India was about to collapse, they believed what they were told and brought forward the date of the transfer of power. When they were informed that the country would have to be partitioned, they preferred to ignore the advice and carry on as if power could be handed over to an undivided India. Their suspicion of the Indian experts, whom they thought tainted with Tory imperialism, led them to prefer a gifted amateur like Mountbatten to someone with real knowledge of India's problems. Above all, being politicians themselves, they thought political decisions could change everything, like a magic wand in a fairy tale. As the honest and sincere men they undoubtedly were, they viewed the bloody shambles of the Punjab with horror and loathing, but did not seem to understand how much they had contributed to it themselves.

But, in the Punjab, some British were still trying to carry out their responsibilities. British officers of the Boundary Force still managed to hold their men together and do battle, and many lives were saved because of them. The streams of refugees had now become a torrent, and in the first fortnight of independence it was estimated that over 500,000 actually crossed the frontiers. There were many more still on the move. They travelled on foot, in bullock-carts, in lorries and in trains. Some of the convoys stretched for fifty miles, and from the air they looked like fat slowly-crawling snakes. Both trains and convoys were constantly attacked by bands of armed men who cut off stragglers and abducted women.

Many men who were in the Punjab at that terrible time thought that, if Jinnah and Nehru had toured the country before independence and exercised firm discipline and control, if they had arrested the ringleaders and generally acted with determination, peace could have been achieved. This belief has often been repeated during the long inquest which still goes on to this day. But it was the present author's opinion at that time, and subsequent investigation has only confirmed it, that personal appearances by the leaders would have had little effect. Immediate action by the armed forces of the two new dominions, on the other hand, could have had a decisive result. The crux of the matter lies in the authorities' misplaced trust in the capabilities of the Boundary Force. This was partly the result of assurances given by the military officers responsible for the Force, which were uncritically accepted by the viceroy and the nationalist leaders. But the responsibility, though legally it still lay with the viceroy, belonged fundamentally to the successor states, which existed in embryo before 15 August. If Nehru and Patel, Jinnah and Liaquat Ali, had been less concerned with division of the assets of British India and more with the welfare of the people, steps could have been taken to minimize violence in the Punjab. But suspicion between the leaders had not been diminished by the imminence of freedom. In fact, it had been increased. Jinnah was prepared to quarrel over what he believed to be his rights, down to the last typewriter ribbon which he was convinced Congress would try to trick him out of. Nor did he trust Mountbatten, especially as he was to be the first governor-general of India. Jinnah's suspicions were reciprocated by Congress, and the transfer of power took place, not in an atmosphere of goodwill, but with the parties treating each other with the wary tension of two all-in wrestlers frightened of being caught off guard.

If the new governments did nothing before 15 August, they must be given credit for acting after the celebrations were over, even if what they did then was vitiated by pettiness and spite and not particularly effective. When independence arrived, the leaders slowly began to realize what freedom meant. The British, the old scapegoats, had gone and it would be no longer possible to blame them for everything that went wrong. Indians and Pakistanis must now shoulder the responsibility. On 16 August the Joint Defence Council met to consider the Punjab problem, but the true seriousness of the problem was still not appreciated. The worst horrors were yet to come. The next day a meeting took place at Ambala in the East Punjab between Nehru, Liaquat Ali, and the governors and ministers of the two Punjabs. The meeting issued a joint statement calling for peace and the Boundary Force was considerably enlarged. But the situation had deteriorated so much that by 20 August the Punjab was completely cut off from outside except by air. Really drastic measures were now necessary.

On 29 August the Joint Defence Council, presided over by Lord Mountbatten and attended by Jinnah, met at Lahore. The Boundary Force was now almost helpless against well-organized Sikh opposition and its commander was being attacked in the Pakistani and, much more virulently, in the Indian press. The Council now decided that the Boundary Force must be disbanded and that the task of keeping order in the frontier areas should be taken over by the armed forces of the two dominions. This was undoubtedly the best move, for it transferred responsibility from a joint force, harassed by the suspicions of both sides, to the two governments and their armies where it should have lain all along. It was decided that the two separate army head-quarters intended to control the boundary areas should both be situated in Lahore. After the meeting, Nehru with Liaquat Ali, and Baldev Singh with Sardar Nishtar, toured the troubled areas. On 1 September, the Boundary Force ceased to exist, and Mountbatten hastily called its commander to Delhi to which the communal war was now spreading.

The main problem which now faced the governors of the two Punjabs was not so much the violence within the territory—for there were now signs of a slight improvement in the situation—as the vast numbers of refugees fleeing from their homes to the protection of their co-religionists in India or Pakistan. At first, both governments had tried to persuade minorities to stay where they were, but this was hardly the sort of advice that people in deadly peril of their lives could be expected to take. Gathering up their belongings, they left their homes, blocking the roads or congregating together in vast camps without shelter, food, or sanitation. To make their situation worse, the monsoon broke and torrential rain added to the refugees' misery. Unfortunately, the refugees carried with them tales of horror which were retold in the press of both countries and given official sanction by the information services of the two Punjabs. Jinnah, even while he appealed for calm and peace, still bitterly attacked the Radcliffe awards as 'unjust, incomprehensible, and even perverse'. Master Tara Singh continued to thunder his denunciations. Nothing was being done to reduce tension.

When news from the Punjab reached Calcutta, the harmony that had been so carefully built up between Muslims and Hindus fell to pieces on 1 September, when rioting broke out again and bombs were thrown in the streets. The authorities acted swiftly and the trouble was not allowed to get out of hand. Vast demonstrations of Hindu–Muslim solidarity continued to take place. But the situation remained fraught with danger and Gandhi, who was still in the city, decided that he would begin a fast to the death which he would 'end only if and when sanity returns to Calcutta'. The entire police force of north Calcutta, Europeans included, undertook a 24-hour fast in sympathy, while continuing with their duties! In this and what followed, the unique Indian-ness of India emerges. Nowhere else in the world could an ugly little man of 77 years of age, growing steadily weaker because he refused to eat, have such an effect. On the basis of this episode alone, so alien to Western understanding, it becomes almost possible to sympathize with the ignorance and incomprehension of India displayed by the British government and Lord Mountbatten. After four days, Gandhi received a pledge from Hindu, Muslim and Sikh leaders to keep the peace in their own areas, and broke his fast. The city became quiet almost overnight.

In Delhi, the old imperial city, tension was growing as increasing numbers of refugees from the Punjab flooded into the city and the surrounding countryside. By 5 September, some 200,000 had arrived and the recital of their sufferings was stirring up feelings against those Muslims who still remained in the city. In the narrow streets of old Delhi, the old pattern of stabbings, hackings and rape began to form. Sikhs and Hindus attacked Muslims who were fleeing along the road to the airport in the hope of escape to Pakistan; others were attacked in the railway station. There, after one particularly terrible affray, the platform actually *did* run with blood, and bodies littered the tracks. Mobs—many made up of refugees who had lost everything in the Punjab—screaming with frenzy, hurled great stones into flimsy Muslim shops, and women and children looted everything within sight. In the early stages, the police—Hindus and Sikhs themselves—looked the other way and occasionally even helped the rioters. But soon a military

force of five thousand men including British and Gurkha troops, with
no communal sympathies whatsoever, began to impose some sort of
order. The streets were patrolled day and night and the men had orders
to shoot to kill. The Muslims of Delhi were collected into large camps
protected by troops, though nothing was done for some time to provide them with food or shelter from the monsoon rains. After four
days of bloodshed during which all communications out of the city
were suspended and nearly a thousand people lost their lives, British
and Gurkha troops finally managed to restore order with the assistance
of Gandhi, who arrived from Calcutta on 9 September.

In the Punjab, however, the apparent improvement had been an
illusion. In the refugee camps, cholera had broken out. Torrential rains
had flooded the country on both sides of the border, breaching railways and roads, destroying food stocks, and drowning the refugees in
their squalid quarters. Attacks on trains carrying Muslim refugees had
increased, and even British officers, who had formerly been spared
because of their white skins, were now being killed with their men.
Both governments were finally forced to suspend rail traffic between
Delhi and Lahore. There were simply not enough troops to protect the
trains or the vast convoys moving along the roads. Some two million
people were on the move and convoys often numbered several hundreds of thousands. By the end of September, relations between the
two dominions were worse than they had ever been.

The newspapers, completely uncontrolled, bristled with atrocity
stories and calls for revenge. Extremist leaders demanded that troops
should be sent across the borders to rescue their co-religionists. The
Pakistan government alleged that India was deliberately driving
Muslim refugees into Pakistan in order to bring about administrative
and economic collapse. It was, Jinnah trumpeted, a deep-laid and well-
planned conspiracy to bring Pakistan to her knees before she had even
properly stood up. Counter-accusations flared back from India, and
even Gandhi gave way and joined in the general bitterness by attacking
Pakistan.

As the last days of British rule had drawn to a close, Nehru, referring
to the time in January 1930 when he and other nationalist leaders had
raised the Congress flag and taken a pledge to win freedom for India,
spoke these moving words: 'Long years ago we made a tryst with
destiny, and now the time comes when we shall redeem our pledge,

not wholly or in full measure, but very substantially.' No one who was present at that brave ceremony over seventeen years before had thought that destiny had so much suffering and bitterness in store for them.

But at least this particular suffering and bitterness could not be placed directly at the door of the British, for they were free at last from the responsibilities of ruling an alien people. The white man's burden had been dropped—on to the backs of the nationalist leaders. Some, but very few, Englishmen were overjoyed at the chaos that seemed to be enveloping the old Indian empire. Had they not always forecast that, as soon as the British left, anarchy and rapine would take their place? Some, but very few, felt a sense of shame. But on the whole the general feeling was one of relief, of having got out of a mess comparatively unscathed. The British had never expected anything from their Indian subjects except, as Kipling put it, 'The blame of those ye better, The hate of those ye guard.' Now, they were awarded an instant friendship and goodwill which, under the circumstances, should have been a cause for embarrassment and heart-searching rather than un-critical pride.

A number of Englishmen, however, had not left India when British rule ended. To these men, India and Pakistan owe much more than they are as yet willing to admit. Lord Mountbatten remained as governor-general of India, Field-Marshal Auchinleck as supreme commander—though his heart was no longer in his admittedly thankless task—while the commanders of both dominions' armies were still British generals, and others of lesser rank but no less value also remained. Some of the old British governors stayed at their posts; so did a few civil servants. The influence of these men was out of all proportion to their number. There is no doubt that when, under the impact of the bloody horrors of the Punjab and the tribal invasion of Kashmir, peace between the two new dominions trembled on a knife-edge, the presence of a few British in key positions drew both countries back from the edge of irretrievable disaster. And then they too left. Behind them, nearly 600,000 people had died in the Punjab and some 14 million had been forced to leave their homes.

The Pledge Redeemed

1 The Inheritance

With the division of India on purely religious grounds, it looked at the time as if the British occupation had left very little of lasting value. 'You found us divided,' said an Indian friend to the author on independence day, 'and you have left us the same way.' Certainly, in the chaos that then surrounded us, the criticism seemed just. In modern terms, the partition of India was an act of madness. The British, once they had achieved control of the whole of the country, had dealt with it as a unit, had, in fact, *created* India out of an anarchy of warring states. The great changes of the late nineteenth century, the development of communications and of industry, had reinforced administrative unity with the interdependence of economic life. Partition cut that life in two. The case of Bengal and jute was duplicated on the other side of the country, where the cotton-growers of Pakistan—who produced over half the total crop before partition—now found themselves cut off from the mills and markets of the new India. There were many other such anomalies.

Partition might not have been disastrous if the two new countries could have been friendly and could have co-operated economically for their separate welfare. But the political pressures that had made partition inevitable were to make co-operation impossible. Both countries had to turn inwards and reconstruct their economies on the basis of what had been left to them. Anger over the disruption of economic life reinforced the bitterness that had grown up in the political life of India before partition.

The administration too had to be rebuilt. The trend of administrative change under the British had been towards decentralization. The 1935 Act had brought in representative government for the provinces, and this had helped to intensify the separatist tendencies which found their final expression in the creation of Pakistan. These tendencies, given even stronger sanction by the Cabinet Mission plan, would have weakened the Centre to such an extent that it would not have been able to function, and the breaking up of India into provincial groupings with almost complete, and possibly even actual, independence would have been inevitable. The creation of the two new dominions put an end to decentralization and encouraged the establishment of strong central authorities. In India, however, centralization has not been taken far enough, and the self-interest of the states which make up the Indian Union seriously inhibits the emotional unity of the country—that sense of belonging to something bigger than one's own village or town which makes a nation. To a large extent, the functional machinery of British rule was retained, basically because there was no alternative. Despite constant nationalist claims that Britain did not associate Indians in the *government* of India, as time went on the British had employed more and more of them in the *administration*. These men had been trained in the British tradition and knew no other. Politicians may cause revolutions and change governments, but generally speaking they know very little about how government works. That, when they are successful, they must leave to a civil service.

When freedom came, the nationalist leaders—appalled by the actual problems of government—could not ignore those Indians and Pakistanis in the civil services whom they had once sneered at as lackeys of the British. During the first few months of power, Congress politicians overruled civil servants on questions of day-to-day administration, simply because they could not rid themselves of the prejudices they had built up when fighting for independence. Good sense, however, prevailed when they discovered that it was not possible to run a country like a political party. Administrative experience was the most important physical legacy which Britain left—and which her successors accepted—in India. Basically, of course, the successors had no real choice. They did not know how to run the administration but the civil servants, who had been trained by the British, did.

The new rulers of India and Pakistan were also the inheritors of nearly thirty years of constitutional reform which culminated, in the 1935 Act, with the establishment of representative government in the provinces. Congress, because its leaders were Westernized in their

political thinking, had rejected traditional Indian forms of government
in favour of the more sophisticated institutions of Western liberal
democracy. They had fought for popular democracy because, through
it, they would achieve the fruits of office for themselves, and—apart
from a few like Subhas Chandra Bose—they had relied on the justice of
their demands to help them convince the British of their democratic
right to rule themselves. From the point of view of the top Congress
leaders, independence was the natural culmination of the years of constitutional reform. They had early placed their faith in democracy, and
they were hardly likely to discard it once it had been achieved. Of
course, the Congress leaders' attitude to democratic forms of government was not entirely an expression of their theoretical belief in its
essential goodness; democracy meant the rule of the majority, and no
one doubted that Congress commanded the support of the majority.
Most of the secondary and lower levels of Congress membership had
little faith in democracy as such but were prepared to accept a democratic form of government because they knew they would not suffer
by it. In fact they did not care what sort of government they got as
long as Congress dominated it. Experience after the provincial elections of 1937 had shown them the advantages. If the top leaders
wanted liberal democracy, they could be indulged without anyone
losing the gains of office.

Democracy as a system had no roots in India, but only an intellectual
and emotional appeal to the Westernized middle class which expected
to gain from it what had been denied to them by British 'tyranny'.
The fact that parliamentary institutions seem to work in India has
deluded many in the West into believing that these were Britain's most
seminal legacy and that, because of them, India is the world's largest
democracy. But these institutions exist only by the consent of those
who profit from them, and even then are fundamentally distorted by
self-interest. As soon as real opposition to Congress dominance
emerges through the medium of democratic procedures, the desire to
abandon parliamentary institutions will increase. India's acceptance of
democracy—and her toleration of it—is based not on any fundamental
belief in its moral virtue, but in the fact that as yet it does not inhibit
the enjoyment of power by the ruling class.

The Pakistanis, however, were positively opposed to democracy.
The Muslims of undivided India, ever since the first reforms of the

late nineteenth century, had feared democracy just because it meant the rule of the majority. As the British granted more and more concessions in response to Congress demands for representative government, so the Muslims became more and more antagonistic. Jinnah, essentially authoritarian in his political thought, attacked democracy because it discriminated against the minority, and the idea of 'Pakistan' was devised, not to gain democracy, but to escape the consequences of it. He and his colleagues did not change their attitude after independence. Muslim nationalists rejected democracy for exactly the same reasons as Congress welcomed it, and, though for a number of years after independence quasi-democratic institutions existed in Pakistan, they were not introduced by constitutional legislation but left over from the 1935 Act. The governor-general of Pakistan still retained extensive discretionary powers, under which he could dissolve the legislative assembly if he chose, without reference to the political parties. A new constitution promulgated in 1956, when Pakistan became a republic, left the president with almost the same powers, and two years later the Pakistan Army took over the government and has ruled ever since. Under yet another constitution introduced in 1962, there has been an introduction of democratic institutions on the very lowest level. By an odd irony, opposition to the military regime has followed the pattern of the Congress fight against the British. Politicians in Pakistan are now demanding parliamentary institutions as the only alternative to military tyranny.

India and Pakistan inherited the old antagonisms between Hindu and Muslim. Though the primary struggle had been against the British, the final stages of that struggle were framed in religious conflict. This conflict was at the root of the political struggle and was strengthened by the pattern of that struggle. With the creation of Pakistan, these antagonisms were institutionalized, and though both countries deny that religion is at the bottom of their disagreements and suspicion, it is nevertheless true that the conflict between the Muslim League and Congress during the years before independence has been perpetuated, and even reinforced, by the governments of India and Pakistan. British rule did not create these antagonisms, but only the opportunity to use them as a political weapon. Tilak had been the first to recognize the power of religious feeling as a weapon against the British; Jinnah learned the lesson and turned it against Congress.

Most apologists for British imperialism point to the fact that those who inherited its estate had been created in a Western image, that political power was handed over to those who most closely resembled —and appreciated—the best in the British political system. The imperial justification lay in the fulfilment of a mission. The great day had arrived which Macaulay had foretold, 'the proudest day in English history', when having tasted the delights of English institutions, Indians demanded them for themselves. Certainly the prophecy had been fulfilled, but the real legacy of the British connexion was rather more than the 'imperishable empire of our arts, our morals, our literature, and our laws'. The British, having made a great renunciation of empire, were forced to justify that renunciation with almost as much vehemence as they had once justified its retention. 'The imperishable empire' was the answer, for it was only by pointing to the triumph of British ideas that the British could claim to be different from other imperial powers.

The legacy of imperialism—whether British, French, or Dutch—was 'Westernization', a concept which implies the acceptance of Western political ideas and values. A better word is 'modernization', which means the acceptance of Western industrial and economic techniques and the patterns of behaviour and values which go with them. Even where Western political institutions have been rejected, and where foreign policies are avowedly anti-Western, 'modern' techniques which originated in the West have not been rejected. The primary response of colonial Asia to the West was to demand the political institutions of the conquerors. The secondary response, and the one most far-reaching in its consequences, was the demand for industrialization and the sort of society which had evolved because of it. The conflict that now exists inside former colonial territories is not so much between political ideologies as between traditional societies and their 'modernizing' minorities. This conflict is on a much vaster scale than the struggle between the nationalists and their former rulers. The struggle for freedom was only a conflict between élites—the alien rulers and the Westernized native minority. Now it is between a way of life sanctified by religion and custom, and the modern world of technology.

A more immediate legacy of the British transfer of power was not to the Indian people at all, but to those of the other colonial empires.

Despite the unwillingness of France, Holland, and in particular Portugal, to give up their empires, the ending of British rule in India made it inevitable that they should do so. The Indian Independence Act of 1947 was a charter of liberty for the peoples of colonial Asia and of Africa.

There was one other legacy and it was shared both by Britain and those who succeeded her in India. There have been many criticisms—as this book has only too clearly shown—of British behaviour towards India during the years of power and in the final days of weakness. But the act of renunciation itself was without precedent or even analogy in history. The Labour government's action, though based upon ignorance and misunderstanding and vitiated by grave tactical errors, was in the final analysis an act of statesmanship. It permitted India and Pakistan to remain friendly with Britain, and though that friendship has often been frayed it has never been broken. All have benefited from it. For India and Pakistan, membership of the Commonwealth brought immediate, and not unwelcome, status in the world outside. It also brought aid and advice—and economic advantage. The reality of this continuing link with Britain needs no further proof than the fact that India, faced in 1962 with a Chinese invasion of her frontier areas, turned to Britain and the Commonwealth for help and received it almost as of right. Cynics maintain that only advantage brought India and Pakistan within the Commonwealth and has kept them there; they are probably right. But the advantage would not have been seen, nor would it in fact have existed, if Britain had not given up India peaceably instead of trying to hold on to it by force.

2 The Inheritors

The mantle of British rule fell upon those who had learned most from the West, upon an élite almost as remote from the mass of the people as the administrators they replaced. Essentially, the freedom movements—Congress and the Muslim League—were not mass parties, despite the fact that Gandhi had given Congress the appearance of being so. Because of Gandhi, the British believed that the struggle for freedom was firmly based upon the mass following of Congress. But did Congress in fact have a mass following? Certainly Gandhi had

demonstrated that the peasant could be manipulated for political purposes, but so too had religious extremists and, on a criminal level, so
had the gangsters who incited mobs so that they could profit from the
loot. Because India was so large and her population so vast, the numbers of those who could be called upon for action were large too. A
Congress membership of four million appears immense in terms of
English political parties, but that number is small when it is related to
the four hundred million or so of India's population.

It is also interesting to examine the caste background of Congress
members. Most of the leadership, during the freedom struggle and
after independence, came from the higher castes of Indian society. In
fact, Congress organization seemed, and still seems, to favour the
traditional Indian-dominant classes, even if their representatives are
disguised behind a Western veneer. The only exception is the Kshatriya or warrior caste, to which in the past most Indian rulers belonged.
Only one major Congress leader, Subhas Chandra Bose, was a
Kshatriya and he was squeezed out by his traditional enemies, the
Brahmins and the Vaisyas—the first represented by Nehru and Patel,
and the second by Gandhi. Subhas took a typically Kshatriya course by
attempting to overthrow the British by violence. In fact the triumph of
Congress in 1947 was a victory in the caste war which had been going
on for centuries, and to this day the Kshatriyas—dispossessed princes,
traditional landowners, and so forth—are to a large extent excluded
from government. In Pakistan, though the traditional structure of
Muslim society differs from the caste system of Hindu India, the
inheritors came almost entirely from the old ruling classes or from
the so-called 'martial' elements. In both countries, however, whatever
the traditional pressures, the élite was fully persuaded of the need for
'modernization'. Because of this, they have engaged in large-scale
economic activities which are undermining traditional patterns of
society. The British had only once deliberately attempted to reform
Indian, and specifically Hindu, society, though by their very presence
and the use of Western administrative methods, codes of law, industrial
techniques and so on, they could not avoid influencing the social order
to some extent. The area in which they had chosen to attempt reform
concerned aspects of the religious life of the people such as suttee, or
widow-burning, but one of the consequences of these attempted
reforms was the Indian Mutiny of 1857 which so frightened the British

that they made no further attempts to change Hindu society. The British were 'modernizers' only insofar as it was to their advantage as rulers and businessmen; their successors are 'modernizers' by necessity, and are consequently involved in the promotion of social change. The British preserved the social order because it was to their advantage not to interfere with it. Their successors have been forced to strike at its very roots. As a result, the mass of the Indian and Pakistani peoples are the inheritors of a process of 'modernization' loosed by the transfer of power.

It was not only the people of India who were changed, and are being changed, by the ending of British rule. The people of Britain too found themselves in a very different world because of it. Vast social changes have taken place in Britain, particularly in the welfare and wealth of the working classes. The propaganda of colonial nationalists and the quasi-Marxist ideology of British socialists insisted that colonial rule was exploitive, that the riches of India were drawn away for the aggrandizement of the conquerors. But if this in fact had been the case, the former metropolitan power should have suffered economically when empire passed away. Yet Britain is better rather than worse off today when she has lost nearly all her overseas possessions. In purely economic terms Macaulay has once again proved to be a remarkable prophet. In a speech in the House of Commons in 1833 he said:

'It would be, on the most selfish view of the case, far better for us that the people of India were well-governed and independent of us than ill-governed and subject to us; that they were ruled by their own kings, but wearing our broadcloth, and working with our cutlery, than that they were performing their salaams to English collectors and English magistrates, but were too ignorant to value, or too poor to buy, English manufactures. To trade with civilized men is infinitely more profitable than to govern savages. That would indeed be a doting wisdom, which, in order that India might remain a dependency, would make it a useless and costly dependency; which would keep a hundred millions of men from being our customers in order that they might continue to be our slaves.'

Trade with India and Pakistan has increased since independence and Britain no longer carries the immense burden of responsibility for their government.

But in one sphere the British people may have suffered by the dissolution of their empire. Many people felt a sense of personal loss as all the pomp of yesterday became one with Nineveh and Tyre. Empires are not merely political and economic realities; their possession becomes part of the national psychology of the imperial power. There is an 'identification' with empire that is not restricted to those of the upper and middle classes who benefit from it. Even those who bitterly attacked the imperial adventure as a symbol of outmoded privilege still seem to feel a sense of constriction as the Union Jack flies over fewer and fewer of the outposts of empire. This feeling has nothing to do with reality, for it is obvious to practically everybody that to attempt to hold on to an empire in present world conditions could lead only to disaster. Because this feeling is irrational it has received irrational expression in such neo-imperial gestures as the attack upon Egypt over the Suez Canal in 1956—which, according to public opinion polls, was supported with almost nineteenth-century emotion by at least half the British population. This, and the attempt to hold on to the island of Cyprus, were part of the price that had to be paid for a readjustment of national attitudes.

The imperial adventure was something that dominated the imagination of men, and attempts to resurrect the glories of the past appeal to the imagination as well. While Britain still had her empire, the propaganda of imperial greatness was just as much a part of it as the Royal Navy and the Indian Army. The empire had its martyrs and its hagiology, its saints' days and its shrines. The rejection of these by the British people made it possible for the Attlee government to dispose of India peacefully. But as the British people's material wealth has increased and Britain's stature in the world diminished, both Labour and Conservative politicians have made appeals to the past as justification for the future. There is great danger in dwelling upon the glories of the past and ignoring the lessons it contains. Though history has warnings for us all, they are seldom recognized and even more rarely acted upon, as the events of the last years of British India so amply testify.

Index